Youth Studies

Youth Studies: an introduction is a clear, jargon-free and accessible textbook which will be invaluable in helping to explain concepts, theories and trends within youth studies. The concise summaries of key texts and the ideas of important theorists make the book an invaluable resource. The book also raises questions for discussion, with international case studies and up-to-date examples.

The book discusses important issues within youth studies, for example:

- educa   and opportunity
- emplo   nt and unemployment
- family   ds and living arrangements
- crime   ustice
- identi
- health   sexuality
- citizer   and political engagement.

Suitab   a wide range of youth-related courses, this textbook provides a theoretical and empirical   duction to youth studies. It will appeal to undergraduate students on inter-national   mic and vocational courses, including sociology, politics, criminology, social policy, ge   phy and psychology.

Andy Fur   Professor of Social Inclusion and Education in the School of Education at the Unive   ty of Glasgow, Scotland. Andy is an educational sociologist with a long-standing specialist   e study of youth and a strong interest in the reproduction of inequalities and in p   s of social change. Since 1998 he has been Editor-in-Chief of the *Journal of Youth St   s*, and his books on youth include *Young People and Social Change* (with Fred Cartm   , 1997, 2nd edition 2007, Open University Press), *Higher Education and Social Justice* (with Fred Cartmel, 2009, Open University Press) and the *Handbook of Youth and Young Adulthood* (2009, Routledge).

Andy Furlong has written an authoritative introduction to youth studies. The focus throughout is on the momentous changes that are currently affecting young people throughout the world. Students and lecturers will welcome the even-handed, lucid accounts of the main sociological and psychological perspectives, and the comprehensive coverage. The book deals with all aspects of young people's lives – family, education, labour market, health, leisure, crime and politics – and is sensitive to differences among present-day countries.

–*Professor Ken Roberts, University of Liverpool*

Andy Furlong has provided an excellent overview of the key debates in youth studies in a concise and clear way, introducing students to the major themes and issues they should be aware of in their studies. It is a book that is long overdue.

–*Professor Alan France, University of Auckland*

A book of this nature is long overdue. Professor Furlong has used his extensive knowledge of the field to produce a highly readable, informative and challenging text. Anyone who is looking for a comprehensive overview of the key issues in youth studies should read this book.

–*Professor Tracy Shildrick, Teesside University*

Furlong provides the most comprehensive introduction yet through the historical antecedents and contemporary strands of youth studies. Those new to the field will gain a depth of understanding from Furlong's effortless summary of the concepts, theories and issues that shape youth studies. The identification of contemporary examples and policy implications keeps the text grounded. Furlong's analysis defines this enduring but fragmented field in a way that the experienced will find enlightening and compelling.

–*Johanna Wyn, Professor in Education and Director of the Youth Research Centre, University of Melbourne, Australia*

Youth Studies

An introduction

Andy Furlong

Routledge
Taylor & Francis Group

LONDON AND NEW YORK

First published 2013 by Routledge
2 Park Square, Milton Park, Abingdon, Oxon OX14 4RN

Simultaneously published in the USA and Canada
by Routledge
711 Third Avenue, New York, NY 10017

Routledge is an imprint of the Taylor & Francis Group, an informa business

British Library Cataloguing in Publication Data
A catalogue record for this book is available from the British Library

Library of Congress Cataloging in Publication Data
Furlong, Andy.
   Youth studies: an introduction/Andy Furlong.
      p. cm.
   Includes bibliographical references and index.
   1. Youth–Study and teaching. 2. Youth–Research. I. Title.
   HQ793.F87 2013
   305.235'071–dc23   2012010623

ISBN: 978-0-415-56476-2 (hbk)
ISBN: 978-0-415-56479-3 (pbk)
ISBN: 978-0-203-86209-4 (ebk)

Typeset in Scala
by Sunrise Setting Ltd, Paignton, UK

MIX
Paper from
responsible sources
FSC
www.fsc.org   FSC® C004839

Printed and bound in Great Britain by the MPG Books Group

For Alina and Harvey

Contents

List of figures

List of tables

list of tables

The author

Andy Furlong is Professor of Social Inclusion and Education in the School of Education at the University of Glasgow, Scotland. Andy is an educational sociologist with a long-standing specialism in the study of youth and a strong interest in the reproduction of inequalities and in processes of social change. He completed his PhD on youth transitions and unemployment in the 1980s and has since worked on a wide variety of youth-oriented research projects. Since 1998 Andy has been Editor-in-Chief of the *Journal of Youth Studies*, one of the leading journals in the field. He has produced several books on youth, notably *Young People and Social Change* (with Fred Cartmel, 1997, 2nd edition 2007, Open University Press), *Higher Education and Social Justice* (with Fred Cartmel, 2009, Open University Press) and the *Handbook of Youth and Young Adulthood* (2009, Routledge); his work has been translated into 12 languages. Andy has held visiting positions at Deakin University, the University of Melbourne and Monash University, and has held an invitation fellowship from the Japan Society for the Promotion of Science. He is an academician of the UK Academy of Social Sciences and has recently been awarded a Doctor of Letters by the University of Leicester. An up-to-date listing of activities and publications can be found at http://andyfurlong.com/.

Acknowledgements

I would like to thank the following friends and colleagues for commenting on various aspects of this book or supplying me with references and materials: Fred Cartmel, Rob MacDonald, Tracy Shildrick, Howard Sercombe and Howard Williamson. Some of the material used in Chapter 12 is drawn from a report – 'Evaluating Youth Work with Vulnerable Young People' – written with colleagues Fred Cartmel, Janet Powney and Stuart Hall; their contribution is acknowledged.

chapter 1

Youth and the life course

Contents

What is youth?

Youth is a socially constructed intermediary phase that stands between childhood and adulthood: it is not defined chronologically as a stage that can be tied to specific age ranges, nor can its end point be linked to specific activities, such as taking up paid work or having sexual relations. Youth is a broader concept than adolescence, which relates to specific developmental phases, beginning with puberty and ending once physiological and emotional maturity is achieved, and it tends to cover a more pro-tracted time span. The term adolescence was coined by G. Stanley Hall in 1904 in an ambitious two-volume book entitled *Adolescence: Its Psychology and its Relations to Physiology, Anthropology, Sociology, Sex, Crime, Religion and Education*. For Hall, the physiological changes associated with adolescence meant that the experience was essentially traumatic: characterized by 'storm and stress'. Adolescence was a period which involved risky behaviour, mood swings and conflict with parents. Subsequently, psychologists such as Bühler (1921) and Erikson (1968) recognized that there was an important cultural dimension to adolescence and that physiological explanations were somewhat limited. In recent years there has been something of a resurgence of interest in developmental theory and the physiology of adolescence as researchers have begun to use modern brain imaging technology to study differences in the brain activity of young people and adults. The argument here is that the brain's frontal lobe cortex, which plays an important role in judgement, does not mature fully until young people are in their early or late twenties. As a result, young people may exercise poor judgement and are prone to risky behaviour (Evans *et al.*, 2007; Bessant, 2008). Bessant notes, however, that some neuroscientists are highly critical of this reductionist tendency and argue that young people's experiences, well-being and relationships also have a powerful impact on development and on decision-making processes.

G Stanley Hall was born in Massachusetts in 1844. Educated at Union Theological Seminary and Harvard University, he held a Chair at Johns Hopkins University before being appointed as the first president of Clark University. An influential psychologist, he founded the *American Journal of Psychology* and was the first president of the American Psychological Association. As well as his work on adolescence (he is sometimes referred to as the 'father of adolescence'), he played a leading role in the development of educational psychology. He died in 1924.

The sociological tradition in youth research has always placed a strong emphasis on the way in which experiences (which obviously vary across time and space and between social groups) are central to definitions of youth as they link to patterns of dependence. Whereas adolescence can be tied reasonably accurately to a specific age range and the completion of a set of developmental tasks (whether or not these are explicitly linked to the physical structure of the brain), as a socially constructed category youth can be difficult to define. It is essentially a period of semi-dependence that falls between the full dependency that characterizes childhood and the independence of adulthood. Defined in this way, it is clear that youth is constructed differently across time and between societies. In some societies young people become independent at a relatively young age, while in others dependency can last well into their second decade of life, and even beyond. As Heinz argues:

> The coordinates of this period of life vary according to the economy and the educational and social policies of the state: the life course and its component 'youth' are path-dependent social structures. Modern societies differ in their institutional arrangements concerning life transitions: education and training provisions, labour market regulations, exclusion mechanisms, social assistance rules, and the extent to which there is an explicit youth policy (2009: 6).

Thus Heinz argues that the youth period is not self-contained and is impossible to indentify clearly 'except in terms of the legal definitions of the maturity age' (2009: 4). Of course in legal terms, the age of maturity varies across time and between countries: in the United Kingdom the age of majority was 21 until 1970 when it was lowered to 18. In most countries, the age of majority is now 18, although it is not universal. In Canada there is variation between provinces: 18 in Ontario but 19 in British Columbia. Even in countries where the legal age of majority is set at 18, some rights are not granted until a later stage: in the United States, young people are not able to purchase alcohol until the age of 21, while in the UK full entitlement to social security assistance is not granted until age 25. In most countries rights and responsibilities are granted in a piecemeal fashion, beginning well before the legal age of majority and ending sometime later. In England, for example, young people may be regarded as responsible for criminal behaviour from the age of 10, allowed to work part time in a limited range of occupations at age 13 but not allowed to drive heavy goods vehicles until 21.

While recognizing that member states use different chronologies to define youth, the United Nations defines 'youth' as persons between the ages of 15 and 24 with all UN statistics based on this definition. The UN also recognizes that a useful distinction can be made between teenagers (i.e. those between the ages of 13 and 19) and young adults (those between the ages of 20 and 24). While seeking to impose some uniformity on statistical approaches, the UN itself is aware of contradictions between approaches in its own statutes. Hence under the 15–24 definition (introduced in 1981) children are defined as those under the age of 14 while under the 1979 Convention on the Rights of the Child, those under the age of 18 are regarded as children.

In some respects the identification of a clear youth stage in the life course has become increasingly problematic as a result of changes in modern societies. Young people spend longer in education, enter full-time employment at a later stage and can remain dependent for greater periods of time. Moreover, many young people have non-linear sets of experiences in which events occur in a non-traditional order: they may have children before they have completed their education, for example, or may return to education after several years in employment. As a result of the growing protraction and complexity of youth as a stage in the life course, researchers have begun to argue we must recognize a new phase that they have termed 'young adulthood' (EGRIS, 2001), 'post-adolescence' (Keniston, 1968) or 'emerging adulthood' (Arnett, 2004).

Why study youth?

People study youth for a wide variety of reasons and do so from within a range of social science disciplines such as sociology, politics, criminology, social policy, geography and psychology. Within these subject areas, researchers may be interested in events or experiences that are predominantly manifest among young people (such as leaving school, entering the labour market for the first time or negotiating sexual identities), may wish to explore the youth dimension of a generalized phenomenon (such as voting behaviour or unemployment) or may wish to draw on the experiences of youth to explore broader questions relating to the nature of social change. The study of youth is both broad and dynamic and is frequently at the cutting edge of theoretical debate within different subject areas.

Unsurprisingly, the issues that engage youth researchers are frequently of great interest to policy makers. Often researchers are attracted to a field of study because it is very topical and stimulates widespread debate, although frequently they become involved because they harbour doubts about the veracity of popularist explanations. The link between the policy agenda, media concerns and the research agenda has been evident

youth studies: an introduction

throughout much of the history of youth research. In terms of policy-related themes, two interlinked areas stand out particularly prominently: crime and youth cultures. For a variety of reasons (which are discussed in Chapter 9), young people are more likely than adults to engage in forms of behaviour that attract the attention of law enforcement agencies, and, as such, much of the work of criminologists focuses on youth. There has also been a long-standing interest in youth cultures, especially when particular subcultures are seen as posing a threat to the established order, when they are regarded as having anti-social or criminal tendencies or when their consumption habits suggest new markets to be exploited.

In many respects, it would not be unfair to suggest that there is always a high level of interest in young people when they are perceived to be a problem because their behaviour causes concern to those with power and influence (the recent urban disorders in the UK are a good example), when their actions are seen as posing a risk to themselves (through their use of alcohol or drugs, for example) or when there are concerns about social integration and economic efficiency (manifest in terms of high levels of long-term unemployment or mismatches in the supply and demand for labour).

In youth research there has been a long-standing rift between what can be termed the 'transitional' and 'cultural' approaches (discussed more fully in Chapter 7). Those working within a 'transitional' perspective have tended to focus on the relationship between education and work and the ways in which social inequalities are reproduced as part of the transition from youth to adulthood. Many (but not all) of those working within a 'cultural' perspective have tended to focus on lifestyles and youth subcultures, especially those that are highly visible and challenge the cultural standpoints of older generations.

Youth research, though, is not simply about policy, about the concerns of the powerful or about understanding cultural change. The examination of young people's lives provides a unique window on processes of social and economic change and facilitates the exploration of some of the big theoretical concerns in social science.

> It is important to study youth, because the points where young people engage with the institutions that either promote social justice or entrench social division are significant points of reference for every society. Hence, the study of youth is important as an indicator of the real 'costs' and 'benefits' of the political and economic systems of each society.
>
> (Wyn and White, 1997: 6)

In this context, youth research is concerned with social justice, class, 'race', gender and spatial divisions. It focuses on issues of power and privilege on the one hand, and deprivation and exclusion on the other. Sociologically it provides a focus for discussions of structure and agency, illustrating the ways in which young people are constrained by factors such as social class or gender and highlighting the ways in which they can help break down barriers through their own actions. For psychologists the study of adolescence provides an ideal window for the exploration of identity development. Hence many of the 'big names' in social science have, at various points in their careers, held an interest in youth: Aristotle, Freud, Jung, Rousseau, Comte, Mannheim, Parsons and Elias, to name but a few.

Youth and the life course

For many youth researchers, discussion of change tends to centre on transitions from one status to another, such as the transition from school to work, embedded within a broader discourse of life course dynamics. It is useful here to make the distinction between *life course* theory that developed out of the work of Glen Elder, and earlier work that used the term *lifecycle*. The idea of embedding the experiences of youth within the lifecycle is a positivistic approach in which the individual's journey through life is presented as normative and de-contextualized. In other words, key sets of experiences are closely linked to age-related stages in a developmental process. Conceptualized in this way, the lifecycle is essentially linear with one set of age-related experiences (such as leaving school) being closely related to another (gaining full-time employment or getting married). Elder's contribution (1974) was to place individuals' experiences within contexts that were presented as both dynamic and linked to the lives of others. For Elder the key principles of life course theory 'are historical time and place, the timing of lives, linked or interdependent lives and human agency in constrained settings' (1997: 5). As Elder describes it, 'The life course is age-graded through institutions and social structures, and it is embedded in relationships that constrain and support behaviour – both the individual life course and a person's developmental trajectory are interconnected with the lives and development of others' (1998: 951–2).

In elaborating life course theory, Walter Heinz suggests that it rests on five principles:

1 each life phase affects the entire life course: life-span development;
2 individuals actively construct their biography: human agency;
3 the life course is embedded in historical events: time and place;

4 social circumstances and events influence transitions: timing of decisions;
5 social relationships and networks contribute to the shaping of biographies: linked lives.

(Heinz, 2009: 4)

While the central principles of Elder's work continue to underpin work on the life course, research relating to transitions from youth to adulthood has moved through a number of phases, each characterized by a shift in emphasis from one component factor to another. In some periods of time there has been a strong emphasis on the ways in which young people's transitions are shaped by structural factors, such as social class or gender, while in other points in time there has been a much greater emphasis on factors underpinning individual agency, such as motivation and resilience.

These changes in emphasis come across fairly clearly in the metaphors used by researchers to summarize the general principles that characterize transitions in different periods of time (Evans and Furlong, 1997). In the 1960s, work on youth transitions tended to have a strong psychological underpinning with processes of integration seen in terms of clear routes leading to occupational 'niches'. Influenced by the work of Havighurst (1948) and Erikson (1968), there was an emphasis on 'growth task' models in which young people's routes were linked to the successful accomplishment of a developmental project which resulted in the establishment of a vocational identity. In the 1970s, with a rise in youth unemployment resulting in more complex transitions, 'routes' and 'pathways' became the favoured metaphors. This shift in thinking did not simply reflect changes in transitional contexts, but also reflected new ways of thinking that were influenced by sociology and which placed less emphasis on subjective orientations in shaping transitions, and more emphasis on opportunity structures (e.g. Roberts, 1975). By the 1980s, with transitions apparently having become increasingly complex and protracted and unemployment continuing to rise, 'trajectory' became the predominant metaphor. Underpinned by structuralist interpretations, the term implied that transitional outcomes were strongly conditioned by factors such as social class and cultural capital and were therefore largely beyond individual control. By the 1990s, with the rise of postmodern perspectives, structural explanations fell out of fashion and new metaphors were introduced that revolved around the idea of 'navigation'. Individual agency was given much greater prominence, and transitional outcomes were increasingly linked to factors like judgement, resilience and life management skills (Evans and Furlong, 1997).

In one sense, the shifting metaphors highlighted by Evans and Furlong (1997) represent changes in theoretical fashion among youth researchers, which can be identified in social science more generally. Here we can observe a move from functionalism to structuralism and from structuralism to postmodernism, although of course changes in theoretical paradigms are never quite as neat as this. While researchers may move towards a new model of understanding, they tend to develop hybrid models and the metaphors represent something of a caricature. In the 1980s, for example, few researchers supported a determinist model in which agency was totally absent. Likewise today, for many researchers the adoption of navigation models does not involve the wholesale abandonment of structural perspectives. Evans (2002), for example, presents the idea of 'bounded agency' as a way of highlighting the extent to which reflexive agency occurs within contexts that restrict the scope for life management.

These changes, and the assumptions that different models rest on, are important and worth illustrating. The key concerns of youth researchers have actually changed very little over the last 40 years or so, although both the lived experiences of young people and the way in which social scientists interpret them have. From a sociological perspective, the transmission of advantage and disadvantage across generations has always been a key topic of interest. How is it that children from poor families tend to end up in low-wage jobs – and what are the processes that occur during the youth period that result in the reproduction of advantage? Underpinning this question are issues relating to structure and agency: are inequalities reproduced mainly as a result of the resources people have access to, or does the answer lie mainly in differences in individuals' motivation and the ways they try to manage their lives?

Structure versus agency

In common with other social scientists, youth researchers have frequently changed their position in relation to the resolution of the structure–agency question. To an extent their positions have been influenced by broader theoretical debates within their subject areas, but they have also been affected by observations of the lives of young people, the constraints they face and the extent to which they seem able to influence outcomes. One of the factors that has a strong bearing on young people's experience relates to the nature of opportunities that are available at a given point in time. In times of high unemployment, for example, young people may have far fewer opportunities than they might in periods when the labour market is buoyant: as a result their scope to exercise agency might be restricted. Other factors also help shape the contexts in which young people's lives are lived: social policies and welfare regimes, for example, may constrain opportunities, while the assumptions embedded in cultures can promote agency or reinforce barriers.

Implicit in the idea of pathways is the assumption that, while routes are structured by factors such as gender or social class, there are various points at which people make decisions regarding routes. They may, for example, decide to extend their education, or, based on their educational attainments, make decisions about the sort of job they would like to take up. The metaphor therefore highlights the importance of both structure and agency. In contrast, the idea of a trajectory suggests very limited scope for agency: the term implies that destinations can be predicted with a high degree of accuracy using information on origins. In modern contexts, it is recognized that individuals make key decisions within contexts that constrain choices. Agency is 'bounded' (Evans, 2002), but, while the pathway model highlighted the ways in which individuals were, at various points in time, forced to make decisions that could alter the course of a transition, navigation models recognize that the capacity to act, the skills which individuals develop to enable them to read signals, anticipate problems and develop life management strategies, are significant and have a bearing on outcomes.

The emphasis on reflexive life management in the navigation model is associated with biographical methodologies in which individuals are asked to provide accounts of their lives and to interpret sequences of events. Biographical approaches attempt to represent 'consciousness and subjectivity, as well as the objective constraints that shape individual lives' (Rustin and Chamberlayne, 2002: 3). With life presented as a project with uncertain outcomes, constantly being revised by individuals, a distinction is frequently made between the 'normal biography' which was prevalent prior to the 1990s and the 'choice biographies' which are frequently seen as characteristic of modern transitions.

In modern times, the human life-course is increasingly becoming a 'project' in which the beginning (birth) and end (death) are stage-managed as much as the periods of life in between. What used to be phases of development – small child, schoolchild, adolescent, adult – have turned into parts of the project which have an autonomous status and which, put together, do not necessarily result in a coherent course of life. [...] 'Projects' are drafts for a desirable future, a future which clearly will never become reality in the way it was planned.

(du Bois-Reymond, 1998: 63)

As du Bois-Reymond makes clear, the idea of a 'choice biography' does not necessarily involve free choice; paradoxically, the freedom to choose may itself be a constraint. Young people may not feel prepared to make choices or may find choices blocked or constrained at times when they want to take action.

> 'Choice biographies' are by no means purely based on freedom and own choice, but are determined by a paradox which is typical in modern life: although (western) societies provide more options to choose from, modern (young) people are forced to reflect on the available options and justify their decisions. They might also get frustrated because they realize that there are many options available; perhaps they do not feel ready to make a good choice, or perhaps they would like to make a choice but are prevented from doing so. It is the *tension between option/freedom and legitimation/coercion* which marks 'choice biographies'.
>
> (du Bois-Reymond, 1998: 65, original italics)

While a focus on transition is compatible with the idea that individuals are constantly revising and re-interpreting their biographical projects, it does introduce a greater fluidity into the process and makes it increasingly difficult to identify end points. In this context, youth, young adulthood and adulthood are all statuses that must be negotiated: there are no clear beginnings or finishing posts that unambiguously define these stages of the life course. As Henderson and colleagues put it, 'adulthood does not exist, it has to be invented' (2007: 20). 'Youth is problematic largely because *adult status itself is problematic*' (Wyn and White, 1997: 9, original italics). Consequently, transitions are increasing portrayed as non-linear, as involving breaks, gaps and reversals: as individualized.

The process of individualization, as applied to youth, has its roots in the work of Ulrich Beck (1992). For Beck, late modernity is characterized by a process of individualization whereby risk permeates all aspects of life, and categories like social class become redundant. In these circumstances, young people find it increasingly difficult to identify others who encounter the same sets of experiences as themselves, while lifestyles, attitudes and forms of consciousness lose their association with social class. In Beck's view, individualization is a process whereby agency takes precedence and structures assume a secondary position. In late modern contexts, in all aspects of their lives, people constantly have to choose between different options, including the social groups with which they wish to be identified (Beck, 1992).

youth studies: an introduction

The idea of generation

Perhaps surprisingly, it is relatively rare for youth researchers to use the term generation as a way of distinguishing the experiences of a group of people born in a particular era from those born in earlier or later periods. This is partly because the term is thought to lack both precision and an adequate theoretical grounding. While discussions about supposed generational differences are frequently associated with journalists and popular writers (such as Douglas Coupland in his novel *Generation X*) the term does crop up in academic writing, especially in the field of marketing. Indeed, the idea of generation was introduced and developed by respected social theorists such as Auguste Comte (1798–1857) and Karl Mannheim (1893–1947), but with one or two notable exceptions (such as Dwyer and Wyn, 2001, Edmunds and Turner, 2002 and Wyn and Woodman, 2006), has not been developed so as to account for contemporary situations.

Early theorists were primarily concerned with social dynamics and change and, in different ways, generational groups were presented as agents of change or as associated with distinctive forms of knowledge and consciousness. Comte's position was that conflict between generations ultimately led to social change as the conservatism of the older generation was challenged by the younger age cohort. Comte failed to develop or elaborate these ideas and Mannheim can perhaps be regarded as the first social scientist to fully engage with the idea of generation. In his essay 'The Problem of Generations' which he wrote in 1923, Mannheim suggested that groups of people who grew up at particular points in time tended to share a set of formative experiences, develop common 'modes of behaviour, feeling and thought' (1952: 291) and a unique consciousness.

Karl Mannheim was born in Budapest, Hungary, in 1893 and studied sociology and philosophy in Budapest, Berlin, Freiburg and Paris. Mannheim's first academic post was an unpaid lectureship in Heidelberg, subsequently taking a Chair in sociology and economics at Frankfurt. Dismissed under the Nazi regime in 1933 he came to Britain and obtained a lectureship at the London School of Economics, before moving to the Institute of Education at the University of London to accept a Chair in 1945. During his career he came into contact with a number of influential academics; he was taught by Husserl and Lukács and worked with Alfred Weber (brother of Max) and Norbert Elias (who worked as his assistant). He is best known for his work developing the sociology of knowledge. He died aged 53 in 1947.

For Mannheim, the process of identifying as belonging to a particular generation is conditioned through the way in which social change results in the emergence of new experiences which, in turn, encourage the new generation to challenge the values of the older generation. The pace of change is an important precondition of generational consciousness (which is by no means inevitable), while social, economic or political crises can represent a 'trigger action' (1952: 310) which helps promote an awareness of common interests. When a clash of values occurs, the result can be a generational consciousness in which people become aware of their membership of a particular generation and of the nature of the values and experiences that make their group distinct. Mannheim argued that the distinctiveness of experiences and the challenge to the values that are transmitted as a part of the process of socialization start to become apparent at around the age of 17 as the young person begins the attempt to interpret the world through their own experiences rather than those relayed to them indirectly through the experiences of significant others.

Mannheim also recognized the significance of differences in formative experiences and their impact on the development of a generational consciousness. While he did not attempt to link his theory of generation to his ideas about social class directly, the clear implication is that the sub-groups he referred to as 'generational units' relate to different class locations which result in stratified sets of experiences in the formative years. These generational units have the potential to become agents of social change, although there can also be antagonism between units.

Dunham summarizes Mannheim's generational theory as follows:

1 intergenerational continuity results from socialization into societal values by one's parents;
2 when fresh contact occurs, those values are challenged by generational experiences;
3 the development of a generational consciousness results from this process; and
4 generational units are formed which become a political force for social change.

(Dunham, 1998)

To take an example to illustrate this process, today's teenagers are growing up in a world that is significantly different to that experienced by their parents' generation. They are expected to remain in education for longer

youth studies: an introduction

periods and come to encounter a labour market in which opportunities have become much less clear cut, and perhaps more precarious. They no longer expect, and in some cases do not want, a job for life or to see their lives clearly mapped out for them with defined markers to represent life's milestones. As they become aware that their parents' experiences cannot be used as a road map, they begin to re-think core values. Social change does not lead to the emergence of a new generation who adapt or rebel in uniform ways, because all generations are internally divided, or stratified. Some groups of young people, who may be thought of as a generational unit, may regard some of the circumstances they inherit as threatening (climate change, for example); they might identify radical solutions to the situations they face (direct action to prevent airport or road development) and may identify closely with others who share their views ('green' political groups, for example). Other segments of the same generation might hold different values and support different causes (such as political groups who identify the primary threat to well-being as linked to immigration policies) which may be in direct opposition to those held by other groups of young people.

Mannheim's ideas have been developed by some writers in the Marxist tradition in ways that link directly to social, economic and political change. Feuer (1969), for example, regarded the generational struggle as the driving force of history. This interpretation holds that changes in the equilibrium between the material base and ideological superstructure are affected by youth as key agents of change, and suggests that generational conflict equates to the idea of a 'youth-for-itself', in much the same way that Marx had argued that capitalism would be overthrown when the proletariat ceased to be a 'class-in-itself' and became a 'class-for-itself', as they came to recognize their common interests and their inevitable conflict with the interests of the bourgeoisie.

Also drawing on the work of Mannheim (as well as being influenced by the ideas of Pierre Bourdieu), Edmunds and Turner develop a sociological approach to generation rather than pursue a chronological one, which they regard as 'not sociologically interesting or fruitful' (2002: 116). The theory they develop rests heavily on the idea that generations are shaped by their exposure to traumatic events that have a lasting effect on their culture and consciousness. They also recognize the link between a shared habitus, cultural identification and the ability to engage in political action that promotes generational interests and values.

> A generation can be defined in terms of a collective response to a traumatic event or catastrophe that unites a particular cohort of individuals into a self-conscious age stratum. The traumatic event uniquely cuts off a generation from its past and separates it from the future. The

event becomes the basis of a collective ideology and set of integrating rituals.

(2002: 12)

As examples of the formation of generations out of trauma, they highlight the impact of wars (such as the generation who lived through the First World War and the generation who came of age during the Vietnam War) as well as the impact of economic catastrophe (such as the Great Depression), although clearly any traumatic event has the potential to lead to the formation of a generation. Edmunds and Turner also make a distinction between 'active' and 'passive' generations, with the former actively shaping its cultural milieu: a condition that is explicitly linked to the presence of traumatic events. In this context Edmunds and Turner speculate about the implications of the 11 September 2001 attack on the World Trade Center, which they suggest has the potential to create a generational consciousness among the current cohort of young people.

In comparison to the sophisticated sociological analysis of generations developed by Edmunds and Turner, the ways in which generational groups are constructed by popular writers and market researchers tend to be much more simplistic, although they do frequently have an intuitive appeal. Popularist approaches are essentially functionalist and are largely based on chronology rather than being framed by social and historical events within a time frame that has both quantitative and qualitative dimensions (Pilcher, 1994). They also tend to draw heavily on stereotypes and patterns of consumption and overlook the ways in which class divisions can cross-cut generations.

A wide variety of labels have been used to describe post-war generations: terms such as 'boomers', generation X, 13th generation, generation Y, millennials, and the igeneration, to name but a few. 'Boomers' is a term frequently applied to the generation born in the immediate post-war 'baby boom': typically 1946 to 1964. Essentially it is a demographic descriptor, although commentators suggest that they share certain conditions and, therefore, have an outlook that is partly shaped by their circumstances. In the US, for example, this generation (or at least those born before 1959), were eligible to be drafted to serve in the Vietnam War.[1] The boomers also grew up in a period characterized by relative economic affluence with employment conditions being fairly stable.

The following generation, often referred to as 'generation X' are typically regarded as being born between 1965 and 1980. Taking a very US-centric approach, Howe and Strauss (2000) refer to this generation as the 13th generation: the 13th generation since America gained independence. Sometimes referred to as the 'baby bust' generation, they represent the demographic downturn that began in the early 1960s. 'Generation X'

youth studies: an introduction

though, are not simply defined in terms of a demographic trend, but they are characterized by a set of attitudes that are shaped by the era they grew up in and through rebellion against the perceived passivity of the 'boomers'. In contrast to the affluent lifestyles enjoyed by the 'boomers', generation X experienced the recession of the 1980s and 90s and came of age during the ascendancy of the 'new right' in a period shaped by the leaders such as Ronald Reagan and Margaret Thatcher. Harsh economic circumstances combined with the trimming of welfare regimes can be seen as constituting the sort of trauma identified by Edmunds and Turner (2002) as leading to the establishment of an 'active' generation. The cohesion of 'generation X' therefore has its origins in the opposition to the perceived complacency of the 'boomers' and becomes manifest in the development of anti-establishment views among some 'generational units'.

The generation born between the early 1980s and 2000 are frequently referred to as 'generation Y', as the 'millennials' or the 'igeneration'. According to Howe and Strauss (2000), the term 'generation Y' was coined by the journal *Advertising Age* and is a term strongly rejected by members of the generation who feel that it associates them too closely with 'generation X'. The term 'millennials' is preferred by members of this generation. The 'millennials' experienced a very different upbringing to that of the previous generation and grew up in more affluent circumstances. Whereas 'generation X' experienced a laid-back, laissez-faire style of parenting, the millennials were subject to far greater control and surveillance and enjoyed a level of affluence unknown to the previous generation (Howe and Strauss, 2000).

In contrast to the rebellious and alienated nature of 'generation X', the millennials are presented as optimistic, engaged and accepting of authority. They are viewed as team players who place a premium on achievement both in the classroom and in the world of work. Hence the increased involvement in education has not simply been achieved through the expansion of places, through parental expectations or through a 'tightening bond' between qualifications and jobs; the millennials are presented as conformists who value learning and are committed to 'making something of themselves'. In the context of employment, Trinca and Fox (2004) even suggested that the millennials are so committed to achievement that they sometimes regard work as 'better than sex'. According to Howe and Strauss, the millennials 'have a solid chance to become America's next great generation, as celebrated for their collective deeds a hundred years from now as the generation of John Kennedy, Ronald Reagan, Joe DiMaggio, and Jimmy Stewart is celebrated today' (2000: 5).

A generation can be defined as a society-wide peer group, born over a period roughly the same length as the passage from youth to adulthood (in today's America, around twenty or twenty-one years), who collectively possess a common persona. The length need not always be the same. A generation can be a bit longer or a bit shorter, depending on its coming of age experiences and the vagaries of history.

Howe and Strauss (2000: 40)

Howe and Strauss have written extensively about the characteristics of post-war generations (1991, 1993, 1997, 2000), but their analysis goes beyond the descriptive and contains a theory of social dynamics in which recurring characteristics of generations are linked to social change. The core characteristics of the post-war generations are identified in successive generations from 1459 to the present day. For Howe and Strauss (1997), the characteristics of all generations can be reduced to one of four types (in much the same way that the Chinese horoscope assigns personality types to sets of birth years!): prophets, nomads, heroes and artists. A prophet generation is highly moralistic with strong core values that they vigorously defend; a nomad generation is cynical and tough; a hero generation conformist and highly motivated; and an artist generation emotional and indecisive. For Howe and Strauss, the 'boomers' would be representative of a prophet generation, 'generation X' of a nomad generation, 'millennials' representative of a hero generation and the 'silent generation' (born between 1925 and 1942 and growing up during the Second World War) representative of an artist generation.

While Howe and Strauss develop an imaginative and highly illustrated theory of the relationship between generations and social change, their work is light on theory and lacks the sort of rigour normally found in academic discussions. Essentially they develop a series of historical stereotypes, make 'pop-psychology' links to child-rearing practices and fail to link to economic history or to traumatic events which tend not to follow such a regular pattern.

While the use of generation as a concept through which we can understand the changing experiences of modern youth has not tended to enjoy widespread currency in the social sciences, there has recently been a debate as to whether the idea of generation offers possibilities for theoretical advance. Wyn and Woodman regard the idea of 'social generations' (2007: 375) as providing a way of conceptualizing youth which overcomes the shortcomings in the transition approach. This, they argue, portrays youth as a 'developmental stage of life' (2006: 497) within a model

youth studies: an introduction

based on linear progression from one status (e.g. school) to another (e.g. employment).

> [T]o move beyond the conception of youth as transition, it is neces-
> sary to develop an understanding of how each generation is located
> within its social, political and economic milieu, because, as many soci-
> ologists have pointed out, the meaning of age is constructed through
> the prevailing social and economic relations of society (2006: 497).

Wyn and Woodman argue that the post-1970s generation are confronted by economic and political conditions that are very different from those that shaped the lives of the previous generation, the baby boomers, and represent a 'clear break' (2006: 501) with earlier patterns of life. Importantly, they argue that the tendency to benchmark the experiences of generation Y against those of the baby boomers tends to lead to the conclusion that contemporary transitions are, in some way, defective.

In responding to the ideas of Wyn and Woodman (2006), Roberts (2007) accepts that there have been significant changes to the life contexts and experiences of young people, but argues that youth must still be regarded as a life stage underpinned by transition. Youth research in a transitional perspective, he argues, is not preoccupied with the transition from school to work but has always involved an interest in other aspects of young people's lives, such as family formation, housing and consumption. He also suggests that transitions, which he regards as socially constructed, are not necessarily linear but have always involved a degree of complexity. For Roberts, there is no need to choose between transitional and generational perspectives: they complement each other.

> Inviting youth researchers to choose between transition and gener-
> ation is like insisting that diners choose either fish or chips. The
> transition and generation perspectives are not mutually exclusive: they
> can be used complementarily (2007: 265).

Roberts suggests that comprehensive transitional perspectives (which would examine the ways in which childhood origins shape routes and destinations) are relatively uncommon in youth research, which is more likely to be characterized by cross-sectional or short-term longitudinal studies (involving, for example, tracing movements from unemployment to employment). While this is true, many countries do support birth cohort studies and these have been used to examine the experiences of young people over a long period of time and in the context of families and localities. Through these studies researchers have been able to examine the ways in which various aspects of the family and childhood experiences impact on factors such as educational performance, on outcomes in the labour market, on health and on subjective orientations (e.g. Ferri *et al.*, 2003). By comparing cohorts born at different points in time, researchers have also been able to study changes between generations. Cohorts are not necessarily synonymous with generations in a sociological sense (a cohort can be defined as one born in a particular time frame, but such individuals do not necessarily differ significantly from an earlier cohort in their experiences or values, nor do they necessarily develop a generational consciousness), but are often treated as such.

I n Britain, there are three large-scale cohort studies which have been used extensively to comment on the changing experiences of 'generations'. The prime mover behind the British birth cohorts was Neville Butler, a paediatrician and professor of child health at the University of Bristol. Butler's interest was in perinatal mortality and the first cohort, comprised of all babies born in one week in March 1958. While he never intended to launch a survey which would follow the cohort throughout their lives, by seizing a number of opportunities he increased the scope of the study to cover a broad spectrum of human experiences, from health to education, employment, family establishment and beyond. The 1958 cohort has been surveyed nine times, most recently in 2008 at the age of 50. The second birth cohort began in 1970 and included all 17,200 babies born over the course of one week in April. That cohort has now been surveyed nine times, most recently in 2012 at age 42. For the third cohort, the millennium cohort study, the population comprised babies born over a 12-month period beginning in Autumn 2000 with 18,818 selected through a stratified sample design, based on electoral wards, to make sure that deprived groups and ethnic minorities were adequately represented. Surveys have been conducted at 9 months, 3 years, 5 years, 8 years and 12 years (2012). Full details can be found at the Centre for Longitudinal Studies website (www.cls.ioe.ac.uk/page.aspx?&sitesectionid=26&sitesection title=About+the+Centre+for+Longitudinal+Studies).

Psychological perspectives

In many ways, social psychologists with an interest in youth share the same concerns as other social scientists, while clinical psychologists tend to focus on cognitive disorders and the physiology of brain development.

Social psychologists are interested in a broad range of experiences (such as education, employment, health, the family and consumption), and are also likely to take account of the objective constraints which shape subjective experiences. There are, however, certain dimensions of the youth experience that tend to attract greater attention, such as the formation of identity, relationships, sexuality, well-being and psycho-social disorders.

Lerner and Steinberg (2004) argue that three stages in the psychological study of adolescence can be identified. The first stage, characteristic of the period prior to the 1970s, tended to involve 'grand theory' and was marked by a concern to describe the processes which led to the transformation from dependent to fully developed forms of consciousness. For Jung, adolescence involved a 'psychic birth' or a 'psychic revolution', set against a backdrop of the 'eruption of sexuality' that characterizes puberty (Frankel, 1998: 114). Adolescence is 'a process of experiencing, reorganizing and integrating one's past psychological development within a new context of physical sexual maturity' (Laufer and Laufer, 1984, quoted in Frankel, 1998: 31). Writers such as Hall (1904), Erikson (1968) and Anna Freud (1958) regarded adolescence as a period of great psychological disturbance, a period of 'storm and stress', of 'universal and inevitable upheaval' (Lerner and Steinberg, 2004: 3) associated with this 'psychic birth' (Frankel, 1998: 115). Adolescence involves a process of individuation, of separation and emerging independence which is associated with discomfort or trauma. It is important to note that the idea of individuation used by psychologists is very different from the process of individualization used by Beck (1992), which is discussed in Chapter 2.

> [Individuation] is the process by which individual beings are formed and differentiated; in particular, it is the development of the psychological individual as being distinct from the general, collective psychology. Individuation, therefore, is a process of differentiation, having for its goal the development of the individual personality.
>
> (Jung, quoted in Frankel, 1998: 115)

The second stage in psychological interpretation stretches from the 1970s to around 2000 and is characterized by mid-range theory developed so as 'to account for person-environment relations within selected domains of development' (Lerner and Steinberg, 2004: 2). The focus here is on an empirical understanding of adolescent psychological development within their social and historical contexts. This nested approach to fields of experience was most fully developed in the work of Bronfenbrenner (1979) whose 'Ecological Systems Theory' attempted to map the relationship between individuals, families, schools and peer groups, external environments and broader socio-cultural contexts.

The third stage identified by Lerner and Steinberg begins around 2000 and involves the emergence of a more practical and policy-oriented psychology which aims to transfer knowledge in ways that 'advance civil society and promote positive development' (2004: 3) among young people. It is at this stage that the shared assumptions and interdisciplinary agendas start to become clear, involving a strong convergence of psychology with other social science disciplines. In common with other disciplines, psychologists focus on young people's lives in virtually all contexts, and they have also started to accept the validity of approaches that suggest the emergence of a new phase of life that stands between adolescence and adulthood, which sometimes involves a developmental moratorium (Côté, 2000; Arnett, 2004). These developments justify the decision to avoid unnecessary distinctions between psychology and other social sciences in this book.

Policy perspectives

In many countries, it is difficult to identify a coherent set of policies that relate to youth. Youth policy tends to be fragmented and articulated within broad thematic areas, such as employment, health, criminal justice and education, with marked variations to adult policy acknowledged where appropriate. Youth policies tend to relate to defined age groups, rather than by the types of transitional markers used by social scientists. Moreover, the age ranges used to signify youth frequently vary according to government departments: they are higher in welfare-related areas (such as social security) where there is an assumption that the young person is dependent on their parents, and lower in areas where the state wants to be able to hold an individual accountable for their actions (such as criminal justice).

> Youth policy in Britain has developed in a largely piecemeal and uncoordinated way, with each different Department of State addressing only those aspects of 'youth problems' which it sees as falling within its domain.
>
> (Coles, 1995: 1)

Here Britain is far from unusual and it is rare to find either a holistic approach to youth policy or a consistent set of principles that underpin policies. To an extent, youth research can also be fragmented and focused on discrete areas of young people's lives. In each of the chapters of this

youth studies: an introduction

book, the implications of youth-related policies are explored and significant gaps are highlighted. However, it is also important to begin to think about some of the implications of changes in the life course described in this chapter for effective youth policy.

While much youth research has been driven by policy concerns, it would be fair to say that, in a macro perspective, academic understandings of changes in the experiences of youth have yet to lend shape to government policy in any of the advanced societies. This is not to say that youth research has not influenced policy in numerous ways, but that the holistic knowledge of changes in the life experiences of modern youth has not fully permeated the policy agenda in a meaningful way.

The key messages for policy that emerge from our knowledge of changes in the life course relate to the protraction of transitions and to the process of individualization. If policies are underpinned by research, then they should not be based on an assumption of linearity, they must avoid one-size-fits-all approaches and should provide respect for youth and young adulthood as a time of experimentation, rather than attempt to expedite rapid transitions. An acknowledgement of the prevalence of non-linear transitions requires the facilitation of backtracking and new starts, and the opening up of second (and third) chances in all policy areas, especially education and training. The individualization of routes means that it is necessary to provide bespoke support for biographical projects and imaginative, youth-centred policies that encourage practitioners to work with young people to help them fulfil their aspirations.

The protraction of transitions provides opportunities for experimentation and, with appropriate safety nets in place, can facilitate a process of meaningful exploration and identity development. In this context, Rustin and Chamberlayne speak of 'capacity building' replacing 'welfare as the object of social policy' (2002: 11) and suggest that 'transitions can only be made well, and with lessened risk of human damage, where there is social and mental space to think out their implications' (2002: 4).

> The theory of 'risk society' suggests that enhanced 'reflexivity' is a necessary concomitant of the social environment that faces individuals in risk society, since it offers a better survival strategy than collective identification and affiliation. As individuals become more exposed to changes in their lives, with the disappearance of 'jobs for life', the insistence on flexibility, and the demand for repeated retraining, reflexive self-monitoring and individualized life strategies becomes necessary for survival. This has become the guiding norm of the new social order, a new kind of 'governmentality' in Focauldian terms.
>
> (Rustin and Chamberlayne, 2002: 11)

In modern contexts, the policy environment for youth and young adulthood requires a radical re-think. Holistic approaches to policy, grounded in an understanding of changes in the lives of young people, can help support the social justice agenda and provide the social space in which barriers can be broken down and opportunities opened up.

Summary points

1 Youth is a socially constructed category, a period of semi-dependence, falling between childhood and adulthood. It should not be defined in chronological terms as it is constructed differently across time and between societies.

2 The examination of young people's lives provides a unique window on processes of social and economic change and facilitates the exploration of power and privilege.

3 Elder developed life course theory as a way of overcoming normative approaches and setting lives in contexts that are dynamic and linked to the lives of others.

4 In youth research, the metaphors used to represent transitions have changed to reflect new contexts as well as to incorporate theoretical developments. Contemporary models have tended to place an increased emphasis on the role of agency.

5 Although the idea of generation is not commonly used in youth research, it does have strong theoretical roots, especially in the work of Mannheim. Although contested, in recent years generation has begun to receive more attention, especially in the work of Edmunds and Turner, and Wyn and Woodman.

6 Psychologists have tended to focus on distinct aspects of young people's experiences, especially in the area of identity studies. Recent trends show something of a convergence with other social sciences and the emergence of interdisciplinary agendas.

Further questions

1 Explain why contemporary youth researchers prefer to use the term 'life course' rather than 'lifecycle'.

2 To what extent can generations be said to drive social and political change?

3 How do the terms 'youth' and 'adolescence' differ?

4 In what ways can youth be said to be socially constructed?

5 Outline the main differences between the baby boomers and generation Y.

6 What are the factors that shape a generation?

Further reading

Coleman, J. C. (2011) *The Nature of Adolescence*, 4th edn, Abingdon: Routledge.

Furlong, A. and Cartmel, F. (2007) *Young People and Social Change: Individualization and Risk in Late Modernity*, Maidenhead: Open University Press.

Heinz, W. R. (2009) 'Youth transitions in an age of uncertainty', in A. Furlong (ed.), *Handbook of Youth and Young Adulthood: New Perspectives and Agendas*, Abingdon: Routledge.

Henderson, S., Holland, J., McGrellis, S., Sharpe, S. and Thomson, R. (2007) *Inventing Adulthoods: A Biographical Approach to Youth Transitions*, London: Sage.

Howe, N. and Strauss, W. (2000) *Millennials Rising: The Next Great Generation*, New York: Vintage Books.

White, R. and Wyn, J. (2004) *Youth and Society: Exploring the Social Dynamics of Youth Experience*, Melbourne: Oxford University Press.

Internet links

Web links and YouTube clips on generation Y:
www.usatoday.com/money/workplace/2005-11-06-gen-y_x.htm
www.youtube.com/watch?v=2ZUPYI975GQ&feature=related
www.youtube.com/watch?v=vknHKTy1MLY

YouTube clip of Neil Howe talking about generations
www.youtube.com/watch?v=BGGa-9d-50Q

YouTube clip on Bronfenbrenner's theory
www.youtube.com/watch?v=me71030IE-g&feature=related

chapter 2

Divisions in youth

Contents

Conceptualizing divisions

Although they belong to a common age cohort, young people do not represent a homogeneous group. The same divisions exist among young people as among older age groups: class, gender, 'race', ethnicity and so on. In time, young people will leave behind their youth and become recognized as adults, but the socio-economic divisions that shaped their lives as young people will often characterize their adult lives. The interest of youth researchers is often stimulated by the enduring question of how – despite the desire to provide young people with a wide range of opportunities – social inequalities are frequently reproduced across generations. Youth, which should be a time of opportunity, or flux and transformation, is all too often about assuming roles that are in keeping with their social and economic origins. Youth in itself, though, is an important division, and one people will escape through the process of ageing, but nevertheless a subordinate category and, like childhood, one that defines a section of the population that can 'legitimately' be discriminated against. In all advanced societies, young people's exclusion from certain key aspects of citizenship is enshrined in legislation. They may be prevented from marrying, living independently or from drinking alcohol. They may be forced to engage in various activities against their will, such as education, and may have certain activities closed off to them, such as work in specific occupations. Discrimination may be temporary, but it still involves the state-sanctioned denial of various rights and obligations of citizenship.

The justification for the restrictions we place on youth can involve benevolence and regard for their security and long-term well-being. The prevalent view is that young people are incapable of making crucial decisions and need protecting from their tendency to act impulsively. Restrictions can also be linked to the state's concern with the development of human resources, to a perceived need to promote conformity through a lengthy period of secondary socialization and to a desire to manage the size of the labour force by retaining sections of the population in the holding devices of education and training.

Traditionally researchers have focused on three key divisions that are said to shape and differentiate young people's experiences: gender, social class and 'race' or ethnicity. Across different dimensions of their lives, young people's experiences are clearly shaped by gender. From early childhood, girls and boys are treated differently in the home and school (Oakley, 1981). Although lacking any scientific underpinning, boys and girls are often thought to possess different characteristics: boys may be portrayed as aggressive or assertive, while girls may be thought of as emotional or submissive. From an early age, the leisure experiences of boys and girls tend to differ and they may develop different interests and tastes. At school, their preferred subjects may differ. As young people, they may develop different aspirations and expectations with regard to their lives as adults, and their employment careers and domestic lives may take different shapes.

These differences are not just important because they affect people's lives qualitatively, lend shape to day-to-day experiences and impact on the assumptions of people with whom they fall into contact: they also lead to crucial quantitative differences. Males and females perform differently at school and may follow different educational pathways; they enter different occupations and face different career structures and wage prospects. They may be treated differently in public and social policy, by the courts and by health professionals. In other words, structured inequalities are built on the foundations of gender, even though there is nothing in their biological essence that explains or justifies such divisions.

While gender tends to be firmly embedded in our consciousness, social class affects young people's core experiences even though they may not recognize the existence of such divisions or have ideas about which class they belong to. Class is often thought of as an old-fashioned category, as something linked to 'old world' societies like the UK or France and as having far less relevance in the supposedly more open, 'new world', societies such as the US or Australia. While invisible to some, class has a powerful impact on the lives of young people in all developed societies. There is a strong correlation between social class and the area we grow up in, the relative wealth of our families, the schools and colleges we attend, the jobs we enter and the regularity with which we become unemployed. Government statisticians, sociologists and political scientists all use social class as a way of describing and understanding unequal outcomes and differences in the pathways people follow, or the ways in which they behave. Psephologists use class to understand and predict voting behaviour; sociologists may use class to explore differential educational outcomes; and market researchers use class to predict patterns of consumption or to pitch marketing campaigns effectively.

Of course people think of class and operationalize class in different ways. The person on the street may see class in simple terms, as a division between rich and poor or between a working class, a middle class and an upper class. They may have given little thought to what it is that might determine class membership or to what class they themselves belong to (in fact most will describe themselves as middle class). Social scientists also conceptualize class in different ways, sometimes on the basis of the theoretical traditions they subscribe to; at other times, pragmatically, in terms of the ways in which official data is presented to them. Like the person on the street, although for different reasons, many contemporary social scientists have come to challenge the existence of class.

As a set of categories that often involve visual differences, 'race' or ethnicity can be a division that people recognize and identify with more readily than class. As with class, those with different ethnic origins may be disadvantaged or advantaged in a variety of ways: in school, in employment and in encounters with the criminal justice system, for example. But 'race' or ethnicity are complex categories and, as Webster has argued, 'it cannot be presumed from the outset that race or ethnicity will be the overriding or main factors determining black or minority experiences' (2009: 66).

youth studies: an introduction

Sociologists often put the term race in inverted commas in order to highlight their belief that 'race' is a socially constructed category. In other words, there is no scientific or genetic distinction that marks someone out as belonging to one racial group or another. Most of us, whatever the colour of our skin, have a complex genetic make-up, reflecting historical patterns of migration and inter-marriage. The use of the term ethnic tends to suggest a common culture, and while that might apply to certain minorities, in the main those who may be allocated to a certain group on the basis of visual characteristics tend to identity with the 'mainstream' cultures of the society in which they live. While a young person living in northern Europe might have a black or brown skin colour, it does not mean that they identify with an African or Asian ethnic culture.

A further complexity is that 'race' is often cross-cut by other factors that are associated with disadvantage. New immigrants may face greater difficulties than those who are well established, some may not speak the language of the country in which they have come to reside, others may lack a work permit. Some immigrant groups may be subject to greater discrimination than others, while certain groups are less likely than others to come to a new country with professional or business skills. In some countries, aboriginal groups face discrimination in a wide range of institutional settings, despite having roots in a country that stretch back much further than the white settlers.

In addition to the 'big three', there are many other divisions that are often overlooked. Various disabilities can lead to inequalities and to exclusion, as can sexual orientation. There are various spatial inequalities that impact on life chances: third world versus first world, north versus south, urban versus rural, affluent cities or neighbourhoods versus deprived cities and neighbourhoods. In the following sections these divisions will be explored: we will highlight some of the ways in which such divisions might be changing and draw attention to the implication of these changes.

Class, mobility and exclusion

If we are to use social class to help us understand the structured inequalities that shape young people's experiences, we first have to be clear about what we mean by class. In sociology, the theoretical roots of class are to be found in the work of Karl Marx and Max Weber and these perspectives (especially the Weberian position) shape modern thinking on class and the way in which we operationalize class in official statistics. Marx thought of classes as objective structures which impact on our experiences and life chances. For Marx, there are two major classes in capitalist society, the bourgeoisie and the proletariat, together with a third class, the petit bourgeoisie, which stands between them (and which he thought would become swallowed up by the other two classes over time). Marx thought of class as a relationship to the means of production: the bourgeoisie own and control the means of production, while the proletariat have nothing to sell but the exchange of their labour power. With relationships between classes underpinned by exploitation, classes are in a state of constant conflict: and class conflict is the driving force of history.

The history of all hitherto existing society is the history of class struggles.

Freeman and slave, patrician and plebeian, lord and serf, guild-master and journeyman, in a word, oppressor and oppressed, stood in constant opposition to one another, carried on an uninterrupted, now hidden, now open fight, a fight that each time ended, either in a revolutionary reconstitution of society at large, or in the common ruin of the contending classes.

In the earlier epochs of history, we find almost everywhere a complicated arrangement of society into various orders, a manifold gradation of social rank. In ancient Rome we have patricians, knights, plebeians, slaves; in the Middle Ages, feudal lords, vassals, guild-masters, journeymen, apprentices, serfs; in almost all of these classes, again, subordinate gradations.

The modern bourgeois society that has sprouted from the ruins of feudal society has not done away with class antagonisms. It has but established new classes, new conditions of oppression, new forms of struggle in place of the old ones.

Our epoch, the epoch of the bourgeoisie, possesses, however, this distinct feature: it has simplified class antagonisms. Society as a whole is more and more splitting up into two great hostile camps, into two great classes directly facing each other – Bourgeoisie and Proletariat.

From *The Manifesto of the Communist Party* (Marx and Engels 1848)

While Marx thought of classes as determined by economic position, Weber, while agreeing that economic classes were the prime source of inequality, also thought that status and party were central to the way in which power is distributed. On the economic level, Weber adopted a broader view than Marx and argued that key resources included not just capital but ownership of skills and credentials, as these were assets that are traded on the market in ways that secure advantage: one's position in a market has a powerful impact on one's life chances. Status and party are divisions that tend to reflect economic position, but offer the potential for alternative lines of stratification. Those with economic power, for example, tend to enjoy high status, while those who lack economic resources tend to have low status. However, people who lack economic power do sometimes enjoy high status: for example, clergy may enjoy high status without having significant economic power, while a member of the aristocracy who has fallen on hard times might still enjoy high status. By party Weber refers to groups, such as political parties, who organize themselves in ways that allow them to influence agendas and seek power: as with status groups, party members can potentially enjoy a level of power that goes beyond that derived from economic position.

Essentially the socio-economic classifications used in the official statistics of many countries are built on a Weberian tradition. While occupations are used as the basic building blocks, individuals are assigned to socio-economic classes not simply on the basis of the typical economic standing of occupations, but also of the skills and credentials of occupational incumbents and, to an extent, patterns of prestige. In the UK, since the 2001 census, the system of classification (referred to as NS-SEC, shorthand for National Statistics, Socio-Economic Classification) has been a fivefold one which is used in all official statistics and surveys. It is common for the first three classifications to be referred to as middle class occupations and the later two as working class occupations.

- Managerial and professional occupations
- Intermediate occupations
- Small employers and own account workers
- Lower supervisory and technical occupations
- Semi-routine and routine occupations

When social class is used to explain inequalities among young people, researchers typically base their classifications on the occupations held by the young persons' parents. This usually still applies in the early stages of a young person's employment, partly because young people frequently begin their working lives in low-skill, low-status jobs and may take several years to fulfil their occupational potential. Students, for example, frequently work in routine jobs while in education and may continue to work in these jobs for some time after graduation.

As youth researchers are often interested in patterns of social reproduction, they focus on the relationship between class origins and destinations. The study of patterns of social mobility leads to an examination of the extent to which, and the ways in which, the social position of the family affects the lives and careers of young people. In Chapter 4 we will show that, despite changes in patterns of educational participation that affect all social classes, young people's family of origin remains a strong predictor of occupational destinations. The study of social mobility is complex because patterns of opportunities change from one generation to the next: the proportion of professional and managerial jobs has been expanding while the proportion of unskilled jobs has been contracting. As such, absolute levels of social mobility have increased, while the relative chances of young people from a particular social class accessing certain social positions may have remained static or even declined.

> Sociologists make a distinction between absolute and relative social mobility in analysing intergenerational mobility. Absolute social mobility is concerned with the absolute number or proportion of people in a social group who are upwardly or downward mobile. Relative social mobility is concerned with the chances people from different backgrounds have of attaining different social positions.
>
> (Aldrige, 2001: 6)

This seemingly contradictory distinction is well illustrated in the 2009 report of the UK Panel on Fair Access to the Professions. The panel noted that the proportion of professional and managerial jobs in the UK increased from 1 in 14 in 1911, to 1 in 8 in 1951 and 1 in 3 in 2001. As a result of this expansion in professional and managerial occupations, in absolute terms, social mobility increased resulting in a significant growth in the number of young people from working class families who entered these occupations. At the same time, they provide evidence to support the claim that in relative terms mobility is becoming more restricted; 'access to society's top jobs and professions has become less, not more, socially representative over time' (Panel on Fair Access to the Professions, 2009: 12).

> Evidence we have received on the family background that professionals grew up in (measured by their family's income when they were growing up), confirms that senior professionals have increasingly come from wealthier-than-average backgrounds. Professionals born in 1970 typically grew up in a family with an income 27% above that of the average family, compared with a figure of 17% for professionals born in 1958. Doctors born in 1970 typically grew up in families with incomes 63% higher than the average family's income, and lawyers in families

youth studies: an introduction

with incomes 64% above the average family's income. [...] Despite a sharp growth in professional employment opportunities over recent decades, access to the professions is becoming the preserve of those from a smaller and smaller part of the social spectrum.

(Panel on Fair Access to the Professions, 2009: 14)

Many youth researchers are particularly interested in patterns of immobility and in understanding why, despite the creation of new occupational opportunities, some groups fail to make any headway and get trapped in low-paid and insecure positions. In this context, a distinction is sometimes made between young people who are included and those who are excluded. The idea of social exclusion has enjoyed widespread recognition and, in Europe, has underpinned youth and employment policies developed by the European Commission. In policy terms, exclusion is often applied in the context of employment. Those without jobs are regarded as at risk of exclusion, and measures must be introduced to facilitate inclusion. In the 1997 Luxembourg Summit, member states agreed to commit to ensuring that 'every unemployed young person is offered a new start before reaching six months of unemployment, in the form of training, retraining, work practice, a job or other employability measure' (European Council, 1997). The 2000 Lisbon Summit went further with a commitment to address poverty and social exclusion.

For social scientists, the idea of social exclusion is somewhat problematic, especially in the loose way it is used in policy circles where exclusion is seen as linked to long-term unemployment and poverty and, especially, to multiple disadvantage. Social exclusion can be thought of as a possible consequence of long-term unemployment, especially in countries that provide weak welfare safety nets, where disconnection and poverty can lead to disempowerment. In the UK, the definition proposed by Levitas and colleagues is widely used by government agencies:

Social exclusion is a complex and multi-dimensional process. It involves the lack or denial of resources, rights, goods and services, and the inability to participate in the normal relationships and activities, available to the majority of people in a society, whether in economic, social, cultural or political arenas. It affects both the quality of life of individuals and the equity and cohesion of society as a whole.

(Levitas et al., 2007: 25)

David Miliband, as UK Minister of State for Communities and Local Government, suggested that degrees of social exclusion could be identified and coined the term 'deep exclusion' to refer to those excluded in multiple ways. As examples of deep exclusion he proposed 'the person struggling with basic skills seems definitively socially excluded if they are also long-term unemployed, the child in poverty seems more likely to be socially excluded if their housing is poor, and their parent suffering mental illness. The homeless person on drugs and without skills or family is definitively on the edge of society' (2006: 7).

Understood in these terms, the social exclusion of young people can be regarded as linked to the inadequate provision of resources by the state. Long-term unemployment, for example, is less likely to lead to exclusion in countries that provide generous welfare benefits (Furlong and Cartmel, 2001; Heikkinen, 2001). Similarly, the young person living in a poor, inadequately housed family is excluded as a direct result of inadequate welfare benefits and a lack of high-standard public housing. Yet social exclusion is often linked to class cultures, individual deficits and fecklessness: what Levitas (1998) refers to as a 'moral underclass discourse' or what Westergaard has called the 'moral turpitude' thesis (Westergaard, 1992).

This cultural deficit model has a long history and has frequently been applied to young people who are seen as excluded on account of their own (in)actions. In other words, the social exclusion of young people is presented as a moral deficit issue, with the excluded often represented as an 'underclass' holding alternative, often criminal, value systems. Seen in these terms, one of the key divisions among young people relates to whether someone is part of the overall class structure, or whether they lie beneath it, representing what Marx (1947) would have referred to as a 'lumpenproletariat'.

The implications in labelling sections of the young population as an underclass have been explored extensively in the literature on youth, perhaps most comprehensively in MacDonald's (1997) book, *Youth, the 'Underclass' and Social Exclusion*. MacDonald defines the underclass as

> a social group or class of people located at the bottom of the class structure who, over time, have become structurally separate and culturally distinct from the regularly employed working class and society in general through processes of social and economic change (particularly de-industrialisation) and/or through patterns of cultural behaviour, who are now persistently reliant on state benefits and almost permanently confined to living in poorer conditions and neighbourhoods (1997: 3–4).

The underclass thesis has been pursued most vigorously by commentators associated with the New Right, and developed in the UK and US during the Thatcher/Reagan era. An American academic, Charles Murray (1990), was particularly influential in right-wing circles and in parts of the press. Murray argued that in a context of over-generous welfare systems, a rise in unemployment (some of which he regarded as self-inflicted), and a rise in crime

youth studies: an introduction

and illegitimacy had created the conditions for the growth of an underclass that threatened the social order. Young people were growing up in families without fathers, were choosing to support their lifestyles through crime rather than employment and were exploiting the welfare system by having illegitimate children as a way of qualifying for social housing.

Murray's views were strongly opposed by sociologists such as Bagguley and Mann (1992) who highlighted the lack of empirical evidence to support the underclass thesis. More recently, research in poor neighbourhoods by Shildrick and colleagues (2012) has cast doubt on the idea that 'cultures of worklessness' helped explain the transmission of severe disadvantage across generations. The term underclass increasingly became unfashionable in the late 1990s as European policy makers embraced and refined the idea of social exclusion in ways that allowed the identification and targeting of 'degrees of severity' (Levitas *et al.*, 2007: 9), ranging from 'wide' to 'deep' exclusion (Miliband, 2006). As MacDonald and Marsh suggest, 'underclass theory has become subsumed into the even more widespread and influential political, policy and academic discourse of social exclusion' (2005: 21).

From class to capital

For a number of researchers one of the key divisions among young people relates to the possession, or lack of, human, social and cultural capital. Essentially, these capitals can be seen as a class-based resource and as a dimension of the process through which social divisions are reproduced. The terms human, social and cultural capital should not be confused. Human capital is often thought of as having its roots in 1960s economics (e.g. Field, 2003), although the idea (if not the term) can be traced back to Max Weber. Human capital is typically used to refer to things like knowledge, skills and credentials that are typically traded for advantage in a labour market and through this process frequently transformed into economic capital. Whereas human capital can be thought of as an individual attribute, social capital highlights the value of collective relations. As Field puts it, 'the central idea of social capital is that social networks are a valuable asset' (2003: 12). We derive considerable benefits from the social groups with which we are involved; they may provide us with crucial knowledge, put us in contact with people who can help us or provide various types of support.

The term cultural capital tends to be associated with Bourdieu (1977) who used it to illustrate the ways in which people are able to use status and markers of distinction, such as taste, to secure advantage. Cultural capital can be used, for example, to secure educational advantages which in turn can be traded in the labour market. The middle class parents' knowledge of how education systems work, how to deal effectively with teachers and how to ensure that their offspring receive a good educational experience are factors linked to cultural capital. Moreover, a family who have fallen on hard times economically may still be able to benefit from their cultural capital. 'Shaped by family circumstances and school tuition, cultural capital can to some extent operate independently of monetary holdings, and even compensate for lack of money as part of an individual's or a group's strategy to pursue power and status' (Field, 2003: 14).

In youth studies, the idea of social capital was introduced by the American sociologist James Coleman. Stemming from his work on social background and educational equality, Coleman argued that the relationship between social class and educational attainment was mediated both by peer relations within schools and by the ways in which educational establishments were integrated within local communities. Young people who were part of school-based peer groups that reinforced educational values enjoyed advantages over those from the same social class who belonged to groups where those who worked hard were subject to peer ridicule. Similarly, young people attending Catholic schools outperformed those from a similar class background who attended non-religious schools; a factor explained by levels of community integration and shared norms.

> Coleman argued that the most important factor in explaining this pattern was the impact of community norms upon parents and pupils, which functioned to endorse teachers' expectations, and he concluded that communities were therefore a source of social capital that could offset some of the impact of social and economic disadvantage within the family.
>
> (Field, 2003: 23)

James S. Coleman (1926–95) was born in Chicago, studied at Purdue and Columbia universities and taught at Stanford, Chicago and Johns Hopkins. He is best known for his work on social theory, especially in refining rational choice theory, and in the field of sociology of education where he wrote the highly influential report *Equality of Educational Opportunity* (1966) (widely known as the

youth studies: an introduction

'Coleman Report'), which highlighted the relationship between social background and educational attainment. He also wrote several important books on youth, notably *The Adolescent Society* (1961), *Youth: Transition to Adulthood* (1974) and *Becoming Adult in a Changing Society* (1985).

In his book *Bowling Alone*, Putnam (2000) made a distinction between 'bridging capital', which can work to reduce the impact of social and economic divisions through facilitating access to new social networks, and 'bonding capital', which can reinforce social divisions. Bonding capital

is based on community solidarity, but creates boundaries through which it becomes difficult to pass. It may be a characteristic of poor communities or disadvantaged groups. It is protective, allowing the community/group to tolerate negative labelling by outsiders, but protection comes at a price. Staying on in a disadvantaged community means increasingly restricted access to wider opportunities.

(Jones, n.d.: 4)

Gender

Despite changes in patterns of educational performance, the division between males and females remains significant and impacts on virtually all contexts of young people's lives. Obviously gender is cross-cut by other divisions, such as social class or 'race', some of which might be regarded as of greater importance. The young woman from a professional family who lives in an affluent neighbourhood and attends private school may have more in common (both subjectively and in terms of future life chances) with a young man who enjoys similar advantages than with a young woman living on a social housing estate in a welfare-dependent family.

Gender differences add a layer of complexity to experiences and outcomes and represent a persistent source of inequality that we ignore at our peril. In education males and females tend to specialize in different subject areas, and in the labour market they are concentrated in different sectors and are differentially placed within organizational hierarchies (Delamont, 1980; Arnot, 2002). Parents treat boys and girls differently, while employers promote males more rapidly and provide them with superior remuneration. As adults, males and females still tend to undertake different domestic and caring roles and may experience different treatment by social, welfare and criminal justice systems.

The important differences that are attributed to gender cannot be explained in terms of their location in the class structure; therefore other explanations must be sought. The first set of explanations rest on subjective differences in expectations, attitudes, assumptions and preferences, many of which are acquired as part of the process of gender socialization, involving the development of gendered identities. Many authors have highlighted the differences in the ways boys and girls are treated in the family, with boys encouraged to be more outgoing and assertive and girls more caring and submissive (Oakley, 1981). From an early age, occupational aspirations are differentiated by gender, partly reflecting contemporary images of females in the labour market and, in particular, family role models (Sharpe, 1976). Changes in patterns of participation in the labour market that have led to greater female participation, combined with new forms of educational participation, have helped raise aspirations. Yet gender still has an impact on the fields of study chosen, with females frequently selecting courses providing routes into low paid, feminized, industries: forms of employment that 'draw on the stereotypical attributes of femininity including docility, empathy with the needs of others, and an ability to produce a courteous "smiling" performance in exchanges with customers and clients' (McDowell, 2009: 60).

The second set of explanations can be characterized as objective rather than subjective: forms of difference that are structured and relate directly to resources or power structures. On this level inequalities may be maintained through direct discrimination or through structuring opportunities in ways that limit their appeal to either males or females. While many countries have made direct gender discrimination illegal, it does still occur, although is often applied on a level that is subtle enough to bypass legislation. Antisocial shift work, for example, may not be regarded as 'family friendly' and may be rejected by those (largely females) who take the heaviest share of the domestic burden. In the contemporary labour market, characterized by 'feminized' service industries, employers may reject young males who are seen as having inappropriate attitudes or appearances (McDowell, 2009).

Another set of explanations builds on the idea of social capital, in particular the ways in which norms, values and forms of support within peer groups impact on patterns of behaviour. In the labour market, for example, bridging social capital can lead to employment through informal, gendered networks and sources of advice. In education, some have argued that social capital can be thought of as an important resource that has impacted on gender differentials in patterns of attainment (Schuller, 2007). 'Girls help each other to do well by building peer groups that reinforce educational achievement as valuable, and at the same time provide practical information and assistance' (Schuller, 2007: 191). Bonding social capital can also be seen as reinforcing gender divisions and restricting opportunity. Young

youth studies: an introduction

men, for example, may identify so closely with working class masculinity that they regard work in the expanding service industries as 'women's work' (McDowell, 2009).

'Race'

Official statistics relating to a wide range of situations, such as health, employment and education, show powerful inequalities that are distributed along the lines of 'race'. Even though social scientists regard race as a term that has no biological credibility, statistics clearly show that a wide range of outcomes cluster in ways that suggest a 'race' effect. There are various ways we can explain this.

The first explanation can be thought of as the structural position, and one interpretation is to focus on the impact of colonialism, diasporas and intersections with class structures. Indeed, one of the greatest difficulties faced by those who wish to examine inequalities attributable to 'race' or ethnicity, is separating the 'race' effect from the class effect. Indian families in the UK, for example, are more likely to be middle class than are those from Pakistani or Afro-Caribbean families. The tight relationship between 'race' and class can be linked to patterns of immigration and to labour market opportunities in the host country. In the UK, immigrants from the Caribbean in the post-war period were explicitly recruited to fill low-skill positions in the labour market. In the US, industrial labour was recruited from ex-slaves, from migrants from Ireland and Eastern Europe and, more recently, from the Caribbean, Mexico and South America.

Once absorbed into the lower working class positions in the new country, these minority groups found opportunities for upward mobility blocked in the same way as the white members of the lower working classes. Labour market segmentation and the geographic clustering of new immigrants in the industrial centres resulted in blocked opportunities. In many countries, members of ethnic minorities are heavily concentrated in poor neighbourhoods and in parts of the country that have been hit badly by processes of deindustrialization (Mason, 2003). Here Wacquant (2008) refers to 'hyperghettos', 'stigmatized neighbourhoods situated at the very bottom of the hierarchical system of places that compose the metropolis' (2008: 1), among them the black ghettos in the US and the French *banlieue*. Racial discrimination also restricts movement. For the children of migrants, the lack of economic, cultural and social capital restricts intergenerational mobility through education, in the same way as for the white working classes.

Of course not all immigrant groups find mobility is blocked in the same way. In particular, skilled workers have been encouraged to migrate to 'new world' countries such as Australia and Canada from Europe and Asia, while

Indian professionals have migrated to the UK. Just as the context of their migration differs from that experienced by less skilled groups, so do their economic fortunes in the new country. There is also an issue of visibility and language, with some groups better able to blend in. Irish immigrants to the UK have faced discrimination at various points in time, but their low visibility and common language makes it easier for them to assimilate.

In many developed countries, the demographic profile of certain minority groups is skewed more heavily towards young people than is the profile of the majority population. In the UK, for example, the Chinese, Bangladeshi and Pakistani populations are relatively youthful. Many are second or third generation and regard themselves as British. Indeed, collecting information about ethnicity in surveys can be fraught with difficulties and loaded politically. In the UK census, information is collected under five major groups (white, mixed, Asian or Asian British, black or black British and Chinese or other ethnic groups), each of which is subdivided into major national categories (the mixed category, for example, is broken down into white and black Caribbean, white and black African, white and Asian and other mixed background). Even with this degree of detail, categories can be contested. In the 1991 UK census, British Muslims were encouraged to refuse to complete the ethnicity question because Muslim – the category they identified most strongly with – was not listed as an option (nor was ethnicity based on religion offered to any other group, such as Jews or Sikhs) (Peach, 1996).

A second explanation for inequalities of 'race' links both the ways in which members of minority groups view themselves and their relationship to the white majority, as well as the ways in which they are regarded and treated by the majority. Those whose identities are firmly embedded in a minority culture may have no desire to adopt Western cultures. Others might take on an ethnic identity in response to racist treatment as a form of psychological protection. Yet the evidence suggests that second-generation minority groups come to think of themselves as belonging to the country they were born in. In the UK, for example, Modood (1997) showed that most second-generation immigrants think of themselves as British, although they also recognize that their claim to be British is not recognized by all of their fellow citizens.

For many members of ethnic minorities identity is complex and multilayered. People may variously identify as Asian, as Muslim, as male and as British. While some commentators regard fluid, multiple and contradictory identities as a feature of postmodern society (e.g. Rattansi and Phoenix, 1997), others have suggested that a reinforcement of cultural racism in Western societies has served to reinforce ethnic identities. Young Muslims in particular have retreated into their communities in the face of the rise of Islamophobia in the wake of 9/11. In the UK following 9/11 there was a 300 per cent rise in the number of young Asians stopped and searched by the police (*Guardian*, 2004), while in France Muslim women have been prevented from wearing burkas in public places.

Disability

As with 'race', disability can be thought of as a socially constructed category: an impairment becomes a disability because of the ways in which communities respond to diverse needs (Coles, 1995). While frequently thought of as affecting a small minority of the population, in developed countries around one in five young people have a long-standing illness or disability, with these conditions limiting the activities of about 50 per cent of this group (West, 2009a). However, it is a much smaller number, in the region of 2 per cent of 16–19 year-olds, who are officially recognized as disabled (West, 2009a). In addition, young people may suffer from a range of mental impairments (sometimes in addition to physical impairments) that limit their social interactions or single them out for special treatment.

Both physical and mental impairments can lead to discrimination and social exclusion. In the case of young people, disabilities can lead to a protraction of transitions to adulthood and even entrap them in a childlike state of dependence; a situation that may have worsened as transitions have become more complex (Riddell, 2009). With disabled young people experiencing difficulties securing employment, they frequently face poverty and long-term exclusion. In a study that aimed to identify factors that helped disabled young people make successful transitions to employment, Pascall and Hendey found that the most crucial and significant factor was having what they described as 'exceptional parents' (2004: 166). 'Parents were crucial as carers, in developing confidence and independence, in mediating with professionals and in providing material help in accessing housing' (2004: 181). Indeed, 'only those with the most resourceful and resourced parents were likely to access jobs and independent living' (2004: 182). In this context we have another good example of 'bridging capital' (Putnam, 2000) being used to secure advantage in the absence of effective social policies.

As well as leading to exclusion on a structural level, disability can form an important part of a young person's identity. Someone with a physical disability, for example, might socialize within a disabled community, take part in disabled sports and identify with political movements fighting for enhanced rights for disabled people. Disabled athletes might spend much of their time training with other disabled people who share an interest in sport. In the deaf community, a distinction is frequently made between those who are deaf but mix and identify with people who have normal hearing (written using a small 'd') and those who regard their deafness as an important part of their identity and who may largely socialize with other deaf people (written using a capital 'D').

Big D, small d and d/Deaf

Generally, the 'small d' deaf do not associate with other members of the deaf community, strive to identify themselves with hearing people, and regard their hearing loss solely in medical terms. 'Big D' Deaf people identify themselves as culturally deaf, and have a strong deaf identity. The big D Deaf tend to have attended schools/programmes for the deaf, while the small d tend to have been mainstreamed and/or never attended a school for the deaf. When writing about deafness, many writers will use a capital D when referring to aspects of deaf culture, and a lower case d when speaking solely about the hearing loss, and some just simply use d/Deaf. See About.com: Deafness: http://deafness.about.com/cs/culturefeatures1/a/bigdorsmalld.htm (accessed 12 April 2010).

Disability researchers recognize that there are a variety of approaches to negotiating identity among disabled people. Oliver and Barnes (1998), for example, make the distinction between those who grow up largely isolated from other disabled people and who, as a consequence, may lack positive role models; those who mix with other disabled people from an early age; those whose disabilities are not congenital and who may need to renegotiate aspects of their identity; and those who try to hide a disability.

Sexuality

In most societies, heterosexuality is regarded as the norm and those with other sexual identities may be regarded as abnormal and face various forms of discrimination. In many countries homosexuality and bisexuality is now accepted legally, although lesbian, gay, bi-sexual and transsexual people (LGBT or GLBT are the preferred terms) still face discrimination in a number of areas of social life. LGBT young people are known to face homophobic bullying at school and find that 'coming out' as gay is often traumatic (Owens, 1998). In this context, it has been argued that 'queer youth are often cast as victims of homophobic violence or heterosexist exclusion in ways that inscribe them within tropes of victimization and risk' (Driver, 2008: 3–4).

The division between LGBT and the 'straight' population is complex and cross-cuts gender inequalities more generally. Despite liberalization

of legislation, Western societies are often underpinned by heteronormative values, and the sexual activities of members of the LGBT community
are sometimes seen as unnatural, immoral or threatening. The essentialist
approach to sexuality is challenged by social scientists who regard sexuality as socially constructed and culturally diverse (Jackson and Scott, 2010)
and to an extent, fluid (Waites, 2005). From a post-structuralist perspective,
'queer theory', which is grounded in the work of Foucault (1981), challenges
the immutability and stresses fluidity of sexual identities and celebrates the
richness of gay LGBT cultures. Through the adoption of the term 'queer',
'youth affirm their gender and sexual differences, [...] they use "queer"
as an adjective to suggest a rich and layered sense of self' (Driver, 2008).
Queer theory challenges the gay/straight dichotomy by embracing other
sexual identities such as sado-masochism and fetishism.

From a youth perspective, sexual participation is frequently proscribed
by legislation relating to an age of consent. The age of consent varies
between countries (in the cases of Western societies, usually 15 or 16 for
penetrative sex), by sex act and by gender (Waites, 2005). Until relatively
recently, in many countries the age of consent for heterosexual acts was
lower than for homosexual acts. In some countries, such as the UK, legislation further limits relationships by someone occupying a position of trust
(such as a teacher), while in others, lower limits apply when lovers are of a
similar age (such as Canada). Age of consent laws are based on the claim
that those of a certain age lack the capacity to 'give meaningful consent'
and are regarded as a source of inequality (Waites, 2005: 18).

Spatial divisions

Where a young person lives can have a huge impact on their life. Some
people grow up in affluent societies with strong opportunity structures and
comprehensive enabling social policies. Others grow up in poor countries
or in ones with such under-developed social and welfare policies that only
the socially privileged can thrive. Within countries there are also important
spatial divisions between rich and poor neighbourhoods, between strong
and weak labour markets and between urban and rural residences. Patterns
of residence can affect access to education, the quality of employment and
training opportunities, the availability of housing and the type of friends
one is likely to meet.

There is obviously a strong intersection between social class and spatial
divisions and the two can be difficult to disentangle. Some communities
are extremely homogeneous and provide contexts in which class cultures
are validated and reinforced. Others are relatively diverse and provide
opportunities for cross-class socialization and cultural assimilation. In
socially exclusive poor communities, young people's aspirations may be

restricted. Many of their neighbours and the families of their peers may be out of work, while those who are employed might work in low-paid and insecure jobs. In contrast, in a socially diverse community, young people brought up in poor families may be stimulated by the aspirations and expectations of those around them.

Changes in the occupational structure have resulted in some important changes in patterns of communality. Communities that once had strong occupational bonds, such as mining towns, steel towns and fishing or farming villages, have been affected by the decline of traditional industries, with a consequent rise in unemployment and by a re-structuring in a context of diversification and deregulation. These changes have resulted in a process of urban polarization (Byrne, 1999), which has important implications for young people, affecting patterns of solidarity and cohesion in a community and creating sense of uncertainty. In a classic piece of sociological research, Tönnies (2001) made a distinction between two societal types, each of which was linked to personality types. The German term *gemeinschaft* was used to describe a form of community that was tightly regulated and cohesive, where people shared core values and whose lives were closely tied to those around them. The term *gesellschaft* was used to refer to a type of community that he considered as becoming more prevalent: one characterized by weak cohesion and driven by self-interest.

For Byrne, the evidence that urban communities are undergoing a process of polarization is 'overwhelming', especially those 'fully subject to liberalizing post-industrial capitalism' (1999: 112). In this context, class is 'expressed through spatial residence' (1999: 111) which is a form of stratification immediately recognizable to all of us in our day-to-day lives. City residents are aware of the way in which patterns of deprivation are mapped onto the urban landscape, and are often knowledgeable of the ways in which neighbourhoods are sub-divided. Moreover, young people are often held responsible for patterns of urban decline; contributing to the physical condition of the neighbourhood through vandalism and graffiti and to personal risk through involvement in crime (Wacquant, 2008).

Within a country, some communities are likely to be much more cohesive than others and forms of social solidarity can be linked to the forms of social capital outlined by Putnam (2000). At a broader level, nation states are also characterized by different levels of inequality and develop welfare models in accordance with prevalent views concerning levels of inequality that are considered acceptable. In statistics collected by organizations such as the United Nations and the World Bank, the Gini coefficient is used for comparative purposes to represent levels of income inequality within countries. If a country was characterized by perfect inequality, it would have a Gini score of 100; if it was perfectly equal, the score would be zero. With relatively high levels of inequality, South American countries such as Brazil and Chile have Gini scores of around 57, while countries with relatively high levels of equality, such as the Scandinavian countries, have scores of around 25. The UK has a Gini score of 34, Australia has 30 and Japan 38. Up-to-date Gini scores are available in the FBI World Factbook (www.cia.gov/library/publications/the-world-factbook/index.html, accessed 12 April 2010).

Esping-Anderson (1990) has provided a useful typology of welfare regimes which can help provide an understanding of young people's experiences of transitions from youth to adulthood in different countries. Welfare regimes provide the framework in which young people live out their lives; these contexts can facilitate opportunity by providing support for exploration, extended participation in education and training and family formation. In some countries (typically those with low Gini scores), welfare regimes provide generous levels of support and encourage autonomy and active life management among young people. In other countries (such as those in the Mediterranean), minimal support is provided and the family is expected to meet the needs of its members. As we shall see in later chapters, this has an important impact on young people's experiences.

Are structured divisions becoming less relevant?

In this chapter we have explored some of the social divisions that impact on young people's lives. However, in social science there has been a tendency to begin to challenge the idea that we can use information on people's location within social structures (such as class, gender, 'race', place) to predict outcomes and experiences. Those who adopt postmodern perspectives argue that life in contemporary societies has become much more fluid, with people free to interpret and re-construct their lives in ways that transcend traditional divisions. The German sociologist Ulrich Beck has been extremely influential here: he argues that social class has become a 'zombie' category (Beck and Beck-Gernsheim 2002: 201); an idea that lives on in the minds of sociologists but one which has no relevance in late modernity.

> With the decline of class and status groups the individual must become the agent of his or her own identity making and livelihood. The individual, not his or her class, becomes the unit for the reproduction of the social in his or her own lifeworld.
>
> (Beck and Beck-Gernsheim 2002: 202)

Beck is not arguing that social inequalities have become weaker or have ceased to exist; his argument is that with experiences having become more diverse, inequalities are now manifest at the level of the individual rather than at the level of the social class or group. As subjects become disembedded from social class, they are forced into situations where they must reflexively construct biographies as a way of interpreting a diversity of experiences in situations where risk is all-pervasive. The process of disembedding that Beck describes is referred to as 'individualization' (Beck, 1992). Individualization involves 'variation and differentiation of lifestyles and forms of life' (1992: 88) and is a process through which people become less constrained by social structures and forced to become more reflexive.

The potential for using Beck's idea of individualization to develop a deeper understanding of young people's experiences in modern societies has been explored in detail by Furlong and Cartmel (1997, 2007). Furlong and Cartmel suggest that with young people following a much greater variety of educational and labour market routes, they are increasingly encouraged to seek solutions on an individual, rather than a collective, basis, even though outcomes are strongly conditioned by factors like social class and gender. To understand this apparent contradiction, they introduce the idea of the 'epistemological fallacy', which refers to a growing disjuncture between objective and subjective dimensions of life, leading to a process whereby underlying class relationships may become obscured. This does not signal the death of class or invalidate approaches that utilize information on structural location as a way of understanding outcomes, nor does it suggest that young people lack a knowledge or awareness of the link between resources and life chances.

Many youth researchers are reluctant to abandon analysis that draws in information relating to structural divisions; mainly because, as we will see in subsequent chapters, there is plenty of evidence that social divisions such as class and gender continue to shape life chances, but also because research continues to show that many young people do have a basic knowledge or awareness of the ways in which their lives are shaped by unequal opportunity structures (e.g. MacDonald and Marsh 2005). This awareness (which can be expressed by individuals in rather vague terms) relates not just to the inequalities that can be attributed to individual circumstances, but to the structural patterning of inequalities along the lines of class, gender, 'race' and so on.

While few youth researchers have fully embraced postmodernism, since the 1990s there has been an increased tendency to think of modern youth transitions as biographical projects (Evans and Furlong, 1997). Perhaps expressed most clearly in the work of du Bois-Reymond (1998), researchers began to argue that there had been a shift from 'normal biographies' (regarded as structured and linear) to 'choice biographies' which were much more fragmented and driven by choices made by young people as active, engaged and knowledgeable agents. However, many youth researchers, including du Bois-Reymond, recognize that the scope to construct choice biographies is shaped by factors like class and gender. In other words, biographical approaches are being used as a way of understanding how individuals make sense of their lives within the dynamic processes of transition and change and embedded within a set of circumstances that they may be unable to control or influence.

Biographical projects are not free-floating, but are shaped by factors such as social class and locality. MacDonald and Marsh (2005), for example, argued that among young people in poor neighbourhoods in the north-east of England, biographical narratives were 'saturated' by class cultures. At the same time, biographies can help us understand young people's lived experiences and help us come to terms with the ways in which outcomes are not simply linked to the material resources of class, but also to knowledge and a set of subjective capacities through which individuals are differentially equipped to manage their lives.

Policy perspectives

While youth is a temporary phase, the young population is divided in a number of ways and young people's lives are affected by a range of inequalities that will become entrenched over time. Youth policy needs to be focused on preventing marginalization and on opening access to opportunities for all, irrespective of social background, gender, 'race' or other divisions that impact on their lives. Some inequalities, such as gender, 'race' and disability are recognized and addressed by policy (although not always effectively); others, such as class and geographical divisions, are not commonly addressed so directly. While youth tends to be a stage in the life course where inequalities are reproduced, we must begin to recognize the opportunities to redress inequalities that may be lost if action is delayed.

Addressing social exclusion has been a priority in many countries, often with a focus on the world of work and, specifically, workless youth. As we will argue in Chapter 4, many approaches are based on deficit models and are relatively ineffective. Yet effective approaches to social justice do not simply involve targeting policies towards the most disadvantaged segments of the population (although this is clearly crucial); it is also necessary to place restrictions on those who are privileged. Elite positions are becoming more socially exclusive, even though we have a more educated population, and hard-working young people are being denied the fruits of their labour due to the ways in which privilege is protected.

Summary points

1 Youth can be thought of as an important, although temporary, form of social inequality. It is cross-cut by a range of other social divisions, such as gender, class, 'race' and disability status, many of which will continue to shape adult lives.

2 Although, in many developed countries, there has been an expansion in the number of professional and managerial jobs, access to professional jobs remains heavily skewed towards those from affluent families. There are also widespread concerns about levels of social exclusion among young people.

3 Gender inequalities also remain firmly entrenched and these divisions are maintained on a structural level through employment policies as well as on a subjective level through social capital and aspirations.

4 Divisions relating to 'race' are complex because of the ways in which they overlap with class-based inequalities. 'Racial' divisions are strongly linked to patterns of migration and residence, while the identities of minority groups can be fluid and contradictory.

5 Young people may receive different treatment on the basis of their sexuality. Parental surveillance and legislation relating to age of consent may place restrictions on young people's sexual behaviour. Heteronormative values can also lead to discrimination and homophobic bullying.

6 Patterns of residence are an important source of inequality among young people. Such divisions include those between affluent neighbourhoods and ghettos as well as those between countries.

7 Although some social scientists are beginning to question the extent to which lives are structured by divisions such as class, gender and 'race', others suggest that while traditional divisions continue to shape life chances, they have become somewhat obscure.

Further questions

1 In what ways is social class relevant to the lives of young people in modern societies?

youth studies: an introduction

2 What is meant by the terms 'social exclusion' and 'underclass'? How do they differ?

3 Outline some of the reasons for the persistence of gender inequalities.

4 Explain some of the difficulties social scientists have with the terms 'race' and 'ethnicity'.

5 Define the terms 'human capital', 'social capital' and 'cultural capital'.

6 Describe the ways in which your town or city is divided according to social class.

Further reading

Several chapters from Furlong, A. (ed.) (2009) *'Handbook of Youth and Young Adulthood'*, Abingdon: Routledge are useful. See Roberts, K. 'Socio-economic reproduction'; Weiss, L. 'Social class, youth and young adulthood in the context of a shifting global economy'; McDowell, L. 'New masculinities and femininities'; Webster, C. 'Young people, "race" and ethnicity'; Bassani, C. 'Young people and social capital'; and Riddell, S. 'Disability, exclusion and transition to adulthood'.

Furlong, A. and Cartmel, F. (2007) *Young People and Social Change: New Perspectives*, 2nd edn, Maidenhead: Open University Press.

Holland, J., Ramazanoglu, C., Sharpe, S. and Thomson, R. (2004) *The Male in the Head: Young People, Heterosexuality and Power*, London: Tufnell Press.

MacDonald, R. (ed.) (1997) *Youth, the 'Underclass' and Social Exclusion*, London: Routledge.

Internet links

Discussion paper on social mobility:
www.cabinetoffice.gov.uk/media/cabinetoffice/strategy/assets/social-mobility.pdf

The report of the Panel on Fair Access to the Professions:
www.cabinetoffice.gov.uk/media/227105/fair-access-summary.pdf

chapter 3

Education and opportunity

Contents

Education and youth studies

Young people spend much of their lives in educational settings, and their experiences in schools, colleges and universities can shape much of their subsequent lives. Inevitably, youth researchers have an established interest in young people's educational experiences and have been at the forefront of discussions around the impact of changing patterns of participation on the lives of young people. While youth studies is multidisciplinary, research in the area of education has traditionally had a strong sociological focus and partly shares an agenda with the sociology of education. In youth studies, researchers have tended to focus on four overlapping themes:

- Mobility: education as a stage in the reproduction of inequalities, linked to the transmission of advantage between generations and as a process through which groups of young people may be marginalized.
- Skill development: education as a process through which young people acquire qualifications; the 'hard skills' that often determine transitional routes and the 'soft skills' that help them become effective navigators with the ability to shape outcomes.
- Lifestyles: education as a setting that lends shape to lifestyles and impacts on patterns of peer interaction and influence.
- Identity: education as an arena in which young people engage in a process of identity making and learn to reflexively negotiate the complex landscapes of late modernity.

Youth researchers often adopt a holistic approach, rather than viewing education systems in isolation, seeing them as connected to young people's broader life contexts in a dynamic sense. Exploring, for example, the inter-relationship between changing experiences in education and broader transitional processes, and vice versa, and highlighting the connections between educational transitions and inter-related transitions in other areas of life such as in housing and the domestic sphere (Henderson *et al.*, 2007). In this context, youth researchers have questioned whether educational arrangements, which retain a structure developed in the immediate post-war decades, can be considered suitable for the twenty-first century (Wyn, 2009a).

Much recent work in the field of education has been driven by an interest in how the profound changes in patterns of educational participation that have occurred in all advanced societies have impacted on outcomes in the labour market, particularly on the overall distribution of inequalities and on processes of marginalization and inclusion. In the previous chapter we noted that although some far-reaching social and economic changes are in evidence, advanced societies are not in the process of becoming more egalitarian. Indeed, as we will show in Chapter 4, in many countries there is a concern that changes in patterns of demand from employers have left those who fail to thrive academically vulnerable to a process of marginalization and exclusion. In the context of education, youth researchers have had a long-standing interest in processes of disconnection occurring within educational systems and the link between resources – especially cultural resources – and marginalization, and their impact on other life transitions.

Changing patterns of educational participation

In all advanced societies, education is subject to an ongoing process of change as policy makers and practitioners reflect on the effectiveness of systems for different groups of people in contexts that are continually being transformed. Many of the changes implemented are concerned with modes of delivery, levels of teacher autonomy and accountability, the curriculum, the structure of institutions and patterns of management. While activity on this level is near constant (accompanied by frequent airings of teacher frustration as they try to find time to implement the next round of changes), it is much less common to find examples of far-reaching structural change that impact on educational frameworks. Indeed, there is much merit in the idea that contemporary education systems have changed so little that they still bear the hallmarks of their post-war origins. As Wyn (2009a) argues,

> secondary education has been more expanded than transformed, retaining older models and assumptions about the nature of learners and the form education should take. [...] The expansion of post-compulsory education has mainly involved an increase in participation by older students, leaving the educational frameworks and assumptions that have been inherited from an industrial era intact.
>
> (2009a: 98–9)

Although many commentators would agree that the expansion of educational systems has not been accompanied by meaningful and far-reaching reform, expansion has had significant implications for young people's lives. The number of years the average young person spends in educational institutions has continued to increase, and, in many countries, the number of hurdles they are forced to jump has multiplied. Educational achievements and the development of core skills have become increasingly important in a world where unskilled jobs are in decline. Moreover, the emphasis placed on the development of 'soft skills', a strong emphasis on conformity and a willingness to accept educational knowledge as legitimate, contrasts strongly with earlier contexts in which resistance by students heading for unskilled jobs was frequently taken for granted by educationalists (Willis, 1977). Indeed, forms of stratification in education, that once involved clear lines of differentiation between groups of students heading from different class origins to distinct class destinations, have become increasingly blurred and complex (Biggart and Furlong, 1996). Related to this trend, the protraction of educational careers has opened up the possibility of developing new lifestyles and encourages reflexive negotiation of a world where the prescription of opportunities can appear to have weakened.

Before discussing the implications of changing forms of educational engagement, it is worth highlighting the extent to which patterns of participation have changed. The first point to note is that back in the 1970s, in many developed countries, a large majority of young people ceased full-time education at the age of 15 or 16 and entered employment fairly directly. Others, who tended to come from more privileged families, remained at school or in vocational college for another year or two, with a smaller number progressing to university. Patterns of participation in the US were somewhat out of kilter with the rest of the developed world: by 1960 almost four in ten young people were completing high school (37 per cent in New York, for example, and 44 per cent in Boston) (Bureau of Labor Statistics, 2006). Over the following decades, the picture changed significantly: some countries made more rapid progress than others but by the new millennium, in virtually all advanced societies, it had become a relatively small minority who left school without progressing to the upper secondary stage of schooling or entering a formal process of vocational education and training. In the UK, in 2007 15 per cent of males and 11 per cent of females were classed as early school leavers; a figure slightly below the average for the European Union (EU) of 17 per cent of males and 13 per cent of females (Eurostat, 2009a). This change was not brought about by any radical alteration in the minimum legal leaving age (where changes took place, these often lagged behind changes in practice), but was largely triggered through changing opportunity structures both in education and the labour market. As the Organisation for Economic Co-operation and Development (OECD) observed, an upper-secondary education had become a minimum requirement for many employers and 'those who leave without an upper secondary qualification tend to face severe difficulties when entering the labour market' (OECD, 2009: 46). While recognizing that many early leavers may be vulnerable to prolonged or repeated unemployment, it is also important to note that not all early leavers are disadvantaged but that some leave early in order to take advantage of employment opportunities (especially jobs offering quality training) or may follow alternative pathways due to personal preferences (Eurostat, 2009a).

Educational policy makers in different countries have responded to changing patterns of participation in a variety of ways, including expanding capacity at the upper-secondary and tertiary level, introducing courses regarded as 'more suitable' for the 'less academic' student and enhancing vocational provision. In many European countries it is now common to find more than eight in ten young people remaining in education for at least one post-compulsory year and more than seven in ten remaining for at least two post-compulsory years. Rates do vary significantly; countries characterized by high participation, where more than nine in ten young people completed at least one post-compulsory year in 2006, include Sweden, Germany and France (Eurostat, 2009a). The UK is among the European countries with lower rates of post-compulsory participation: in 2006 almost 72 per cent remained in education until the age of 17 and less than half completed two years of post-compulsory education (Eurostat, 2009a).

Although the UK can be described as a low-participation country, significant changes have taken place. In 1985 30 per cent of young men and 34 per cent of young women between the ages of 16 and 18 were in full-time post-compulsory education; by 2007 this had increased to 59 and 67 per cent respectively (Hughes *et al.*, 2009). In many European countries, as well as in Australia and Japan, more than 60 per cent of a school year cohort will now graduate from upper secondary school with a standard of qualification that will allow them to progress to higher education (UNESCO, 2009). As a consequence, participation in further and higher education has also expanded significantly, with the upward trend in the UK being particularly sharp from the early 1990s (Figure 3.1). Again, Europe has lagged behind the US in the expansion of tertiary education: as early as the 1960s around one in four Americans were engaging in some form of post-secondary education, whereas in Western Europe and Japan significant growth only occurred in the 1980s (Altbach *et al.*, 2009).

> The number of students pursuing tertiary education has sky-rocketed over the last 37 years, growing five-fold from 28.6 million in 1970 to 152.5 million in 2007. This translates into an average annual increase of 4.6%, with the average number of tertiary students doubling every 15 years. But a closer look at the data reveals that the expansion has been particularly intense since 2000, with 51.7 million new tertiary students enrolled around the world in just seven years.
>
> (UNESCO, 2009: 10)

In all forms of post-compulsory education the gender gap has continued to expand in favour of females (Eurostat, 2009b). These trends are repeated worldwide with female students outnumbering males in a wide range of countries. In global terms, by 2003 men and women had roughly equal chances of progressing to tertiary education; since then trends have led to increased female advantage. Perhaps surprisingly, these trends are not confined to North America, Europe, Japan and Australia, but in Latin America, the Caribbean and Central Asia women take a greater proportion of places in tertiary education. Even in the Arab states, participation levels are very similar for males and females (UNESCO, 2009).

Among those who participate in post-compulsory education, some follow academic routes leading towards higher education, while others

youth studies: an introduction

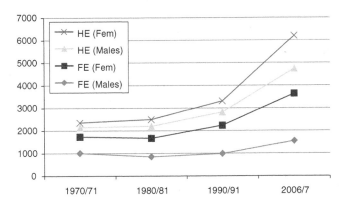

Figure 3.1 Trends in the numbers of students enrolled in further (FE) and higher (HE) education by gender: UK (thousands).

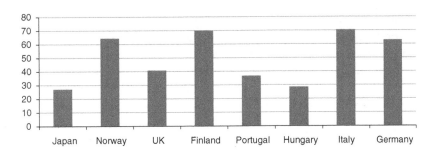

Figure 3.2 Pupils in a vocational stream within upper-secondary education.

Source: Eurostat (2010).

embark on vocational courses that often lead towards skilled forms of employment but may also offer opportunities to embark on tertiary courses. Choices between academic and vocational pathways are strongly conditioned by the policies implemented by individual states: some countries (such as Germany) have had a long tradition of developing vocational pathways, while in other countries (such as the UK and Japan) vocational routes are less developed. In Italy, Finland and Germany, for example, more than six in ten young people who are enrolled in upper-secondary education follow vocational pathways. In the UK around four in ten take vocational courses while in Japan and Hungary less than three in ten are on vocational tracks (Figure 3.2). At the institutional level, the distribution between pathways is often justified on the grounds that some young people are thought to have little interest or aptitude for an academic curriculum.

education and opportunity

The expansion of higher education has led to a situation where significant numbers of young people remain in education until their mid-to-late 20s. The change has led to a transformation of higher education from an elite to a mass experience, although it remains a highly stratified system with important divisions between the elite universities and lower status institutions, some of which have firm roots in vocational education (Furlong and Cartmel, 2009). In several countries, there is also an important division between public and private universities which are particularly prevalent in North America, Japan, South Korea and Indonesia and are expanding in Central and Eastern Europe (Altbach *et al.*, 2009). Other important divisions exist between high and low-status courses and between those which provide clear routes to lucrative sectors of the labour market and those leading to less rewarding sectors of the economy.

To an extent the growth in participation in higher education represents a response to a process of qualification inflation whereby employers are able to seek graduates for positions that could once be accessed with a high-school diploma. Expansion has also been fuelled by a process of professionalization, whereby a range of careers once associated with sub-degree forms of training (such as nursing and a range of medical semi-professions) began to require or prefer those trained to degree level. For young people, the move to a mass system of higher education has other consequences. The period of semi-dependence on parents becomes prolonged and the entry to the world of employment becomes graduated as people increasingly spend several years combining education and work.

In many countries, higher education has also become a process whereby young people run up significant debts that impact on lifestyles, on their ability to get a foothold in housing markets and to start families. Countries vary significantly on funding arrangements for higher education students, and this, in turn, impacts on the numbers of young people who participate and on the burden of debt carried by graduates. In Figure 3.3, patterns of support implemented in a range of countries are described, together with average levels of participation.

While patterns of participation and attainment have changed in all countries, one significant change that is frequently overlooked by policy makers concerns the delinearization of patterns of participation and the blending of statuses. Young people increasingly combine education and work. Rather than making linear, step-by-step movements through school and further through higher education, the sequences of their participation may be adjusted. They may leave education for employment, subsequently returning for further study and perhaps combining study with jobs. In these circumstances, we cannot assume that education is prioritized over work, or vice versa, or even that either of these are prioritized over leisure or family (Ball *et al.*, 2000).

Group 1: low tuition fees, generous student support packages	
Denmark, Finland, Iceland, Norway, Sweden, Czech Republic, Turkey	60%
Group 2: high tuition fees, well-developed student support packages	
Australia, Canada, Netherlands, UK, US, Chile	68%
Group 3: high tuition fees, less-developed student support packages	
Japan, Korea	45–59%
Group 4: low tuition fees, less-developed student support packages	
Austria, Belgium, France, Ireland, Italy, Portugal, Spain	48%

Figure 3.3 Typology of country's student support regimes, and typical HE participation rates.

Differences in academic engagement and performance

While commentaries of educational change are often full of graphs highlighting upward trajectories in patterns of participation, levels of attainment and national resources devoted to educating young people, a more interesting picture emerges when attempts are made to explore variations between social groups. In many cases, a picture of *absolute* growth masks a persistence of *relative* differentials. For sociologists, education is a process which has the potential to facilitate upward social mobility, yet often reinforces disadvantage and protects the privileged.

It was noted earlier that patterns of participation among young women had grown to such an extent that, in a wide range of countries, they have become more likely than young men to participate in upper secondary and tertiary education. In terms of performance, at all levels women are increasingly taking the lead. In 22 member countries of the OECD, women are out-performing men academically (Field *et al.*, 2007). Statistics covering England, Wales and Northern Ireland show that, in 2008, in terms of GCSE attainment males were lagging behind females by around 10 percentage points. Figures for Europe show that young women are significantly less likely to follow vocational pathways in the secondary school (Eurostat, 2009a). Females are also more likely to study at the tertiary level and leave university with higher classes of degree (Hills *et al.*, 2010). Despite these gains, women in higher education tend to be over-represented on low status vocational courses (such as nursing and teaching) and are clustered within a narrow range of subjects (Self and Zealey, 2007).

> Women in secondary and post-secondary education continue to be overrepresented in traditionally female fields, e.g., education, nursing, social work, humanities or social sciences. They remain underrepresented in areas such as engineering, math, physical sciences, and computer science, as well as dentistry, medicine, or law. Even academically gifted school girls are less likely to choose careers in male-dominated areas such as physical sciences or mathematics.
>
> (Tyyskä, 2009: 79)

While gender differentials in education have been changing, social class has proved to be a much more deeply entrenched inequality. In all OECD countries young people's educational attainment and patterns of participation are strongly affected by the class position of their parents. In the UK in 2006, around eight in ten young people whose parents worked in higher professional occupations passed five or more GCSEs at grades A*–C. This compares to four in ten young people whose parents worked in routine occupations (Hughes et al., 2009). While the differentials are huge, in the context of developed countries, they are not untypical. There is also some evidence that the gap is narrowing: in the UK the GCSE performance of young people with parents in routine occupations increased by 16 percentage points between 1999 and 2006, while the corresponding rise for those with parents in higher professional occupations was 6 percentage points (Hughes et al., 2009). The gulf, however, remains extremely wide. Furthermore, it is also important to note that the higher average performance of young women can mask a strong diversity of performance among those from working class families whereby a significant group of lower working class females perform poorly (Walkerdine et al., 2001; Biggart, 2002).

In some countries, the extensive use of vocational pathways can represent a structural barrier that constrains the progress of those from working class families. Although vocational routes often provide for the possibility of progress to higher education, in practice it is not a well-trodden pathway. At the same time, there are clear benefits in providing high-quality vocational alternatives. If we look at countries that have a strong separation between vocational educational routes and academic pathways, such as Germany, there is strong evidence that the vocational alternative reduces unemployment among young people and smoothes transitions to employment; in other words, a strong vocational track helps reduce marginalization. However, there is also evidence that these same

youth studies: an introduction

processes limit the opportunities for upward social mobility (Shavit and Müller, 2000).

Despite the increase in participation in higher education by young people from working class families, inequalities are huge. In the UK, among those born in 1979, around one in ten of those whose parents' income placed them in the lowest quartile had obtained a tertiary degree by the age of 23. In contrast, among those whose parents' income placed them in the top quartile, more than four in ten had degrees (Hills *et al.*, 2010). Moreover, whereas just over one in five young people with parents in unskilled occupations entered a top university (one of the so-called Russell Group), more than four in ten young people from professional backgrounds entered one of these universities (Hills *et al.*, 2010).

In terms of basic skills, the international PISA surveys also show that patterns of literacy and numeracy are affected by social class. In the UK, for example, young people from the lowest SES quartile were more than three times as likely as those in the top quartile to show poor levels of attainment in maths; in Canada, they were two and a half times more likely to fall into the bottom quartile for attainment in maths than their more advantaged peers (Field *et al.*, 2007).

Differences in educational participation and performance that are linked to social class are also manifest in the clear associations between parental education (which can be regarded as a proxy for class) and a range of outcomes. Figures published by Eurostat clearly show that in all European countries the majority of those with poor educational achievements have parents who are poorly educated. Where parents have completed upper secondary education, the chances of their son or daughter finishing upper secondary education are high: in most European countries around 85 per cent of those whose parents complete upper secondary education do so themselves (Eurostat, 2009a). Across the OECD countries, young people with educated parents are 'between two and six times more likely to complete tertiary education' (Field *et al.*, 2007: 39).

In a review of trends in participation in higher education in the EU countries, it has been argued that 'a constant factor in all member states for which data are available, is that while absolute participation rates have increased for all socio-economic levels, the relative rates have rarely changed' (Green *et al.*, 1999: 204). Drawing on data from several countries, Raftery and Hout (1993) proposed a theory of 'maximally maintained advantage'. Essentially, their argument is that educational expansion tends to occur in a way that results in little change in class-based differentials until a 'saturation point' is reached. In other words, working class gains will only occur once middle class participation has reached the point when virtually all young people from middle class families are benefiting.

There is also clear evidence of an association between poverty, family income and patterns of educational participation and attainment (Wotherspoon, 2004; O'Reilly and Yau, 2009). In Toronto, a recent school census highlighted a strong relationship between family income, parental education and ethnic origin, and performance in reading, writing and maths (O'Reilly and Yau, 2009). As the UK National Equity Panel discovered, in the most deprived neighbourhoods around three in ten young men achieve examination results that place them in the top half of the attainment range; in the least deprived neighbourhoods the corresponding figure is seven in ten. For young women, 50 per cent of those in the least deprived neighbourhoods can be placed in the top quarter of the attainment range, compared to a fifth of those in the most deprived areas (Hills *et al.*, 2010).

There are also significant educational inequalities associated with ethnic background, although in many cases these inequalities strongly intersect with social class. Some ethnic groups, for example, are heavily concentrated in working class occupations and over-represented among the unemployed. This can make it difficult to fully disentangle the effect of ethnicity from social class, but also means that the differences *between* ethnic groups are so strong that we cannot simply talk of an ethnic disadvantage. In the UK, for example, boys with Chinese and Indian backgrounds significantly outperform white British boys, while black Africans and Pakistanis perform less well. The rank order for girls is similar, although the overall attainment gap is much narrower (Hills *et al.*, 2010). Recent UK trends have seen the gap between ethnic groups narrow, with strong increases in performance noted among Pakistanis and Bangladeshis (Hughes *et al.*, 2009). The educational performance of young people from different ethnic groups tends to vary by country, in accordance with the history of migration and colonialism. In Canada and Australia, aboriginals have tended to be over-represented among early school leavers and have underperformed relative to their white peers. In the US, Hispanic immigrants and black Americans experience educational inequalities, although as in the case of the UK, women from all ethnic groups are outperforming their male peers (Lopez, 2002).

There are also a range of groups, often labelled as having 'special needs' or 'additional needs' who are subject to a range of initiatives that aim to promote the inclusion of groups who have often been marginalized in education systems. Those with additional needs are a diverse group, including those with physical disabilities, those with moderate or severe learning difficulties, those with specific issues, such as dyslexia and those with emotional and behavioural difficulties. As many as one in five young people in England are identified as having some sort of special need, in most cases of a moderate nature (Hills *et al.*, 2010). In the UK as in other countries, approaches have changed over time, with policy gradually moving away from practices that confined those with additional needs to 'special schools', to inclusive approaches whereby they are educated in mainstream schools. This trend is reinforced by the United Nations Convention on the Rights of the Child (1989), which recognized the forced educational separation of those with additional needs from their peers as a breach of their human rights. Needless to say, many of those with additional needs underperform educationally and researchers have noted a strong link between the existence of a special need and living in a deprived neighbourhood (Hills *et al.*, 2010). Figures from the US show that for many of those with disabilities, rates of education progression beyond high school are low: around one in four of those with any recorded condition will receive any post-secondary education (Blum, 2005).

Explaining persistent inequalities

Without doubt, changes in patterns of demand for labour have been a prime driver of the increase in educational participation and have had a significant impact on changing qualification profiles among all groups of young people. Educational inequalities, though, have proved persistent. As Feinstein and colleagues argue, 'the intergenerational transmission of educational success is a key driver of the persistence of social class differences in westernised societies' (2008: 17). Many of the reasons for the entrenchment of inequalities can be found within the family and relate to the various resources to which they have access. Inequalities in youth cannot be understood without some appreciation of their transmission in childhood. Children's early experiences within the family provide them with an essential preparation for formal processes of education and lay the foundations for patterns of inequality and marginality. Some children begin school able to read simple words, identify colours, count and do simple arithmetic. Others have to acquire these skills within the school environment and may be regarded by teachers as less bright from the outset. Some children may be used to sitting quietly, and paying attention to an adult who is providing instructions, while others might not.

Throughout their time in education, those from more advantaged families often have access to educational resources in the home environment and support from family members who have some knowledge of the curriculum and who can help them with homework. In addition, middle class families frequently stress the importance of education, highlight potential benefits and are able to use their knowledge to secure advantages in an educational marketplace. By contrast, working class families may have narrow occupational horizons, less direct knowledge of educational benefits and may be unable to support their child beyond the end of compulsory education.

Hess and Holloway (1984) (quoted in Feinstein *et al.*, 2008) highlight five factors that help explain the link between family environments and educational outcomes. These are 'verbal interaction between mothers and children; affective relationships between parents and children; discipline and control strategies; expectations of parents for achievement; and parents' beliefs and attributions' (p. 48). These factors can be regarded as dimensions of a family's 'cultural capital' (Bourdieu, 1984). For Bourdieu, cultural capital is one of the key mechanisms that 'helps to enclose the underprivileged class in the roles which society has given them' (1974: 42). The school and middle class parents tend to share a 'habitus' – a set of core assumptions and a common language that ultimately represent a form of capital that purchases educational advantage. Thus the symbolic representations of a shared class background affect the school's view of its pupils and help reproduce advantage. In this context Bourdieu (1974) argued that middle class advantages in the educational system are largely due to the similarity between middle class culture and the dominant culture, with the mode of learning employed in schools being similar to that practised in middle class families. In essence, education systems are shaped by a powerful cultural elite who promote their own culture as superior, leading to the framing of what counts as educational knowledge in ways that are favourable to their own positions. Bernstein (1971) takes a similar approach; he regards the 'lingual codes' used by children and young people from different social backgrounds as central to the ways in which teachers develop impressions about pupils' abilities.

Basil Bernstein (1924–2000) argued that children from different social class backgrounds acquired different lingual codes, with their use of language affecting the school's view of their ability. Children from middle class families tend to use 'elaborated' codes in which meaning is communicated effectively to those who lack 'insider' knowledge. In contrast, working class children tend to use a 'restricted code' whereby effective communication is dependent on shared meanings. A restricted code can work effectively in closed communities, such as a family or a peer group, and all of us use it on some occasions. However, educational systems use, value and reward elaborated codes, partly because they are controlled by the middle classes, but also because the nature of the enterprise means that they are concerned with the transmission of knowledge that transcends shared meaning.

Bernstein illustrated these differences through the use of a cartoon showing a group of boys playing football in the street. One of the

youth studies: an introduction

boys kicks the football and smashes a house window. Subsequently one of the residents of the house comes outside and shouts at the boys who then run away. Bernstein presents this cartoon alongside two sets of verbal descriptions of the sequences of events that are being played out. The first represents a restricted code, under which meaning is only clear if the reader has access to the drawings being described, the second represents an elaborated code which conveys a clear interpretation to the reader, whether or not they have access to the cartoon.

Restricted code

They're playing football and he kicks it and it goes through there. It breaks the window and they're looking at it and he comes out and shouts at them because they've broken it so they run away and then she looks out and she tells them off.

Elaborated code

Three boys are playing football and one boy kicks the ball and it goes through the window the ball breaks the window and the boys are looking at it and a man comes out and shouts at them because they've broken the window so they run away and then that lady looks out of her window and she tells the boys off.

Through these processes, and others, the school may help reinforce family disadvantage. Teachers may have lower expectations regarding the ability of working class pupils and may fail to offer adequate levels of encouragement. In turn, working class pupils are more likely to be placed in lower ability streams where they may mix with pupils who share their class background, reinforcing pre-existing perspectives and limiting their opportunities to familiarize themselves with the assumptive worlds of their middle class peers. Research into the impact of streaming, or tracking as it is sometimes referred to, shows that placing a child into a stream can result in a self-fulfilling prophecy. In a classic study by Rosenthal and Jacobson (1968), it was shown that, irrespective of ability, pupils who were placed in high streams where teachers expected them to do well made far better progress than those placed in low streams where teachers tended to have low expectations. Recent research has also shown that almost nine out of ten pupils who were placed in ability streams at the start of primary school remained in those same streams throughout their school careers (Boaler, 2005). The process of schooling can lead to an increase in inequalities. There is evidence, for example, showing that a child from a lower class background assessed as high ability is likely to be outperformed by a child from a more privileged family initially assessed as having inferior ability (Hills *et al.*, 2010).

In a study of the relationship between parents and primary schools in the US, Lareau (1989) suggested that another way in which cultural capital impacted on educational outcomes was through the degree of connection between parents and their child's school – in other words, the extent and ways in which parents involved themselves in the formal process of learning through interactions with teachers. Lareau found that middle class parents tended to see themselves as partners in the educational process; they were seen as involved, informed, and even demanding. In contrast, working class parents had a much more limited involvement with the school, regarding education as the job of the teacher rather than being a core parental role. In Lareau's study, working class parents regarded teachers as professionals who, by virtue of their specialist training, knew how to educate children effectively. In the words of one parent, teachers 'are right up there next to God and doctors' (1989: 112). In contrast, the middle class parents 'monitored their children's schooling, intervened in their children's classroom program, criticized the actions of teachers, and worked to supplement and reinforce the classroom experience' (1989: 61). In addition, middle class mothers frequently helped out in the classroom so as to get a better picture of their child's progress and the work they were involved in. As one mother put it, 'my main motive for doing that [volunteering as a classroom helper] was not particularly to help the teacher. I think that was important. It was a really good way to find out where your child was in relation to other children and know what they were working on' (1989: 64).

The cultural affinity between the school and middle class parents underpins what is frequently referred to as the 'hidden curriculum': a term that alludes to the norms and values that lend shape to educational practices and which can be institutionalized in a variety of ways. The hidden curriculum incorporates a wide range of practices and sets of assumptions that ultimately contribute to the reproduction of inequalities through educational practices. In guiding pupils' choice of subjects or future careers, for example, teachers may draw on a set of assumptions relating to a 'fit' between class background, gender or ethnicity and 'normal' or 'appropriate' outcomes. A young woman may be encouraged to aim towards a specific 'gender-appropriate' career, a young person from a working class family might be discouraged from applying for a place at a prestigious university, while a black male may find that his lively behaviour is interpreted as disruptive.

While cultural capital clearly plays a central role in the reproduction of advantage in educational contexts, economic resources are also crucial. In most countries schools are clearly stratified, most obviously into public and private sectors with some parents able to purchase educational success for their offspring by enrolling them in expensive schools that have superior facilities and operate small class sizes. Many of these schools have annual fees that exceed average annual wages. (Eton College currently charges £28,851 a year and expects parents to pay for a wide range of extras such as music and fencing lessons, house subscriptions and tips for domestic staff.) Even within the state sector there are clear divisions: some schools serve affluent neighbourhoods and enjoy high levels of parental support and engagement. Others serve run-down inner city areas and have to deal with the social consequences of poverty, deprivation and family dysfunctionality. Consequently some schools have a poor social mix, contain large numbers of disruptive students, have high drop-out rates and lack a tradition of progression to higher education. As knowledgeable consumers, middle class parents are frequently able to 'play the system' in ways that ensure that their child enters the 'best' state school; sometimes by buying a house in the catchment area or, in the case of church schools, by becoming regular churchgoers. In this context, education is frequently portrayed as a commodity, with parents represented as consumers who use their skills and resources to 'play the market' in ways that ultimately reinforce class advantage while students are expected to regard education as an investment capable of bringing long-term rewards. As White and Wyn argue:

> The privatization and marketing of education go hand-in-hand with the notion of education as a commodity. Education is increasingly portrayed in terms of its 'exchange value' on the market, rather than its 'use-value' as something good in its own right and for its own sake.
>
> (2004: 129)

The protraction of post-compulsory education and the emergence of a mass system of higher education has also created new opportunities for families to use cultural and economic resources to secure advantage for their sons and daughters. Not all families can afford to support their offspring through long periods of post-compulsory education or training and even where state support is available, there are still important lines of stratification. Evidence from the UK shows that young people from less affluent families are frequently debt-averse and are reluctant to take out student loans to finance their studies. Young people from poorer families frequently select courses on the basis of cost: not simply in terms of fees, but overall costs which may include the need to move away from home, travel costs, the length of course and the perceived linkages between their course and future employment (Furlong and Cartmel, 2009). This can result in young people from less affluent families selecting courses in less prestigious institutions, choosing shorter courses and considering courses with strong vocational orientations. In addition, less affluent students frequently work long hours to survive in education; this can interfere with their studies and prevent cross-class social interaction.

While the uneven distribution of cultural and economic capital helps explain class differences in educational outcomes, gender differences and inequalities associated with various ethnic groups are slightly more complex and have also been subject to greater change. As noted above, females now outperform males at virtually all levels, while some ethnic groups have made real gains, in some cases seeing them out perform their white peers. Both gender and ethnicity interact with social class, and part of the explanation can be found in changes in the occupational world that have led to the creation of new opportunities, especially for females in the service industries. Attitudes have also changed. Employment discrimination is still extremely prevalent and effects women and members of minority groups, but has become less overt and, in many firms, is seen as unacceptable. Both women and minority groups now have strong role models, including prime ministers and presidents. Changes in patterns of educational participation and occupational achievement within families are likely to impact on aspirations. Macro-level changes in the position of women and minority groups in society may be filtered through peer groups and can impact on educational motivation and shape learner identities.

Young people's perspectives on education

Young people's orientations towards education have long been regarded as central to understanding experiences and outcomes and, ultimately, as part of the process through which inequalities are reproduced. In various ways, class cultures can impact on educational orientations and are regarded as playing an important role in the reproduction of inequalities and in processes of marginalization. Here many researchers have highlighted the ways in which lower working class cultures can be at odds with the middle class culture of the school. The classic work here is the study carried out by Paul Willis in the 1970s. Willis (1977) argued that boys from lower working class families frequently resisted the authority of the school and rejected school-based values that were based on deferred gratification or placed a premium on academic success; indeed, they frequently valued manual labour over mental labour. According to Willis, the 'lads' that he studied had no desire to enter middle class jobs: they wanted to be able to prove their masculinity through manual labour and full engagement in working class culture and lifestyles without any unnecessary delay. In other words, through immersion in working class culture they were active participants in the reproduction of their own inequalities.

Two of the themes that underpin Willis' work are worth highlighting. First there is the idea of a clash between the culture of the school and lower working class cultures and, linked to this, the idea that this culture clash is manifest in a process of resistance which becomes one of the key mechanisms to restrict social mobility.

In recent years, the idea that class-based resistance is central to the reproduction of inequalities has fallen out of favour, mainly because education has become much more central to the lives of all young people, who participate for longer periods of time and are acutely aware of the restricted range of job opportunities available to those without qualifications. In a five-country comparison (Finland, Sweden, Spain, Portugal and Australia), Rinnie and colleagues (2003) showed that young people strongly believe in the importance of working hard at school, with a majority thinking of themselves as hard-working. In many Western countries, today's youth grew up in a period in which the occupational structure changed significantly and many of their parents experienced upward social mobility. As a result, expectations changed and there was a degree of convergence in class cultures. With a serious decline in unskilled manual jobs in factories and building sites and with education becoming more crucial to labour market outcomes, resistance is no longer such a central part of working class orientations to the school, although it still exists, and instrumentalism has become more common. As Côté and Allahar (2006) suggest, even in higher education, many students can be described as 'reluctant intellectuals'.

However, if instrumentalism is the glue that holds young people in the school system, then they have to have a degree of confidence that their efforts will pay off. Young people living in poor communities who lack role models to demonstrate the link between educational attainment and lifestyles are not going to have any confidence in this 'academic bargain' and may continue to reject the idea of academic conformity. And there is a tension here: in lower working class peer groups it is often not seen as 'cool to be clever' (Williamson, 2004: 26) and therefore the rewards for breaking with peer values have to be obvious.

A study of young people in poor neighbourhoods in the north of England by MacDonald and Marsh (2005), illustrates these processes well. Few good words were spoken by students about school, which was 'seen by the majority as "pointless", "meaningless" and "menial"' (2005: 50). Few felt stimulated by lessons and many were of the view that they were receiving a poor-quality education, characterized by low teacher expectations, a lack of imaginative or engaging class-work and poorly prepared or inadequate teachers. As one of their respondents put it, 'if you didn't show the slightest bit of talent you never got pushed, do you know. If you couldn't be bothered, they didn't bother with you' (2005: 52).

For the young people, fitting into the school peer group was important, with those who attempted to work too hard or who submitted homework being at risk of bullying. As MacDonald and Marsh observed, 'saving face amongst peer groups was often viewed as more important than striving to achieve higher GCSE grades' (2005: 55). There is evidence that a combination of boredom, disinterest and poor-quality teaching, set in the context of peer groups that both reinforce and reward disruptive behaviour or disengagement, have a detrimental impact on the education of working class pupils (MacDonald and Marsh, 2005; McLeod and Yates, 2006; Cotterell, 2007). Moreover, these factors do not simply apply to boys; working class girls often share these experiences (MacDonald and Marsh, 2005). Cotterell's research in Australian schools led him to conclude that classroom behaviour is frequently brought about through frustration and is about 'play and diversion' rather than reflecting 'counter-culture or organized resistance' (2007: 152). For Cotterell, classroom behaviour can be regarded as a 'barometer of adolescent motivation' (2007: 150). 'Goofing off is a group expression, arising from a collective awareness among one's peers of a common state of mind' (2007: 151). Such behaviour takes many forms, 'making noises such as loud sighs and yawns and orchestrated fits of coughing, throwing or shooting things, or acting in unusual ways – the overall effect being that it generally annoys or "bugs" the teacher' (2007: 150–1).

While few contemporary researchers claim that schooling for the working classes is conditioned by a process of resistance through which young people prepare subjectively for working class life outside of the school gates, some have suggested that schools have become feminized environments and that attempts to establish and live out a 'traditional' masculinity within such environments often contribute to failure. At the same time, feminists have argued that recent trends point towards a re-masculinization of schooling involving a 'prioritising of boys' education' and 'the sidelining of gender equality discourses' (Arnot and Mac an Ghaill, 2006). As McLeod and Yates (2006) suggest, 'gendered ways of being certainly do enter how individuals manage their school lives and how they produce, enact, or reject ways of being the "good student" ' (2006: 65). The idea of a clash between working class masculinity and contemporary educational institutions is a theme developed by many writers (e.g. Walkerdine et al., 2001; McDowell, 2003), and one that is also linked to orientations and experiences in modern labour markets. Yet McLeod and Yates (2006) found that the young Australians they interviewed, while agreeing that girls were outperforming boys, did not feel that schools were disadvantaging

youth studies: an introduction

either males or females. However, there was some agreement that boys were more prone to distraction and inclined to 'mess about'. Indeed, it has been argued that 'laddish' behaviour can be often be regarded as a protective strategy through which young men defend themselves both against 'fear of failure' and 'fear of the feminine' (Jackson, 2003: 585).

The idea that class cultures are reference points which shape young people's assumptive worlds and impact on educational engagement is a theme developed most coherently in the work of Pierre Bourdieu. For Bourdieu (1977) these class-based assumptions (what he referred to as a habitus) represent a form of cultural capital which is used in education and the labour market to secure advantages. Those who lack cultural capital run the risk of marginalization while those who possess cultural capital have a valuable asset that can be used to secure favourable outcomes and which will offer a degree of protection in educational and labour market careers. In fact, Bourdieu thought that as educational policies were introduced to reduce the impact of structural resources on patterns of participation, cultural capital would become increasingly central to the reproduction of advantage. This is supported by a lot of school-based research that highlights the ways in which cultural capital is regarded by teachers as a proxy for intelligence while those who lack this capital are seen as stupid or disinterested.

If we hold onto the idea that class cultures serve as a reference point through which educational opportunities are evaluated, then we come to appreciate that active and prolonged engagement in education requires some sort of accommodation of an identity as a learner. Young people have to be comfortable to describe themselves as students and have to work out what that means to them in terms of involvement in their communities, in the here and now, and in the context of their future lives and careers. Here Reay (2005) talks about class-based 'authenticity'. For Reay, the effective participation of working class students is not about casting aside a working class identity, but is driven by a desire to accommodate their new experiences within a framework that respects their working-class roots. As Reay puts it, 'for the working class student authenticity most often meant being able to hold onto a self rooted in a working class past' (2005: 7).

Recent work on youth transitions has highlighted the importance of these subjective accommodations through the concept of biography: sometimes referred to as the 'biographical turn'. Essentially biographical approaches have been used as a way of understanding how individuals make sense of their lives within the dynamic processes of transition and change. As individuals we reflect on past experiences as a way of framing future plans and try to make sense of our lives through putting together a coherent story. In a sense, part of the biographical project of youth relates to the construction of a sense of selfhood in which there is a reasonable degree of congruence between objective and subjective experiences. In the past young people were, to an extent, able to use the experiences of significant others (especially family members or peers from the same class positions, gender, or with similar educational attainments) to help them construct road maps. In the modern world, it is argued that rapid processes of social change and the fragmentation of experiences make it extremely difficult to plan for the future or manage lives (subjectively or objectively) in a meaningful sense. This is an important theoretical shift: class, gender and ethnicity must be reflexively constructed; a process that results in a greater variation in the way such divisions are lived out.

In this context, meaningful engagement with education must involve the incorporation of education into the biography in a way that links positive outcomes in the future to participation and attainment. The concept can also be thought of as a method of coming to terms with the ways in which outcomes are not simply linked to the material resources of class, but also to a set of subjective capacities through which individuals are differentially equipped to manage their lives. Here Ball *et al.* (2000) have tried to highlight the advantages derived by those who are able to act as 'biographical engineers', but they also recognize that some young people have limited 'coping resources'. In this context it can be argued that schools have an important role to play in teaching life management skills and helping build young people's capacity for reflexive action and helping them to become aware of the very real structural barriers that must be negotiated.

Some implications for policy

Concurring with Wyn's (2009a) view that educational structures are often ill-suited to the complexities of contemporary society, and in the clear knowledge that education is doing little to address social inequalities in the modern world, it is worth reflecting on what should be done to bring about change. First of all, it is clear, as Basil Bernstein pointed out over 40 years ago, that 'education cannot compensate for society'. Radical changes, though, can go some way towards improving the educational experiences of all young people, especially those who are marginalized within existing structures. Under what Wyn terms the 'industrial model', young people are still expected to sit down and listen to formal lessons in traditional subjects. While progress has been made, on the whole the teacher is in control and the pupil is the subject rather than an active and empowered participant. It is the teacher – or often the state – that decides what the young person needs to know and how best to impart that knowledge. Despite motivation to learn, for many young people lessons are boring and unimaginative, and teachers who are tied into a market-oriented performance culture lack the freedom to take control over the curriculum. In a world where young people are required to reflexively construct their own biographies, more attention needs to be paid to capacity building, independence and decision making. Recognizing that young people's transitions from school to work are less likely to be linear movements, people need to be able to return to education as the need arises or as their interests shift. As such, a 'one-size-fits-all' model of education no longer meets the needs of young people. There are signs that education is becoming more flexible and imaginative here: there is a greater concern to try and engage young people of all ages, including those who have left early with few qualifications.

Inequality and marginalization is not simply part of the context in which we, as educationalists, operate. It is a core responsibility of education at all levels to actively strive to reduce the impact of social background on educational experiences and outcomes. Some groups will inevitably enter the educational system being much better equipped to learn; and this is not necessarily about ability or resilience – it's about resources and initial advantage. To tackle those inequalities so as to prevent marginalization, it may be necessary to focus on the less advantaged rather than on the more vocal and demanding middle classes. It is certainly necessary to monitor performance at the group as well as the individual level with a view to triggering appropriate interventions where we become aware of underperformance.

Underpinning these issues is the question of how we help working class kids to fit into, and even thrive within, a middle class world. Research shows us that the way to do this is not to encourage them to turn their backs on their own culture or to work in ways that value middle class culture over working class culture: this simply leads to resistance and alienation. Working class students must be able to accommodate new ideas within an existing, class-conditioned, framework to maintain an authenticity. Certainly more working class teachers could help provide effective role models: the sort of changes we have seen in recent years mean that parents may be less able to provide their children with an adequate knowledge of the occupational world or offer suitable guidance. We also need to ensure that schools and classrooms contain a broad social mix to provide a context in which young people can broaden their social horizons.

Summary points

1 Despite far-reaching changes in the economy and in young people's lives, educational change has been somewhat superficial. The

organization of education is often based on the assumption that young people make steady, linear progress and prioritize study over other competing activities.

2 Patterns of educational participation have changed radically in recent years, involving mass participation in post-compulsory higher education.

3 While young men once outperformed young women, in most countries female rates of progression and performance are superior. Although absolute gains have been made by members of all social classes, relative differentials remain relatively unchanged.

4 Although it has become increasingly important for young people to perform well educationally, many have a poor educational experience, feel alienated or adopt instrumental approaches.

5 There is frequently a clash between gender, class and racialized identities and school experiences. To succeed, it is important for young people to adopt learner identities that are comfortably grounded within their own class, gendered or racialized biographies.

Further questions

1 Discuss some of the reasons why increasing numbers of young people are remaining in education beyond the compulsory stage.

2 What are the benefits and risks of an educational system that separates students into academic and vocational streams?

3 Explain what Raftery and Hout mean by 'maximally maintained advantage'.

4 List some of the reasons why social class has such a strong bearing on educational experiences.

5 What is meant by the term 'hidden curriculum'? How does it contribute to the reproduction of inequality?

6 Do young people contribute towards their own failure within education systems through a process of resistance?

Further reading

Biggart, A. (2009) 'Young people's subjective orientations to education', in A. Furlong (ed.), *Handbook of Youth and Young Adulthood*, Abingdon: Routledge.

Cotterell, J. (2007) *Social Networks in Youth and Adolescence*, Hove: Routledge. Chapter 7.

MacDonald, R. and Marsh, J. (2005) *Disconnected Youth? Growing Up in Britain's Poor Neighbourhoods*, Basingstoke: Palgrave. Chapter 3.

McLeod, J. and Yates, L. (2006) *Making Modern Lives: Subjectivity, Schooling and Social Change*, Albany: State University of New York Press.

Wyn, J. (2009) 'Educating for late modernity', in A. Furlong (ed.), *Handbook of Youth and Young Adulthood*, Abingdon: Routledge.

Internet links

The report of the UK National Equity Panel, *An Anatomy of Economic Inequality in the UK*, is available through the link below. A shorter summary document is also available.

www.equalities.gov.uk/national_equality_panel/publications.aspx

Eurostat has produced a very comprehensive statistical overview of young people in Europe, including useful information in education. It is available via the link below:

http://epp.eurostat.ec.europa.eu/portal/page/portal/product_details/publication?p_product_code=KS-78-09-920

chapter 4

Employment and unemployment

Contents

Young people and work: change and continuity

Youth researchers have had a long-standing interest in patterns of work and worklessness among young people, and traditionally many studies in the field have been concerned with processes of employment integration and social reproduction as manifest in early careers. Indeed, the transition to employment has frequently been one of the most active and visible areas of youth studies. One of the earliest studies of the integration of young people into employment was carried out by Norbert Elias in the early 1960s with his primary interest being the investigation of workplace socialization and the adjustments made by new workers in order to fit into a new set of social relationships (Goodwin and O'Connor, 2005). This early work on young people and employment was carried out within a context in which large sections of the population were engaged in traditional manufacturing industries. Most young people moved from school to full-time employment at the age of 15 or 16, and females left their jobs to start families in their early twenties. The transition from education to employment was typically regarded as linear, involving fairly rapid and relatively smooth progress from the status of pupil or student to that of worker or trainee. In contrast, today relatively few young people work in the manufacturing industry, minimum-aged school leavers are in a small minority, and the transition from education to employment is protracted, messy and reversible.

Of course earlier transitions were actually more intricate, and several contemporary writers, such as Goodwin and O'Connor (2005) and Vickerstaff (2003), have argued that young people's employment experiences in the 1950s and 60s were more complex than we thought: frequent job changing in the early years was common and, despite relatively full employment, many lived in fear of unemployment.

To accept that the employment contexts for young people in the post-war era have always been fairly complex is not to suggest that important changes have not taken place. In today's world transitions from education to employment most certainly take longer to accomplish, partly because young people spend so much more time in education. It is not uncommon today for young people to spend much of their twenties either in education, perhaps combining study with part-time employment, or moving between a variety of jobs which may be regarded as temporary. In Mediterranean countries transitions are often even more protracted, young adults often spend their twenties in education, and have to contend with labour market conditions that are extremely precarious. Indeed, as we shall see when we look at patterns of work insecurity, it may be that a section of the population live out their entire lives in a state of flux, never completing a transition to stable employment.

Young people's increased length of involvement in education has led to a process of qualification inflation under which jobs that were once open to minimum-aged school leavers are increasingly reserved for those with post-compulsory education, while occupations that could once be accessed by those leaving education at 18 are being taken up by graduates.

Qualification inflation fundamentally re-shapes the transition to employment and makes conditions for those who lack credentials or who are unable to access resources that would facilitate extended educational participation much more difficult. However, the idea that there is a 'tightening bond' between educational outcomes and occupational success contains a paradox: it may be increasingly difficult to secure a 'good job' without educational credentials, but the possession of qualifications does not necessarily offer much in the way of protection.

Labour market changes affecting young people are not confined to a 'tightening bond' between education and employment; the process of globalization has accelerated the decline of manufacturing jobs in Western societies and has even led to the shift of some routine service jobs (such as call centre operatives) offshore to developing countries. In the post-Fordist society, small and medium-sized enterprises form the backbone of the economy while large employers contract work out to a network of peripheral firms who compete for business.

In the new economy, job security has been eroded and employment opportunities have polarized, with a wide gulf in pay and conditions between unskilled service positions on the one hand and professional, semi-professional and managerial occupations on the other. These conditions represent a breakdown of tradition and can lead to a new set of expectations on the part of young people growing up in what Beck (1992) refers to as the 'risk society'. Precarious employment contexts, together with the introduction of tighter regulations on support for those without work may force greater numbers of young people to survive through work in the informal economy (MacDonald and Marsh, 2005).

Patterns of employment and unemployment

To place young people's labour market experiences in context it is necessary to examine trends in employment and unemployment. To begin it is important to be clear that levels of employment (and of course unemployment) are directly affected by educational and training policies as well as by welfare policies. As young people are expected to participate in tertiary education, the supply of labour is restricted and the potential for mass youth unemployment is reduced. Similarly if welfare policies provide assistance to those who engage in training or work-experience programmes and deny benefits to those portrayed as the 'disengaged' workless, then levels of youth unemployment will be controlled. Unemployment is a term with an internationally agreed definition that is applied in ways that exclude large numbers of workless people.

U nemployment is a term that we all think we understand. It means being in a state of joblessness, lacking employment, enforced idleness. Yet away from the desks of labour economists, its true complexity is often overlooked. To be unemployed in an official sense means not only to lack employment but to be able and willing to work, to be of an age that is officially designated as 'working age' and to be actively engaged in the search for employment. The unemployed have always represented a small proportion of those who are workless. Unemployment is a contested status and both governments and organized labour have frequently been locked in struggle over claims for official recognition of workless status. Recognition is important politically as governments' economic policies are frequently judged on the basis of rates of unemployment. Economically, where benefits are available, they tend to be restricted to those whose claim to unemployment status is officially sanctioned and, socially, the public at large has been encouraged to distinguish between the 'respectable' unemployed worker whose worklessness can be linked to a temporary weakness in the market and those who are regarded as feckless whose position is a consequence of personal failings.

Mainly as a result of changing patterns of educational participation, across the developed countries trends in the post-war era have seen a fairly constant fall in levels of employment among young people. In 2008, in the 30 OECD countries, 44 per cent of 15–24 year-olds were employed (Scarpetta et al., 2010). Following the recession that hit Europe and North America from 2007/2008, rates of employment among young people have fallen significantly: in the EU, in the first part of 2011, it reached an all-time low of 32.9 per cent. With high levels of educational participation among the younger part of the age range (especially among females) and high levels of unemployment among those who leave education at the minimum age, we find that a small minority of 16–19 year-olds are employed full time. In the UK, for example, 15 per cent of males and 10 per cent of females in the 16–19 age range were employed full time in 2009; this compares to 51 per cent of males and 40 per cent of females in the 20–24 age range (Hughes, 2009).

A focus on changing levels of employment among young people provides only a partial picture. The nature of employment among young people has also changed, especially in the initial stages of participation. In particular, young people's early careers are often characterized by part-time and flexible forms of working, frequently combined with other activities, such as education. In the UK, even a decade ago, 60 per cent of Pizza Hut employees and 40 per cent of Kwik Save staff were students (Sparrow and Cooper, 2003).

Among 15 European countries[1] in 2008, of the 15–24 year-olds who were not in education, one in four were working part time; an increase from one in five in 1998. Levels of part-time work among young people were similar in Japan, but far higher in Australia, Canada and the US (40, 45 and 34 per cent respectively) (Scarpetta et al., 2010). The prevalence of temporary forms of working contracts among employed 15–24 year-olds also rose between 1998 and 2008: from 35 to 40 per cent in the EU and from 30 to 35 per cent in the OECD countries (Scarpetta et al., 2010).

The occupational changes linked to the emergence of a knowledge economy have resulted in a range of new opportunities for young workers as well as a new set of disappointments. An expansion of jobs in the professional and managerial sectors has provided opportunities for the growing numbers of young people with upper secondary and tertiary level qualifications, although the demand for qualified labour has not matched the growing supply of motivated and educated young people coming onto the labour market. Within 25 European counties,[2] in 2005, almost four in ten (39 per cent) young workers aged 15–24 were employed in hotels and restaurants and in wholesale and retail trade (European Agency for Safety and Health at Work, 2007). A few of these young workers will be employed full time in managerial or trainee managerial positions, but a large proportion will be employed part time and/or on temporary contracts and employed to carry out low-skill functions. In the UK, 38 per cent of young workers were employed in hotels and restaurants; in the Netherlands the figure is almost one in two (48 per cent) (European Agency for Safety and Health at Work, 2007).

In terms of occupations, in the UK, Sweden and the Netherlands the three occupations that, in 2005, accounted for the greatest number of young workers were service and shop sales, elementary occupations, and clerks: all relatively low-skill positions. In Germany and Italy – countries which retain a stronger manufacturing sector – the three top occupations for young people were craft and related trades, technicians and associate professionals, and service workers and shop sales workers (European Agency for Safety and Health at Work, 2007).

In the US, seven out of the ten occupations that were predicted to see the greatest growth between 2004 and 2014 (Figure 4.1) are regarded as low-skill occupations. Indeed, while the US Labor Department expected to see 7.5 million new jobs in the top 20 growth occupations between 2002 and 2012, 'almost 6 million of those new jobs (accounting for 17 of the 20 largest growth occupations) require job seekers with limited education

youth studies: an introduction

Retail sales
Registered nurses
Post-secondary teachers
Customer service representatives
Janitors and cleaners
Waiters and waitresses
Combined food preparation and serving workers
Home health aides
Nursing aides, orderlies and attendants
General and operations managers

Figure 4.1 10 occupations with largest growth, US 2004–14 (highest number of projected workers).

Source: www.jobsearch.about.com/od/cooljobs/a/topjobs_3.htm (accessed 15 April 2010).

and provide limited training and are typically identified as low-wage jobs' (Hansen, n.d.).

During periods where all-age unemployment rises, such as in times of economic recession, increases tend to be magnified among young people. It is usual for the rate of youth unemployment to be two to three times higher than among adults (Figure 4.2). In 2008, for example, in both the OECD countries and the 15 EU countries, unemployment among 15–24 year-olds was, on average, 2.8 times higher than among adults. In several countries, including Norway, Italy and the UK, youth unemployment was between three and four times higher and, in Sweden and Iceland, more than four times higher (Scarpetta *et al.*, 2010). There are a number of reasons for the higher rates of unemployment among young people: they are more likely to be in the process of transition and therefore seeking jobs at a time when employers cease recruitment; they are more likely to be in temporary positions; and are more likely to be laid off as they are not usually eligible for significant redundancy payments. Unemployment among young people is mainly caused by inadequate demand and there is little evidence to support the idea that the relative wages of young people make them unattractive to employers (O'Higgins, 2001). Indeed, by and large, young and older workers occupy different labour market segments and do not compete with each other for jobs. Employers hold varying ideas about the characteristics of younger and older workers, often based on stereotypes and with little in the way of evidential base. Young workers, for example, may be seen as energetic while older workers may be seen as responsible. As O'Higgins argues, 'the fact remains that young people are rarely seen as good substitutes for older workers (or vice versa) and the formal evidence, where it exists, tends to show that replacing one kind of worker with another, according to age, is limited' (2001: 17).

employment and unemployment

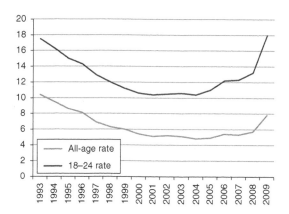

Figure 4.2 Unemployment trends by age range: UK (%).

Source: derived from figures presented in Bell and Blanchflower (2010).

During the recession of the 1980s youth unemployment was a major cause of concern in virtually all developed countries.[3] While economic recovery was accompanied by a fall in unemployment, there was a further rise in the early 1990s, followed by a reduction, and later a rise from around 2008 as economic fortunes deteriorated. Despite the severity of the recession that began in late 2007, in some countries (such as the Netherlands) levels of unemployment among young people did not reach the same heights as in the 1980s,[4] mainly because increased educational participation had removed a large part of the young population from the labour market or removed their eligibility for unemployment benefits, thereby reducing the incentive to register.[5] In 2008, in Europe as a whole, 15.6 per cent of 15–24 year-olds were officially unemployed, although in several countries the unemployment rate was closer to 20 per cent (Figure 4.3). Since then, youth unemployment has risen sharply, especially in Spain, Italy, Ireland and Greece. By 2010 unemployment among those under the age of 25 rose to 19.9 per cent in the Eurozone while in Spain it reached 45 per cent and in Greece 42.9 per cent (Euromonitor, 2010; Eurostat, 2011).

Early school leavers are particularly vulnerable: in the UK in 2009 the unemployment rate among 16 and 17 year-olds was 31.7 per cent (Hughes, 2009). Of course, official figures underestimate the 'true' rate of worklessness because to qualify as unemployed a young person has to meet strict eligibility criteria regarding search activity and availability and has to register.

While the explanations for high rates of unemployment among young people compared to adults are clear, unemployment in the early stages of a career can be particularly problematic. New entrants to the labour market

youth studies: an introduction

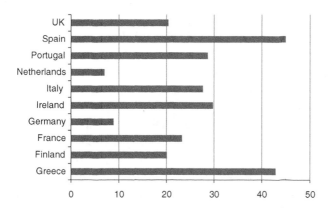

Figure 4.3 Unemployment among 15–24 year-olds, selected countries (%): 2011, second quarter, seasonally adjusted.

Source: derived from statistics collected by Eurostat (2011).

must develop a range of skills, some being 'hard' skills related to the ability to carry out specific work tasks competently, and others being 'soft' skills relating to the acquisition of behavioural traits, keeping good time, learning how to work with colleagues and take orders from managers. Indeed, the recognition of the need for skill development among young workers is frequently used to justify inferior rates of pay. For young workers, there may be long-term implications of being locked out of active labour force involvement at this stage in their lives. When employers stop or significantly reduce recruitment over a period of time they create the potential for the creation of what is sometimes referred to as a 'lost generation' of workers. The logic here is that when employers resume recruitment, they may have a tendency to employ fresh school or college leavers rather than those who have been unemployed for some time, leaving behind the older cohort among whom levels of unemployment may remain relatively high in the long term. There are several reasons why this might be the case. Where legislation sets age-related minimum rates of pay, employers might have to pay more for the services of those who have passed various age thresholds, even though they lack significant work experience or training. There is also evidence that unemployment carries a stigma and that employers might be suspicious of the work ethic of those who have been unemployed for some time. For these reasons, unemployment is said to 'scar' an individual so that the experience causes lasting damage to a career.

Much of the evidence supporting the 'scarring' effect of youth unemployment comes from examination of the careers of those affected by the 1980s recession. Economists have explored the relationship between an early

employment and unemployment

period of unemployment, subsequent earnings and future risk of unemployment. The consensus seems to be that unemployment has a greater impact on earnings than it does on the likelihood of future unemployment, largely due to the impact of reduced work experience on career progression (Ellwood, 1982; Arulampalam, 2001). There is also evidence that early unemployment has a lasting impact on future health and happiness (Bell and Blanchflower, 2010).

The recognition of the lasting damage caused by unemployment, as well as concerns about the relationship between worklessness and crime, has led to the development of a wide range of programmes for unemployed young people, many of which are designed to limit the time young people are without work so as to prevent long-term unemployment. In recent years the policy focus has broadened in an attempt to reach young people who might not be registered as unemployed or meet the strict legal definitions, but who are not in education and are without work. The term NEET, short-hand for Not in Education, Employment or Training, has been widely adopted in a range of countries and represents a broader approach to policy. While there are advantages in adopting a more inclusive approach, it has to be recognized that the large majority of the NEET group meet legal definitions of unemployment. The remainder of the NEET group are extremely heterogeneous, including the long-term sick and disabled, young carers and those taking time out to travel or pursue, for example, artistic or musical interests (Furlong, 2006).

> NEET as a category is extremely heterogeneous. It includes a proportion of young people who are available for work and are actively seeking employment: a group that fits the ILO definition of unemployment. Also included are those who are not available or not seeking work. Groups such as the long-term sick or disabled or those with responsibilities for the care of children or relatives may not be available for work. Some of those who are not seeking work may be pursuing other interests, resting, developing skills in an unpaid capacity through voluntary work or taking time to travel. The usefulness of NEET as a category is therefore compromised through the ways in which disadvantaged people who may lack the resources to navigate transitions or exercise choice are combined with more privileged young people who are able to exercise a significant degree of choice regarding the ways in which they manage their lives.
>
> (Furlong, 2006: 557)

youth studies: an introduction

Like the unemployment rate, the size of the NEET group fluctuates seasonally with a large rise occurring in the summer to coincide with school and college leaving dates. It is important to recognize that unlike unemployment, which has an internationally recognized definition, there are national variations in the ways in which the NEET rate is calculated. In Japan, for example, the formally unemployed are not regarded as part of the NEET group, whereas in most other countries they are a key component of the group.

Statistics on the NEET group are now collected on a Europe-wide basis for 15–24 year-olds. In 2010, 12.8 per cent of young people in the 27 EU member states were NEET, ranging from a low of 4.4 per cent in the Netherlands to a high of 21.8 per cent in Bulgaria. The risks of falling into the NEET group are highest for those with poor educational attainments, with low household income, with a disability, or with those who are immigrants (Mascherrini *et al.*, 2011). In a study carried out for the UK Audit Commission (2010), attempts were made to estimate the costs to the public purse of young people who spend time not in education, employment or training. Taking account of factors such as lost earnings and tax contributions, increased likelihood of subsequent periods of worklessness and the chances of contact with the criminal justice system, in some cases life-time costs were in excess of £2 million per person: costs that could be allayed by effective early interventions costing a fraction of that amount.

Work transitions

Early work on young people's transitions from education to employment tended to regard the process as linear: a one-way street that entailed progression from one status, education, to another status, work. While contemporary researchers have questioned this representation of earlier transitions (Goodwin and O'Connor, 2005), it is clear that, for significant numbers of young people, transitions today are complex and frequently involve reverse movements and periods of uncertainty. Some pathways in particular carry high risks. Those who leave education at an early stage, those who enter employment without training and those who encounter a significant period of unemployment may experience long-term labour market turbulence, especially in periods when overall levels of unemployment are high. It tends to be young people who have extended educational experience, who have performed well educationally and who come from reasonably affluent families who are able to manage to construct linear careers (Furlong *et al.*, 2003).

While Furlong and colleagues (2003) make a distinction between linear and non-linear transitions, a review of transitions carried out on behalf of the OECD made the distinction between young people who were 'poorly integrated' and those regarded as 'left-behind' (Scarpetta *et al.*, 2010). Those regarded as 'left behind' are young people with multiple disadvantages: poor educational qualifications, residence in remote or deprived areas, or those from minority groups. In the OECD countries around one in ten 15–24 year-olds are regarded as 'left-behind', with 'two in three already far removed from the labour market' (Scarpetta *et al.*, 2010: 19). In contrast, 'poorly integrated' young people are those who, despite having reasonable qualifications, find it difficult to secure stable employment and may enter a succession of temporary jobs, frequently interspersed with period of unemployment. This group is relatively large, across the OECD countries representing between one in five and one in three young people, and most prevalent in France, Greece, Italy, Japan and Spain (Scarpetta *et al.*, 2010).

Young people's transitions from education to employment are significantly shaped by educational qualifications which firstly determine the stage at which they move into the labour market and, secondly, provide a signal to employers regarding academic performance and conformity. As young people's engagement with education increases, it has been argued that the bond between education and employment has become tighter. In other words, young people's labour market experiences are increasingly determined by their educational achievements. While such a process may signal a move from a situation where job placement is heavily influenced by social class, to one where merit, as signalled by educational attainments, becomes a key determinant of employment situations, the end result is less clear: as we noted earlier, educational 'success' does not guarantee 'successful' labour market outcomes. Of course, access to education is restricted on the basis of social class, and qualifications can be seen, to an extent, as mere proxies for class position. Moreover, there is a strong body of evidence that challenges the 'increased merit selection' (Jonsson, 1993) hypothesis (e.g. Breen and Goldthorpe, 2001). While employers may screen applicants on the basis of their educational attainments, a range of other factors, which may be associated with social class, can influence recruitment decisions. Employers may, for example, frame advertisements for employment in terms of qualifications, but among similarly qualified applicants may be influenced by factors like accent, dress or demeanour in ways which favour those from middle class families.

The entry into employment has always been conditioned by a wide range of 'soft skills', but it has been argued that, in late modernity, a key skill is the ability to navigate uncertainty. The pace of change means that young people may be left without a clear route map and, to succeed, must be imaginative and entrepreneurial. Drive, resourcefulness and life-management skills become central to the effective accomplishment of transitions. With many of these skills being more prevalent in middle class families, young people from working class families may be doubly disadvantaged: they lose out in the educational marketplace then face marginalization on account of what employers may regard as a deficit in 'soft skills' and underdeveloped reflexivity.

Fragmentation of work and attachment to employment

Despite a wealth of evidence to the contrary, the work commitment of young people is often called into question. Suspicions regarding the lack of a strong work ethic are often made explicit in relation to young people without work, even in contexts where overall levels of unemployment are high. Studies of young people's attitudes to work show clearly that all groups of young people display a strong commitment to paid employment (Noon and Blyton, 2002; Trinca and Fox, 2004; MacDonald and Marsh, 2005), including the unemployed and those in insecure forms of employment (Furlong, 1992; Lawy et al., 2010; Maguire, 2010). Employment commitment tends to be highest among people in their early twenties and then declines with age (Gallie and White, 1993). Commitment to employment is strongest among those with good educational qualifications and is affected by feelings of personal control and success and attachment to an organization (Gallie and White, 1993).

While work commitment among young people is high, they tend to have a weaker commitment to work as a central life activity than older people. By the centrality of work, we mean 'the degree of general importance that working has in the life of an individual at any given point in time' (Meaning of Work Survey, quoted in Noon and Blyton, 2002: 61). The centrality of work tends to be higher among men and is something that tends to increase with age, partly as people acquire greater responsibilities and status at work and partly because other activities, such as peer group socialization, tend to assume less importance (Noon and Blyton, 2002).

Several contemporary commentators have argued that, in the face of technological change, it is necessary for people to fundamentally re-think the place of work in their lives (Gorz, 1999; Rifkin, 2004). When work becomes fragmented and precarious, with workers frequently changing their employment, it is time to explore new balances between work and leisure and to question traditional forms of commitment and the centrality of work in the self-concept. In fluid contexts, described by Bauman (2000) as 'liquid modernity', identity becomes a project that people constantly develop and revise. The development of identity projects and the narratives through which they are expressed require the cultivation of a new set of skills. Young people need to present themselves as desirable commodities in the labour market and be aware of the ways in which some forms of employment expect employees to project a particular image. It may also be necessary to tell a story that places a stable work identity and a coherent trajectory of career development at its centre. Despite having a turbulent career history, a young person may need to present themselves as someone who is in control of their career, who is not simply being bounced around from one job to another without there being any underlying structure or rationale.

The fragmentation and insecurity that sometimes defines young people's employment does have implications for commitment. People are not simply bound to their jobs by money, but may hope for a variety of intrinsic and extrinsic rewards. Employers tend to expect workers to demonstrate a commitment to their job that extends beyond fulfilling formal contractual arrangements: to be flexible at work, to be willing to accommodate the unexpected by covering for a colleague who is off sick or by working extra hours to accommodate a peak in demand. The willingness of employees to be party to a reciprocal, 'give and take' relationship is underpinned by what is often referred to as the 'psychological contract' (Rousseau, 1995). Traditionally, an important 'return' to the employee for their commitment and flexibility came in the form of job security, promotion and access to training. Under conditions of insecurity, the contract is undermined, or at least re-defined. One consequence is that workers put their own interests before those of the firm, although when jobs are in short supply, the reward for effort that goes beyond the scope of the written contract may simply be remaining in work.

These changes can mean that young workers place a value on a different set of rewards, such as flexibility, the gaining of transferable skills or access to new networks with the potential to enhance careers. In some contexts, such as Silicon Valley, transient workers can build a reputation for their skills and, through the development of an individual brand, can command premium wages. In turn this can lead to a new division between 'brand' and 'no brand' workers (Sparrow and Cooper, 2003).

Insecurity can also be a major source of dissatisfaction, mistrust, reduced performance and stress (Sparrow and Cooper, 2003). As Hellgren and colleagues note, a 'concern about losing a job is intimately related to stress symptoms such as ill-health, sleeping problems, and distress, and [...] such problems also tend to transfer to the non-work setting' (1999: 190–1, quoted in Sparrow and Cooper, 2003: 112). There have been few studies that focus specifically on levels of stress among young workers or analyse the extent to which changes in the organization of employment have affected young people's mental health. However, health and safety statistics do show that, as inexperienced employees, young workers tend to have a relatively high incidence of accidents at work. In Europe, the rate of non-fatal accidents among 18–24 year-olds is 40 per cent higher than among those aged 25 or over (European Agency for Safety and Health at

Work, 2007). Young people engaged in shift work and temporary work are especially prone to accidents, partly due to lower levels of supervision and poor bio-rhythmic synchronization (in the case of shift work) and poorer training in health and safety measures (in the case of temporary work) (European Agency for Safety and Health at Work, 2007). Young people also report higher levels of sexual harassment, especially among hotel and restaurant workers (Eurostat, 2004).

Insecurity in the new economy

Although significant numbers of young people will encounter difficulties in making transitions from education to work, relatively few will be locked out of the labour market in the long term. Early careers are frequently characterized by regular job changing, sometimes out of necessity as employment is brought to an end by an employer, and at other times out of choice as young workers move jobs to improve pay and conditions, to obtain greater security or career enhancement or simply to take up a job that is more aligned with their interests and qualifications.

In the US, it has been estimated that, on average, a young worker will switch jobs seven times during the first ten years of their career (usually moving to increase earnings) (Topel and Ward, 1992). While frequent early-career job changing is not a new phenomenon, evidence from a range of countries suggests that in recent years the numbers of jobs held by young people has increased (Pollock, 1997; Auer and Cazes, 2003). As Mortimer suggests, 'workers are increasingly likely to experience multiple job and occupational changes, with the need for "re-tooling", additional certification, degrees, or continuing education to remain viable in highly competitive employment markets' (2009: 150).

One core issue that is difficult to resolve using existing research concerns the extent to which the increase in the number of jobs held by young people reflects heightened levels of insecurity in the labour market (in other words, employers are shedding labour more regularly) as opposed to the emergence of new patterns of engagement among young people that can be linked to preference and choice biographies (reflecting a change in behaviour rather than a change in conditions).

With many young people now engaged with education over a protracted period and having to work to support their studies, it may seem rational to assume that these workers are less committed to such jobs in the long-term. Students may switch jobs to increase wages, to provide space for an extended break in the vacation or to increase hours of employment at times when they are not committed to study. They may also seek variety and get bored quickly with low-skill jobs. Moreover, graduate employers are unlikely to be concerned about frequent job changing among students and may even value broad experience. There is also evidence to suggest that young people do not want to commit to a career at too young an age with 'trendsetters' seeking to avoid traditional compartmentalized patterns of employment (du Bois-Reymond, 1998). Indeed, evidence from Australia suggests that significant numbers of workers prefer non-standard forms of employment (Simpson et al., 1997). Paradoxically, young people may report feelings of security in contexts that are apparently insecure; in contrast, older workers are more threatened by insecurity.

> Young workers focused on their employability in the labour market, and as a result were quite prepared to move between organizations and at the same time report high levels of security. In contrast, some older workers appeared to define security more traditionally in terms of job security and although they had not experienced job loss, insecurity derived from the possible threat of the loss of a long-held job in a specific organization.
>
> (Guest, 2000, quoted in Sparrow and Cooper, 2003: 86)

While increased job changing might be underpinned by the preferences of modern youth, it is also clear that there are new insecurities in contemporary labour markets that have heightened turbulence. Temporary contracts, part-time working and 'survival jobs' (Mortimer, 2009) appear to have become more common, forcing young people to change jobs more frequently. Young people may hold several part-time jobs due to the lack of full-time openings and may be employed under a variety of flexible arrangements such as agency work and 'zero hours' contracts. For many young workers the situation is not ideal, they may have little control over their hours and, where they hold several part-time jobs, may lose a lot of time in travel. As one American worker commented to President Clinton, 'don't tell me about the millions of new jobs created – I've got four of them and I'm not that impressed' (quoted in Beder, 2000: 131).

In such circumstances, young workers may need to be creative and explore effective ways of bringing together the jigsaw pieces of work with other activities, such as education, in a way that allows them to survive and thrive in the modern world. Working in several part-time jobs within the formal economy and coping with the demands of full-time study may leave little space for a social life (Woodman, 2010), especially where there is a lack of financial support from parents. Where it is difficult to find traditional jobs or where low-waged jobs fail to provide an adequate income, then young people may explore less traditional opportunities. Unemployed young people may find what MacDonald and Marsh (2005) refer to as 'fiddly jobs' to supplement benefits, while others may put their entrepreneurial skills to use in the illegal economy, selling drugs or shoplifting.

youth studies: an introduction

Young people may also incorporate legal but stigmatized forms of work, such as participating in medical experiments and sex work, into their job portfolios (Lantz, 2005; Colosi, 2010). Lantz (2005) followed a group of 40 students working in the Melbourne sex industry to help finance their studies. Her respondents worked as lap dancers, in strip clubs and as escorts and prostitutes. Some had few alternatives, such as international students who had large up-front fees to pay and had visa restrictions on the number of hours they were formally allowed to work. Others made lifestyle choices, valuing relatively high wages and autonomy. As one of her respondents put it, 'I can work in McDonald's on minimum wage, long hours and crap conditions, every evening and weekend, or work about two or three nights as a stripper' (2005: 392).

In the context of flexiblization, Beck (2000) speaks of the 'Brazilianization' of labour markets in advanced economies: a term used to suggest that Western labour markets are becoming increasingly stratified with growing numbers of people forced to live under precarious conditions supported by wages from temporary and insecure forms of employment. For Beck, insecurity is not something that is confined to those with few skills, but cross-cuts the entire occupational spectrum.

Temporary contracts are relatively common among young people and their use has increased in recent years. Temporary contracts are particularly prevalent in countries such as Poland, Portugal and Sweden where more than one in two are temporary workers, but more scarce in the UK where fewer than one in five lack permanent contracts (Scarpetta et al., 2010). However, while there is evidence to suggest that there has been an increase in precarious forms of work, especially among younger workers, it has been argued that the trend is often exaggerated (MacDonald, 2009). Indeed, typical transitions have tended to involve early career insecurity, with the (atypical) immediate post-war decades misleadingly used as a yardstick (Pollock, 2002; MacDonald, 2009). In their comparative study of transitions in the UK and Australia, Furlong and Kelly (2005) also advanced a cautious interpretation, suggesting that change was most evident among traditionally vulnerable groups such as the poorly qualified.

> The process of casualisation is not an all-pervasive one. It is a process that is having the greatest impact on the weakest labour market participants. It affects young women more than young men, but is also concentrated in the lowest skilled occupations, and in particular sections of a service labour market. In other words, we are not so much observing a process in which people

are selecting 'flexible' forms of employment that are suited to a modern life style in which work-life balances have become increasingly important. Rather, we are encountering a process by which less advantaged positions in the labour market are made even more precarious through various policy and regulatory processes.

(Furlong and Kelly, 2005: 223)

In countries such as Australia and Japan the growth in precarious forms of employment is more pronounced than in the UK and the 'old' Europe (Campbell, 2004; Inui, 2009). In Japan the term 'freeter' (a combination of the English term freelance and the German word for work, *arbeit*) is widely used to refer to young people holding temporary and part-time jobs (excluding students). Japanese government statistics show that between the early 1990s and early 2000s the number of freeters doubled: estimates vary, but range from two to four million 15–34 year-olds (Inui, 2009). Although the sharp increase in the number of freeters can be linked to a severe reduction in traditional employment opportunities affecting all age groups, in popular debate there has been a tendency to interpret the trend as one driven by the choices made by young people themselves. In this context freeters are often portrayed as parasites who are indulged by their parents and develop leisure-focused life styles.

Interventions and skill development

Leaving aside the debate about whether new forms of working are explained by structural change within labour markets or by preference and choice on the part of young workers, in the context of high unemployment the primary concern is to avoid a process of scarring that may be linked to fragmented labour market experiences among young people. Is any job better than no job, and does experience of poor quality work provide a stepping stone towards a more secure employment trajectory?

If employers place a high value on general work experience and the development of employment-related 'soft skills', then job stability may matter little. Moreover, some work experience may be regarded as better than no work experience. This attitude has underpinned a range of policies developed as a response to youth unemployment. Programmes have been developed to provide unemployed young people with work experience, often with a weak emphasis on skill development. While work-experience programmes can be regarded as well-meant attempts to move young people closer to the labour market, they are often underpinned by a suspicion on the part of officials that those without work are somewhat work-shy. This suspicion is formalized in the 'workfare' approaches that have become popular in a number of countries. The workfare approach makes the provision of benefits conditional upon the uptake of training or engagement in unpaid work. While compulsion is often justified in terms of the need to re-engage young people who have become discouraged and reduced their job-search activity, there is evidence that young people who participate in compulsory programmes may be stigmatized by employers (Fay, 1996). As such, voluntary schemes tend to be regarded as most effective (O'Higgins, 2001).

While there is empirical support for the idea that work experience enhances the employment prospects of the young unemployed, there is also evidence to suggest that, without the provision of quality training or strong links to the education system, young people may be pushed towards the low-skill and insecure sectors of the economy where they become trapped in a cycle of poor jobs interspersed with further periods of worklessness: a process described as churn (O'Higgins, 2001; Watson et al., 2003; Furlong and Cartmel, 2004; MacDonald and Marsh, 2005).

> Labour market churning points to the existence of a particular grey zone of intermittent employment where workers are engaged in employment for limited periods, interspersed with bouts of unemployment and withdrawal from the labour force. This zone exists at the edges of a broader realm of low-paid and low quality, but more longer-term jobs. It includes much casual full-time work and many jobs created through labour market programs, including traineeships. It also includes the large number of short-term casual part-time jobs. Most of these people pay a high price for entering this zone, particularly the instability which continually spills the workers back into unemployment. The highest risk stems from being trapped in this cycle whereby these labour-market disadvantages threaten to accumulate, closing off other options.
>
> (Watson et al., 2003: 41–2)

In this context, in the UK, young people in jobs without training have become a focus of attention because they are regarded as vulnerable to periods of worklessness. In policy terms, those in jobs without training (sometimes referred to by the abbreviation JWT) are defined as not in possession of Level 2 qualifications and working 16 hours or more, in a job where training to Level 2 is not being provided. However in jobs, they are regarded as 'dead end kids in dead end jobs' (Quinn et al., 2008). In the UK around one in ten 16–18 year-olds can be described as in jobs without training (Maguire, 2010) and they are thought to be concentrated in sales process, plant and machine operatives and elementary occupations, and over-represented in temporary and casual forms of employment (Maguire, 2010). However, research has begun to suggest that the JWT group is actually quite diverse and usually committed to working (Lawy et al, 2010; Maguire, 2010). 'They are not "dopes" who sit around on their backsides, but [...] are active co-constructors of their lives, asserting degrees of agency and control over different aspects of their lives' (Lawy et al., 2010: 346).

Government-sponsored programmes providing opportunities for work experience or skill development vary significantly between countries and are constantly evolving. In the UK modern programmes have their roots in the initiatives developed in the mid-1970s and have evolved from schemes that provided short periods of work experience to programmes that guarantee the offer of a range of educational and training opportunities to those who find themselves without work. In the EU an agreement has been reached that requires member states to ensure that all young people who are unemployed for six months are offered a 'fresh start' in the form of training, retraining, work practice, a job or other employability measure.

The measures introduced vary significantly, ranging from programmes underpinned by benefit sanctions that aim to move people into jobs swiftly (such as the UK, the Netherland and France), to those based on vocational training models (such as Germany) whereby accredited training is seen as central to effective labour market integration, to those that place an emphasis on providing educational opportunities (such as Denmark) (Furlong and McNeish, 2000). Where programmes attempt to move people into jobs as quickly as possible through low-level training or work experience, there is a risk that ex-trainees enter low-skill jobs and find themselves unemployed again a short while later. In contrast, countries like Denmark and Germany take a long-term view underpinned by the belief that proper investment in education and training may reduce the need for future interventions. In addition, in Denmark, a universal and general system of youth benefits makes education an attractive option (Fouché, 2010).

One of the key limitations of intervention programmes is that they tend to be most effective in helping young people who are initially advantaged rather than those with more deeply entrenched difficulties (O'Higgins, 2001). As a result, in several countries, special measures have been introduced to address the needs of the most disadvantaged. In the UK, the Gateway programme aims to prepare young people to take full advantage of opportunities available under the New Deal through the provision of counselling and by addressing specific problems such as illiteracy or drug or alcohol abuse. In France the TRACE programme is aimed at disadvantaged young people, especially those considered as 'hard to employ', while in Denmark, under-25s who have not completed secondary education or a formal training programme and who have been unemployed for six months are required to undergo an 18-month course (O'Higgins, 2001).

Experiencing worklessness

The experience of unemployment can have far-reaching consequences for individuals: it can shake confidence and self-esteem and has been associated with a range of psycho-social disorders. Unemployment can also affect relationships with family and friends, lead to isolation and extreme boredom and may sometimes lead people to consider alternative, occasionally illegal, ways of making money. Financial hardship tends to shape the experience, and in countries where support measures are generous, the consequences of unemployment may be less severe (Heikkinen, 2001).

Psychologists have tended to portray the experience of unemployment as involving movement through a series of phases (a variety of models have been used since the 1930s, but most recognize similar stages to those presented in Figure 4.4). On losing a job, an individual first experiences shock at their situation. This is followed by a period of optimism in which the individual assumes that their situation will be temporary and that they will quickly find alternative employment. Morale falls with the shock of unemployment, but soon recovers as they regard the situation as one that is likely to be short-lived. Optimism is subsequently replaced by pessimism as the unemployed person begins to lose faith and morale falls sharply as they come to regard their situation as potentially long term and life changing. Finally the unemployed may adopt a fatalistic attitude whereby they come to see their labour market situation as something that is outside their personal control and begin to structure their lives around other activities (Hayes and Nutman, 1981).

In a classic study of unemployment carried out during the Great Depression, Jahoda and colleagues (1933) highlighted the ways in which time lost meaning for the men who 'idle away the time, doing virtually nothing, with the vast majority not wearing a watch' (1933: 75) (in contrast to the women who were kept busy with domestic chores). The unemployed suffered from a loss of self-esteem and status and had restricted contact with people outside of their household. While few would want to challenge the detrimental impact of unemployment on psychological well-being, sociologists have made a number of qualifications, especially in relation to young people. First of all, for many young people a period of unemployment occurs directly after completing education rather than representing loss of a job

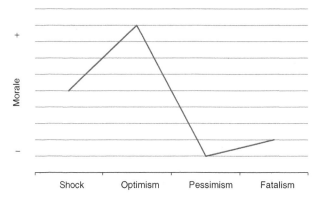

Figure 4.4 Key stages in unemployment careers.

Source: adapted from Ashton (1986).

and a threat to an established occupational identity. Second, a period of unemployment may be regarded as preferable to taking a low-status job without the opportunity to explore alternatives. Third, where peers are in the same situation, the social consequences of unemployment many not be as severe as for older people whose peers are mostly employed. Fourth, in the case of young people, the financial consequences of unemployment may be cushioned by the family (Ashton, 1986). However, family support may not be forthcoming and young people may be ineligible for unemployment benefits due to a lack of prior employment and might not have had the opportunity to build personal savings to fall back on (Economic Policy Institute, 2010).

Marie Jahoda (1907–2001) was born in Austria and obtained her PhD in psychology from the University of Vienna. She was forced into exile in the UK between 1937 and 1945 and shortly after moved to the US where she held posts in New York and Columbia universities. Returning to the UK, she worked in Brunel and Sussex universities. Her book *Marienthal: The Sociography of an Unemployed Community* (1933) was based on research undertaken in an Austrian community where three in four were dependent on unemployment relief. It is a classic study in unemployment and many of her findings relating to the social psychological impact of unemployment are still relevant today.

youth studies: an introduction

Ashton (1986) also makes an important point in relation to the variability of the unemployment experience that has relevance for both younger and older people: work identity as well as identity within the family varies by previous employment experience and by whether the unemployed person is a fresh entrant to the labour market. Those who have worked in professional and managerial jobs, who have a strong work-based identity, face much greater threats than do those in unskilled jobs who have a weaker investment in a work-based identity. New labour market entrants may not experience a threat to an occupational identity, but might face delayed access to adult status and may be forced into prolonged dependence on the family. While accepting that, for different groups of people, work-based identities may occupy a different position in the overall self-concept, it is important to be aware that research evidence shows clearly that the unemployed tend to have a strong work ethic and even show a 'greater commitment to employment than those in work' (Gallie and Vogler, 1994: 124).

Recent research evidence from the UK among 16–25 year-olds shows clearly that, compared to those in jobs or education, unemployed young people suffer from low self-esteem and are less happy and confident. While overall just 15 per cent thought that their lives lacked direction, this increased to 42 per cent among those not in education, training or employment. Arguments with family members were thought to increase and those without jobs lost confidence in their ability to deal effectively with job interviews (Prince's Trust, 2010). This is in line with evidence from a range of psychological studies of young people that clearly shows an association between unemployment and increases in psychological distress and psychological disorders, depression, anxiety and self-esteem, and reductions in happiness and life satisfaction (Banks and Ullah, 1988; Rutter and Smith, 1995).

Young people who cope best psychologically with unemployment tend to be those who have access to social support, especially help with finances and with suggestions about ways of spending time, those who have social contact with other unemployed people and those who remain active (Banks and Ullah, 1988). However, the type of support is important as when young people feel that they are being put under pressure to find a job, levels of distress and anxiety increase (Banks and Ullah, 1988). Young people who place the highest value on finding work and put great efforts into job-search activities may experience the greatest psychological distress (Banks and Ullah, 1988).

Some implications for policy

In many respects, policies focused on the employment of young people can lack grounding in research and fail to take account of the protraction and delinearization of experiences. Many of the assumptions underpinning policy are based on ideas about young people's approaches to work and about employers' demand for young workers that are out of touch with the reality of the situation. Unemployment in the developed world currently stands at a level that seriously damages the morale, living conditions and future prospects of a generation, especially in countries like Spain and Greece. Policies to alleviate youth unemployment must be prioritized, even in the context of austerity. Yet the world is changing in ways that make solutions implemented in past eras less relevant. Many favoured measures are summarized by a term favoured by the European Commission, 'activation': it carries an assumption that the problem that that needs 'fixing' is one related to the supply of labour, rather than to the demand. Clearly, when we have countries where one in two young people are unemployed, the problem is primarily linked to demand.

Several influential writers have outlined a vision of the labour market of tomorrow, characterized by poor jobs, fragmented careers and insecurity. These conditions are likely to be experienced first by young people and require a set of policies to counter trends, facilitate life management and underpin the basic securities that are fundamental to psycho-social well-being. In one sense we see the beginnings of a new approach in the ways in which the term NEET recognizes that vulnerability extends beyond the formally unemployed. In another sense though, NEET is framed in a way which neglects the relatively large group of young people who are constantly churned between poorly paid and insecure positions, sometimes without experiencing significant periods of worklessness. Standing (2011) uses the term 'the precariat' to refer to this growing, vulnerable band of people in varied forms of insecure work. For Standing this group tend to lack work-based identities and find it difficult to sustain a coherent narrative to connect their disjointed lives.

Running counter to the research evidence is one of the approaches taken by the Greek government in the face of growing youth unemployment and severe austerity measures forced on it by richer states within the Eurozone. In Greece the minimum wage rate for under-25 year-olds was reduced from €700 to €592 per month in order to improve their chances of finding employment in a failing economy. Even if we accept that intentions were good, the international evidence does not support the idea that levels of youth unemployment are significantly affected by relative wage rates (O'Higgins, 2001). Another common misconception relates to the ways in which policies influenced by the idea of workfare push people into accepting jobs or training to 'prove' their willingness to work without any regard for the interests of young people themselves: enforced participation on training or work-experience programmes are rarely effective and can be counter-productive.

youth studies: an introduction

Policies that involve enhanced opportunities for education and training are popular with many governments because they reduce the pool of people active in the labour market and can lower politically sensitive headline unemployment rates without the need to create jobs. One of the underlying justifications for such approaches comes from evidence showing lower levels of worklessness among educated populations. It is also true that in the aftermath of the 1998 recession, it was countries that had strong education and training policies (such as the Netherlands) that fared best. While attractive on some levels, the danger is that young people may be placed in a holding pattern, experiencing unemployment and underemployment at a later stage and making it difficult for them to establish relationships or make housing transitions. There is also a danger that rising participation in education puts at risk those who fail to participate and, in the face of mass participation, encourages employers to make selection decisions through recourse cultural capital in ways which restrict social mobility. In some countries there is also a growing tendency to provide internships which favour young people whose families can support them through a period where they are working for no pay.

Summary points

1 With young people remaining in education for longer periods, the entry into employment is delayed and often fragmented, and education is often combined with part-time or temporary jobs. Few young people are employed full time.

2 Young workers tend to be concentrated in a small number of occupations and industries which are often poorly paid. Many of the new jobs being created are in low-skill sectors of the economy.

3 The rate of unemployment among young people is always significantly higher than for older people. Early school leavers and those with poor qualifications are particularly vulnerable to unemployment.

4 Young people, even those who are unemployed, tend to be highly committed to employment, although compared to older people they may have a weaker commitment to work as a central life activity.

5 Employment insecurity can encourage young workers to seek alternative rewards such as flexibility or skill development. However, insecurity has also been linked to dissatisfaction and stress.

6 While governments have developed a range of programmes that aim to help re-integrate those who become unemployed, many schemes provide low-quality training and help push young people into low-skill sectors of the economy. While many programmes involve a degree of compulsion, the most effective tend to be those that involve voluntary participation.

Further questions

1 Describe some of the ways in which young people's labour market experiences have changed.
2 In the context of employment, what is meant by the term 'lost generation'?
3 How useful is the term NEET?
4 What does Beck mean by the term 'Brazilianization'? Does it enhance our understanding of labour market trends?
5 In what ways can the experience of unemployment be regarded as different for young people compared to older people?
6 What is meant by the term 'psychological contract'? What are the implications of changes in the psychological contract for young people's attachment to employment?

Further reading

Furlong, A. and Cartmel, F. (2007) *Young People and Social Change: New Perspectives*, Buckingham: Open University Press, Chapter 3.
MacDonald, R. (2009) 'Precarious work: risk, choice and poverty traps', in A. Furlong (ed.) *Handbook of Youth and Young Adulthood*, Abingdon: Routledge.
MacDonald, R. and Marsh, J. (2005) *Disconnected Youth? Growing Up in Britain's Poor Neighbourhoods*, Basingstoke: Palgrave Macmillan.
Mortimer, J. (2009) 'Changing experiences of work', in A. Furlong, *Handbook of Youth and Young Adulthood*, Abingdon: Routledge.

youth studies: an introduction

Internet links

This is an OECD YouTube clip discussing youth unemployment:
www.youtube.com/watch?v=-bwYnTge7sA&feature=channel

This is a link to the report 'Against the Odds' that discusses unemployment and the NEET group:
www.audit-commission.gov.uk/SiteCollectionDocuments/Downloads/20100707-againsttheoddsfull.pdf

chapter 5

Family, friends and living arrangements

Contents

Dependency, family relations and transitions

Family and friends provide an essential source of stability to young people's lives and represent a resource that helps support processes of change. These relationships are dynamic in nature and change significantly during adolescence and young adulthood. Whereas early youth is a time of dependence on the family, with young people subject to considerable control over most aspects of their lives, by the mid-teenage years boundaries are increasingly subject to negotiation. The protraction of transitions, together with changes in welfare and student funding regimes have made young people more dependent on resource transfers from their parents and have impacted on residential arrangements (Schneider, 2000). Indeed, the transition from co-residence with parents or carers to residence with friends, partners or single living has traditionally been regarded as one of the key markers of adulthood, representing a move from dependence to independence. Whereas this transition once involved a relatively early and fairly straightforward break, changes in the labour market and extended patterns of involvement in education have had a profound effect on residential arrangements and forms of dependency. Marriage, which once tended to mark the first stage of independent living, increasingly occurs later in life, often following the birth of children. Students frequently rely on the financial support of their parents, especially in contexts where state support is weak, while in some countries welfare regimes have been cut back to the extent that the availability of inter-generational resource transfers significantly affect young people's ability to leave home.

Leaving home has become more complex, frequently involving reverse moves back from independent living to co-residence with family. Young workers may take some time to reach a position where they have sufficient income and feel secure enough to set up their own homes. Young people are also likely to experience a greater variety in forms of residence, including shared accommodation with friends, single living and co-habitation with one or more partners.

The changes that have taken place increase the complexity of young people's lives and can be linked to a number of policy concerns. Insecurity and fragmentation of early careers can make it difficult for young people to secure quality accommodation and to become owner-occupiers, especially in contexts where rising prices make affordability an issue. The social housing stock has been allowed to diminish in some countries, while in others a severe lack of affordable housing has increased the prevalence of multi-generation households. Youth homelessness is a cause for concern in many cities, while a shortage of suitable accommodation can inhibit geographical mobility and make it difficult for young people to access jobs in other parts of the country. While young people are delaying starting families, concerns are frequently expressed about teenage pregnancy and welfare-dependent young parents.

In this chapter we examine relationships with parents and peers, patterns of leaving home and residential arrangements, including marriage, co-habitation and parenthood, highlighting significant change and continuity. We also look at potential problems by focusing on the issue of homelessness, the difficulties faced by those who lack effective support networks, such as care-leavers, and at processes of extreme social withdrawal that have been noted recently in countries like Japan and South Korea.

Families

While young people's lives have changed quite significantly, family structures are also very different, leading to changes in the ways in which young people are socialized and prepared for adulthood. Although still common, the nuclear family, consisting of a husband and wife who live together with their children, has declined in importance (Cheal, 2008). In the UK in 2009, around six in ten families with dependent children were comprised of a married couple and their offspring, almost one in four was headed by a female lone parent, 13 per cent involved a co-habiting couple while less than 3 per cent were headed by a lone male parent (Hughes, 2010). Single-parent families were three times more common in 2009 than in 1971 and twice as common than in 1981 (Hughes, 2010). The increased prevalence of single-parent families is largely a result of an increased divorce rate which, in the UK, reached a peak in 1993 (Hughes, 2010). Families have also become smaller with young people having fewer brothers and sisters: in 1971 9 per cent of British households contained three or more dependent children; by 2009 this had fallen to 3 per cent (Hughes, 2010). Family life has become more complex: young people whose parents are separated or divorced may spend part of the week with the non-resident parent, and they may also have to adjust to the presence of a step-parent or step-siblings.

The family provides young people with a crucial foundation for life: it equips them with the life skills and the resilience that help them cope with the changes they must negotiate in the external environment and prepares them for the relationships they will establish with people they encounter outside of the home. The family is also a crucial determinant of future life chances and attainment in the school and the workplace. Families prepare young people for different positions in the socio-economic hierarchy. The family environment can help prepare young people to become confident and competent social actors, but equally can produce ill-adjusted and poorly equipped individuals who find it difficult to organize their lives or relate to others. Research into styles of parenting tends to identify four ideal types which are rooted in class-cultures: authoritative; authoritarian; permissive/indulgent, and indifferent (Tyyskä, 2009: 50). It is authoritative parenting, which 'involves a gradual relinquishing of parental control over the child in a supportive and warm atmosphere that allows the adolescent to gain more control over his or her decisions and actions' that has been 'linked to the most positive outcomes, measured through high levels of adolescent adjustment, psychosocial competence and maturity, high self-esteem, and academic success' (Tyyskä, 2009: 50).

Even where families are regarded as warm and supportive, we can often identify overt and covert forms of conflict which impact on the lives of young people. First and most obviously, age can represent a form of power with younger members subject to greater daily control than those who have gained status and trust through age. Second, power relations within families are often gendered with women subject to greater levels of control and expected to perform specific roles. Third, as young people begin to participate in the labour market and make financial contributions to the family they may enjoy greater status and freedoms.

The material resources of families also have a crucial impact on the lives of young people. Some are able to benefit from an abundance of resources, a rich, stimulating environment and access to world-class private education. Others live in poverty with families concerned to meet immediate needs rather than being able to plan for the future.

> Individuals, families and groups in the population can be said to live in poverty when they lack the resources to obtain the types of diet, participate in the activities, and have the living conditions and amenities which are customary, or at least widely encouraged and approved, in the societies in which they belong.
>
> (Townsend, 1979: 31)

When material circumstances are challenging, there may be pressure on young people to leave school at the earliest opportunity to help with family finances, and investment in education may be difficult or impossible. In England, by the age of three, children from poor families are already nine months behind those from more affluent families: around a third of young people who, on account of family poverty, receive free school meals gain five GCSEs at A*–C compared to more than six in ten of those who do not get free meals (DCSF, 2007). While extreme poverty in advanced societies is often thought of as affecting a small marginal minority, in reality most developed countries' significant proportions of the population live in conditions of poverty. In the UK, more than one in five children live in poverty (22 per cent) (although in some areas around one in two children may live in poverty); in the US the comparable figure is 19 per cent, with 41 per cent living in low-income families (Child Poverty Action Group, 2010; National Center for Children in Poverty, 2010). Denmark and Finland are the only European countries where child poverty rates are below 10 per cent (Child Poverty Action Group, 2009). While poverty can be linked to unemployment, long-term sickness or disabilities, in the UK the majority of children who live in poor families live in homes where at least one parent is working and in households with two parents (Child Poverty Action Group, 2009).

> Studies of children's early physical and cognitive development suggest that family income in the first five years of life is highly correlated with developmental outcomes in early and middle childhood. And similarly, family income is found to be linked to developmental outcomes in adolescence and early adulthood. This includes the probability of completed schooling and early-adult success in the labour market, as well as the probability of having children out of wedlock.
>
> (Cheal, 2008: 31)

In the UK those growing up in single-parent families are more prone to poverty, as are those from large families, those in local authority housing and those from Bangladeshi and Pakistani families (Child Poverty Action Group, 2009). In the US, there has been a significant increase in families headed by female Afro-Americans, many of whom live in poverty (Cheal, 2008). In the Afro-American community, single parents often receive child-care support from grandparents, especially grandmothers (George and Dickerson, 1995), effectively providing children and young people with the support of an extended family. In low-income families it is not uncommon for grandparents to take some of the financial strain, and poorer families are more likely to live in close proximity to other relatives who are in a position to provide mutual support (Cheal, 2008).

Family structures tend to be conditioned by resources with extended families frequently formed to provide support to senior members or to young adults. As such, co-residence is often an indicator of weak socio-economic position (Cheal, 2008). Where extended families are constructed in order to provide assistance to a son or daughter and his or her partner or children, they are often said to be constructed through 'downward extension'; in contrast, where older relatives are incorporated so as to provide support, perhaps due to failing health, they are regarded as having been subject to 'upward extension' (Cheal, 2008: 29).

Friends and lovers

Peer networks are central to the ways in which young people's social horizons are opened up, exposing them to alternative views, values and expectations.

Friendship groups are also central to identity, impact on behaviour, provide crucial psychological support and represent a means through which people express their personality (Pahl, 2000). Yet young people's friendship networks and patterns of sociability have changed quite significantly as a result of a process of individualization and new frameworks that shape youth transitions. In times of rapid social and economic change, peer groups can help individuals understand and come to terms with new situations and can offer a contemporary alternative to the out-dated, and perhaps irrelevant, perspectives of the family. Where patterns of educational participation or labour market experiences have changed significantly, for example, parents may have had little exposure to the structures that their offspring will be forced to negotiate and, as a result, may provide poor advice. It is in peer groups that young people begin to come to terms with what Markus and Nurius (1986) have described as their 'possible selves', anticipating future mobility and lifestyles in modern social contexts.

In their *Inventing Adulthoods* study, Henderson and colleagues (2007) illustrate the ways in which young people's relationships with those outside the family, especially boyfriends and girlfriends, can influence decisions about transitional pathways. They also highlight the ways in which such relationships can both constrain or facilitate mobility. Although somewhat dated, Willis' (1977) study of working class males provides insights into processes of anticipatory socialization within peer groups that are central to understanding the reproduction of inequalities, while Walkerdine and colleagues (2001) highlight similar processes within female peer groups. In the context of mobility, Henderson and colleagues (2007) show how young people may revise their peer networks as they make transitions, letting some relationships wither and establishing new ones in line with their changing statuses. However, in a study of 16–18 year-olds in post-secondary education, Brooks (2002) showed that young people used a variety of strategies to maintain the stability of friendship networks, even when they were aware of growing inequalities between themselves and their peers: strategies included avoiding discussions about career choices and pathways with certain friends and being very selective in which friends they involved in decisions relating to the future.

Relationships with friends also fulfil a range of psychological needs. Cotterell (2007), for example, identifies six key functions:

- providing a network to facilitate the enjoyment of shared activities;
- providing loyalty and availability;
- providing assistance in times of need;
- providing reassurance and sensitivity to feelings;
- providing confidence and self-validation;
- providing comfort sustaining optimism in challenging circumstances.

Cotterell recognizes that young people are part of a variety of social networks, from tight, closely bound cliques to fluid clusters, and that not all of them meet each of the needs he identifies. He is also aware of social class and ethnic differences in networks and of differences between males and females. As Cotterell argues, 'females engage in greater disclosure of their innermost thoughts and feelings than males' (2007: 82). On the other hand, boys, even when discussing relationships, tend to adopt a more neutral stance. The relatively poor social and ethnic mix that characterizes many peer networks, and especially close friendships within them, is partly explained by opportunity structures and institutional constraints on patterns of social interaction. Social-psychological factors also play an important part in that 'reciprocal trust, social support and social connectedness' (Reynolds, 2007: 385) that are often provided most effectively by those who share a similar social background. Young Caribbeans living in Britain, for example, tend to have best friends who share their ethnic background: in turn these ethnically homogeneous friendship networks help them to negotiate ethnic identities and can 'act as a protective buffer and support mechanism in the face of social exclusion and racial discrimination' (2007: 385).

Recent changes have been seen to create the conditions for broader and more close-knit friendships, while others argue that the demands made on young people's schedules are so extensive and unpredictable that friendships suffer (Woodman, 2010). For Beck and Beck-Gernsheim (1995) the process of individualization strengthens primary relationships which are regarded as an essential source of stability in an uncertain world. New technologies make it much easier for young people to keep in regular contact with each other, using mobile phones and social networking. Technology can be regarded as a tool of liberation though which young people can keep in contact or develop relationships with people disapproved of by their parents, circumventing restrictions placed on face-to-face contact and reducing the chances of being eavesdropped during calls to landlines (Henderson et al., 2007). As a downside, they can also extend the parental reach to beyond the domestic sphere and lead to new forms of control through a phenomena referred to as 'iParenting' (Hofer and Moore, 2010), involving constant phone calls and text messages. Young people develop various strategies to prevent what they may regard as intrusive communication and have clear views on what is appropriate. In a study of Facebook 'friends', for example, young people were clear that parents were unwelcome as 'friends' and regarded parental access to public comments on the social networking site as a breach of privacy (West et al., 2009).

While new technologies may facilitate communication within peer groups and between lovers, Woodman (2010) has argued that changes in education and the labour market can make it more difficult to create the space for regular, direct contact between peers. For Woodman, the need to mix work and study and the unpredictability of employment schedules in the flexible economy means that making time for friends becomes increasingly difficult. As Woodman argues, 'the individualised timetables that have emerged with contemporary further education and casualised shift-based work, and their combination, make finding ongoing periods of shared time with the same group of people, at university or at work or with existing friends from secondary school, more challenging' (2010: 135). It is not simply that young people are increasingly busy managing complex lives, but that their 'timetables and rhythms are multiple and are not likely to closely synchronise with those of others' (2010: 155).

There is evidence that some young people, often struggling with the complexities of modern life, are withdrawing from social life. While acute social withdrawal among young people certainly exists in Western societies, it is a process that appears to be most acute in developed parts of Asia such as Japan, South Korea, Taiwan and Hong Kong (regions that have witnessed an extremely rapid pace of change). In Japan young people who completely withdraw from social life for extended periods of time and have no contact with anyone outside of their family are referred to as *hikikomori*: some estimate that they number more than a million (Saito, 1998; Zielenziger, 2006), although others regard this as an exaggeration and put the figure at closer to 200,000 (Inui, 2007). While the figures are disputed, it is generally agreed that numbers have risen since the mid-1990s, corresponding to a period of rapid change in the Japanese labour market and in transitions to employment. Although interpretations vary,[1] it has been argued that in a rigid system that offers few second chances, it important for young people to 'get it right' first time around: the pressures on young people who fail, or who perceive themselves to be at risk of failure, are intense. In Western countries young people are often able to take time out to reflect and change direction, while in some developed Asian countries no such flexibility exists. The *hikikomori* phenomenon highlights the extent to which patterns of sociability among young people and their connections to peer networks can be profoundly affected by processes of change in contemporary societies.

The term *hikikomori* is derived from the Japanese term for social withdrawal. Academic definitions vary somewhat, but Saito, who is considered to be one of the most authoritative practitioners, refers to *hikikomori* as people who have spent six months or more in an asocial state, being outside of education and employment and having no intimate relationships with anyone outside of the immediate family (Saito, 1998). There has been a tendency to think of *hikikomori* as confined to their homes, although some do go out on a regular basis. In fact while many spend most of their time in bed or lying on the sofa, some will go outside late at night or in the early hours of the morning when they expect not to encounter ex-classmates or neighbours. Others will attempt to hide their condition by leaving the house daily, as if going to school or work, but spending their time aimlessly walking the streets or riding trains. Another common mis-understanding is that while withdrawn in a conventional sense, *hikikomori* engage in modern forms of communication involving extensive interaction over the internet. Saito disputes this and argues that less than 10 per cent spend large amounts of time on the internet (Furlong, 2008).

While young people have been developing friendships since early child-hood, in their teenage years they often establish, or attempt to establish, more intimate relationships with others. These may be heterosexual, homo-sexual or bisexual relationships, and they may be fleeting, experimental or long term. The widespread acceptance of teenage sexuality in Westernized societies and the de-coupling of sex and marriage mean that experimenta-tion is common and multiple partnerships are the norm. As Henderson and colleagues suggest, 'relationships no longer follow a linear trajectory on a continuum starting with being single, meeting someone significant, devel-oping a relationship, getting engaged and finally getting married and having children' (2007: 149). Commitment does not always suit young people, nor is it necessarily expected, especially in the early stages of a relationship and where future pathways are unclear. Moreover, even within long-term commit-ted relationships, a variety of arrangements exist: from maintaining separate homes (referred to as living apart together – sometimes referred to as LATs), to co-habitation and marriage.

With respect to relationships, Arnett (2004) argues that young people today expect to have a number of lovers before settling down and that some hold the view that it is necessary to experience several intimate rela-tionships so as to learn what they want, and what they don't want, from a partnership.

> With marriage delayed for most people until at least their late twen-ties, the late teens and early twenties become a time for exploring their options, falling in and out of love with different people, and gaining sexual experience. They clarify for themselves what kind of person they would like to marry by having involvements with a variety of people and learning what they don't want in a relationship as well as what they want most.
>
> (Arnett, 2004: 73)

The protraction of youth and young adulthood and its experiences within a range of contexts opens the door for relationships with a variety of peo-ple and the opportunity to experiment with a range of different people. In practice, young people tend to develop relationships with people who

youth studies: an introduction

share a common socio-economic and ethnic background, who hold similar values and beliefs and are educated to a similar level (Michael *et al.*, 1995). This happens partly because the institutional contexts in which we meet potential partners are stratified, but also because those who share characteristics provide validation for personal values and beliefs and therefore make us feel good about ourselves (Arnett, 2004). As Arnett puts it, 'the more similar your love partner is to you, the more likely you are to reaffirm each other, and the less likely you are to have conflicts that spring from having different views and preferences' (2004: 79). So while new technologies can open a window on new worlds, communications may be restricted in ways that reinforce divisions and people may seek partners who share their own outlook and priorities: Facebook friends, for example, tend to consist of people already known in everyday life (West *et al.*, 2009), while internet dating sites may be selected to make contact with people who share interests (e.g. dating sites for professionals, for people of Asian origin or for those who hold specific religious beliefs).

Leaving home

The stage at which young people leave home has fluctuated over time and displays a strong variation by country. In Northern Europe, North America, Japan and Australia the majority of young people today have typically left home before the age of 30 (in many countries significantly earlier than this), while in southern Europe it is not uncommon for young adults to be living with their parents in their early thirties. In Finland, Denmark, the Netherlands and the UK, one in two young people live independently by the age of 24; in Portugal, Spain, Italy and Greece by the age of 28 fewer than 50 per cent are living independently (Aassve *et al.*, 2005).

The process of leaving home is often fluid and can entail reverse moves as, for a variety of reasons, young people return to live with their families (Jones, 1995: Goldscheider and Goldscheider, 1999). For this reason, researchers may have difficulty reaching agreement on the time at which someone can be said to have left home and at what stage they can be regarded as living independently (Mulder, 2009). Can a young person who moves into college residences be said to have left home, and can someone living with friends whose parents make substantial contributions towards rent be regarded as living independently? Research has shown that the reasons young people have for leaving home are related to the fluidity or permanence of their residential situation. Young people who leave for education or work, for example, are more likely to return to the parental home than are those who leave to live with a partner (De Jong Gierveld *et al.*, 1991; Mulder, 2009).

> In the early postwar decades, leaving home and marriage were closely connected. The age at leaving home declined in association with the age at marriage. From around the 1960s, the age at marriage began to increase again. In North America and Northwest Europe this increase in the age at marriage was partly, but not totally, compensated by a rise in unmarried cohabitation. In the end, postponement of union formation (the formation of co-residential partnerships) was seen in all European and North American countries, pushing up the age of leaving home. Around the same time or a few years later, however, a formerly rare phenomenon began to gain importance in North America and Northwest Europe: living alone or with roommates after leaving home. This trend pushed down the age of leaving home.
>
> (Mulder, 2009: 205)

Changes in the average age of first marriage have had a powerful impact on the age at which young people leave home. For a significant part of the last century, in Western societies, marriage was one of the primary reasons that young people left home with many making a straightforward transition from co-residence with parents to co-residence with a marital partner. A trend towards later marriage, an increase in education participation, changes in patterns of employment among young women and welfare revisions impacted on the age at which young people left home and led to a de-coupling of leaving home and marriage. 'Normative timetables' (Jones, 2009: 90) were undermined as the protraction of transitions opened up a space which began to be filled with a variety of forms of residence and a greater fluidity of arrangements. Co-residence with friends has increased in popularity and single-person households have risen significantly in Northern European and North American societies (Heath and Kenyon, 2001).

The age at which young people first leave home is affected by a range of factors. Females tend to leave home earlier than males, those with divorced parents or residing with a step-parent tend to leave earlier, as do those living in rural areas and in towns that lack a higher education establishment (Mulder and Clark, 2000; Mulder, 2009). Parental resources also have a significant impact on timing. Middle class parents may have the resources to support young people's housing transitions (Jones, 2009) and help accelerate the process through resource transfers, while on the Other hand, 'a caring family climate, or space and privacy in the parental home' may provide a disincentive to leave (Mulder, 2009: 207). Although parents

youth studies: an introduction

may subsidize housing transitions, there is evidence to suggest that leaving home can lead to poverty, especially in the Scandinavian countries where young people leave home relatively early (Aassve et al., 2005).

The tendency for young people living in southern Europe to leave home at a relatively late stage is affected by a number of factors. Low wages and the high cost of housing is one factor. Early employment careers in the south are often very fragmented and do not provide the means for independent living. Compared to the north, young people spend longer in higher education, sometimes switching between full and part-time modes of study, and there is a tendency for students to live at home. The transition of graduates into stable employment can also be fairly protracted and, as a result, graduates may not be in a position to leave home until they are in their thirties. Southern European countries also have relatively weak welfare provision, termed 'sub-protective' by Esping-Anderson (1990), and contrasted with the 'universalistic' provision of the Scandinavian countries. In the south, provision is underpinned by a belief that families rather than the state should be regarded as the main source of support. Consequently, whereas in some parts of Northern Europe the state will promote early home leaving through various subsidies, in the south these support measures are virtually non-existent. Tradition also plays a role. In southern Europe co-habitation is less socially acceptable and leaving home is still strongly linked to marriage (Iacovou, 2002; Jones, 2005).

In post-communist Eastern Europe and the former Soviet Union, patterns of home leaving and family formation have also changed little. With poor wages and a lack of affordable housing, most young people have little choice but to live with their parents, even when they have jobs and frequently after they marry (Roberts et al., 2009: Roberts, 2009). In Eastern Europe, the older generation effectively controls the housing stock and young people are forced to wait until they inherit private property, take over the lease of a state-owned property occupied by family members or work their way up the list for social housing (Roberts et al., 2009: Roberts, 2009).

For many young people, it is financial factors that determine the stage at which they leave home. In a survey of young people in 27 European countries, more than seven in ten (72 per cent) 15–30 year-olds who were living with their parents said that they could not afford to move out or said that not enough affordable housing was available. Just 16 per cent said that they wanted home comforts without the responsibility, while 7 per cent were waiting until they married (Eurobarometer survey, quoted in Hughes, 2009).

In many parts of Northern Europe there have been changes in welfare regimes that have effectively increased young people's dependence on their families and restricted opportunities for leaving home among those unable to rely on financial support from their families. While changes in welfare entitlements and the reduction in the relative value of payments have been partly responsible for the increased financial dependency of young people on their families, employment insecurity, the prevalence of part-time working and low youth wages mean that even when they are in employment, those under the age of 20 tend to remain financially dependent on their families (Schneider, 2000). This has knock-on effects on other status transitions: in a UK survey, one in five 18–44 year-olds said that they were delaying having children because they could not afford to buy a home, while a similar number said that it would take them ten or more years to save for the deposit for a house or flat (Turffrey, 2010).

As providers of financial assistance to their offspring, parents' power to influence young people's behaviour has increased. Parents may try to influence courses of study, job choices and even the development of intimate relationships (Jones et al., 2006). Here Jones and colleagues (2006) argue that, despite a weakening of 'normative timetables', parents often use their own experiences as a benchmark in their attempts to influence young people's behaviour. 'In keeping their children on the "right track", many parents draw initially on their own behaviour when young, describing these as traditional. Some persist with these outdated norms and are faced with a crisis of authority, while others adapt their constrictions of what is "right" to reflect recent trends' (Jones et al., 2006: 377).

Vulnerable leavers

While young people have become increasingly dependent financially on their parents (Schneider, 2000), there are young people who are forced to fend for themselves at an early age and have to survive on benefits. These include young people who have difficult relationships with their families and are effectively forced to leave, those who have suffered abuse within the family and those who have been 'cared for' by the state. These forced early leavers often face extremely difficult transitions and can find it difficult to secure and maintain accommodation (Horrocks, 2002). Indeed, care leavers tend to be strongly represented among homeless populations (Horrocks, 2002). Changes in welfare systems may have been associated with an increase in homelessness in many Western societies, although some researchers argue that the evidence for a significant increase in youth homelessness is weak and often exaggerated (Pleace and Fitzpatrick, 2004).

It is, however, extremely difficult to accurately quantify levels of homelessness among young people. While the popular image of the homeless involves rough sleeping, there are a wide variety of situations that can be indicative of homelessness. The young homeless may have some sort of temporary accommodation such as a Bed and Breakfast or hostel accommodation, or may sleep on couches in other people's homes. Many

youth studies: an introduction

young people do not qualify for re-housing by state agencies and, in such circumstances, are unlikely to be included in official statistics. In the UK, for example, people only qualify for priority re-housing in a limited number of circumstances, usually involving people with dependent children. In their report on youth homelessness in England, Pleace and Fitzpatrick argue that 'none of the homelessness data sources currently available provide the sort of snapshot "stock" figures required to generate [...] a "point-in-time" estimate. Thus it is not possible to even commence this exercise at present' (2004: 4). However, the evidence does show that those who have left local authority care and those with disrupted family life during childhood are particularly vulnerable to homelessness, while females are more likely than males to present as homeless (Pleace and Fitzpatrick, 2004).

Homelessness, and even residence in accommodation provided for the homeless, tends to carry a stigma which can make it difficult for those affected to move on and can impact on psychological well-being and mental health (Stephen, 2000). One of Stephen's respondents captures the stigma experienced by young hostel residents particularly well.

> See they must class us all together or something 'You must be on drugs', 'You must have an alcohol problem'. They think you're all young offenders and that annoys me cause we're no like that. You all get a bad name.
>
> (2000: 451)

Rugg and colleagues (2004) would regard housing careers that include periods of homelessness as 'chaotic' pathways which tend to be characterized by an absence of family support, a lack of planning and the presence of a range of external constraints. They also identify four other housing pathways: an 'unplanned' pathway, often involving constraints (such as pregnancy) but involving some parental support; a 'constrained' pathway which involves both planning and family support but also a range of obstacles (such as a lack of affordable housing or poorly paid work); a 'planned non-student' pathway which may involve a strategy and manageable constraints; and a 'planned student' pathway involving support and a safe introduction to independent living in student accommodation or in the private sector. For Rugg and colleagues (2004), the planned student pathway involving a 'sheltered' experience in the private sector provides a valuable housing education with lasting benefits.

Marriage and co-habitation

While marriage was once an important marker in a 'normative timetable' (Jones, 2009: 90) in many Western societies, for a number of reasons it has lost much of its significance for youth-adult transitions. First of all, marriage occurs much later, often long after a young person has left home, frequently after they have begun living with a partner and sometimes after they have become parents. Marriage as an institution has changed to the extent that it has ceased to be a significant milestone for young people. Fewer people are getting married and those that do are marrying much later. In the UK in 1966, 384,980 first marriages were performed; by 1996 this had fallen by almost 40 per cent to 236,980 (Figure 5.1). Moreover, the age of first marriage continues to increase. In the UK, the average age of first marriage in 1996 was 29.3; in 2006 it was 31.8. In 1996, 21 per cent of marriage partners were under the age of 25: by 2006 this had fallen to 12 per cent. Over the same period, marriages of 25–29 year-olds fell from 31–26 per cent (Hughes, 2009). In the US, although the average age of marriage has been rising since the late 1950s, it remains lower than in Europe and, among certain groups (notably white Americans) it is still fairly common for young people to move directly from the parental home to the marital home (Iacovou, 2002). In the US, the average age of first marriage in the mid-1950s was around 20, rising to 22 by 1980 and to 25 by 2000 (US Census Bureau: www.census.gov/population/www/socdemo/hh-fam.html (accessed 14 June 2010)).

With widespread acceptance of sex outside marriage and, since the 1960s, the availability of effective contraception leading to the control of fertility, attitudes towards marriage have changed. Co-habitation has taken over from marriage as a key rite of passage in the road to independent living, with most couples in Northern Europe who marry already living at the same address (Roberts, 2009). In the US, the majority of couples who marry have previously co-habited (Bumpass et al., 2000), with the

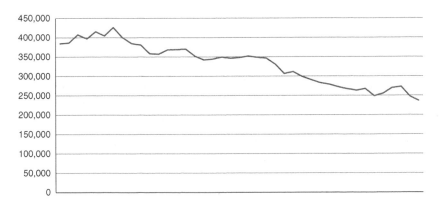

Figure 5.1 Number of first marriages, UK 1966–2006.

Source: derived from Hughes (2009).

youth studies: an introduction

numbers co-habiting having increased tenfold between 1960 and 2000 and by 80 per cent between 1990 and 2007 (US Census Bureau, 2000; 2007). In the UK, co-habitation gained in popularity in the 1970s (Kiernan, 1992) and the numbers of couples living together outside of marriage has increased steadily. Among those born between 1966 and 1970, just over three in ten co-habited between the ages of 15 and 29 while among those born between 1976 and 1980 the figures had reached 50 per cent (Hughes, 2009). The stability of co-habiting relationships vary according to country: in some countries, especially in Scandinavia, co-habitation is frequently long term while in others, such as the UK and Germany, co-habitees tend to get married when they have children (Ermisch and Francesoni, 1998; Blossfeld et al., 1999).

Family formation

The age at which young people become parents has also increased. In England and Wales in 1972 the average age of first-time mothers was 23.8; by 2008 this had risen to 27.5 (Hughes, 2010). While relatively uncommon (and subject to social disapproval) prior to the 1970s, from the 1980s onwards the number of births registered to unmarried women increased significantly so that, by 2008, 45 per cent of all births in England and Wales were to unmarried women. However, around two-thirds of these births were registered by two parents sharing an address (Hughes, 2010). Although births outside marriage are increasing across Europe, North America and Australia, cultural differences mean that overall rates vary substantially: representing more than 50 per cent of births in Estonia, Sweden and France, for example, but less than 20 per cent in Italy, Poland, Cyprus and Greece (Hughes, 2010).

Despite the continued rise in the average age at which women have their first child, in policy circles there are concerns about teenage mothers and young single parents. It is true that, on average, unmarried mothers tend to be younger than married mothers (27.1 compared to 31.5 at the birth of their first child) (Hughes, 2009). However, numerically teenage mothers are not a large group. In the UK in 2007, just 6.4 per cent of births were to women under the age of 20 with those under 16 representing just 0.9 per cent of all births (Duncan et al., 2010).

In the UK the number of births to teenage mothers has been falling, although they remain high in comparison to many other European countries. Teenage mothers, especially those under the age of 16, are a source of concern politically and are frequently highlighted by the tabloid press as a sign of social breakdown. In this context, the moral panic over teenage mothers (it is usually directed at mothers, not fathers) tends to be linked to multiple disadvantage, low levels of educational attainment and depressed aspirations. Also, fears have been expressed about a culture of welfare dependency, including planned pregnancy as a way of jumping the queue for social housing (e.g. Murray, 1990). Summarizing these concerns, Duncan and colleagues suggest that 'what seems axiomatic in this discourse is that teenage parents are necessarily and incontrovertibly *bad people*, *bad parents* and *bad citizens*, condemned to a lifetime of poverty, social hand-outs and economic apathy, and destined to repeat these failures across the generations' (2010: 4) (original italics).

Many of these concerns are either ill-founded or exaggerated. As Hawkes argues, 'teenage motherhood is largely associated with prior disadvantaged family background experienced by the teen before the birth of the child' (2010: 69), rather than teenage motherhood being the trigger for subsequent privations. In the UK, young women with parents working in unskilled manual occupations are 10 times more likely to have a child before the age of 20 than are those from professional families (SEU, 1999). In deprived areas, there is evidence to suggest that people display a greater acceptance of teenage pregnancy than in relatively affluent areas, whereas patterns of acceptance are reversed when it comes to abortion (Turner, 2004). Teenage pregnancy is declining (although not as quickly as some governments would prefer) and there is evidence showing that early pregnancy has remarkably little impact on future employment and earnings (Duncan *et al.*, 2010).

While early pregnancy is often unplanned few young mothers express regrets and many derive significant benefits from motherhood. Motherhood is an identity that symbolizes adulthood (Schofield, 1994; McDermott and Graham, 2005), which may be strongly valued among young women who find other transitional pathways to be blocked. As Duncan and colleagues argue, 'many mothers express positive attitudes to motherhood, and describe how motherhood has made them feel stronger, more competent, more connected to family and society, and more responsible' (2010: 16). Indeed, they suggest that 'for many young mothers and fathers parenting seems to provide the impetus to change direction, or build on existing resources, so as to take up education, training and employment. Teenage parenting may be more of an opportunity than a catastrophe' (2010: 4).

These findings are supported by young mothers interviewed by Yardley who felt positive about young motherhood and described the ways in which it had enriched their lives. These perceptions were often reinforced by their own families were 'there exists a value system within which young motherhood is worthy and esteemed' (2008: 671). In a study of 'planned' teenage pregnancy, Coleman and Cater (2006) found that young women explicitly regarded pregnancy as an opportunity to give a new direction to their lives; often linked to negative experiences in childhood and poor

youth studies: an introduction

educational experiences. In addition, there are some clear health-related benefits to early pregnancy which, for example, reduces the chances of breast cancer in the mother and diabetes in the child (McDermott and Graham, 2005).

At the same time, teenage motherhood has been associated with mental health problems (Berrington et al., 2005) and post-natal depression (Botting et al., 1998; Harris et al., 2005) and many young mothers report that they are treated poorly by the health, education, welfare and housing services (McDermott and Graham, 2005; Yardley, 2008). Young motherhood is also often associated with money problems and social isolation (Coleman and Cater, 2006). Moreover, young mothers tend to feel stigmatized by the public at large and by the media who often portray them as lazy benefit scroungers (Yardley, 2008). The majority of young mothers interviewed by Yardley were able to provide examples of situations when people had criticized them for having children, although within low-income neighbourhoods teenage motherhood was largely accepted and there 'was no likelihood of any recrimination or negative judgement over their decision' (Coleman and Cater, 2006: 603).

1 Young parenthood is not necessarily a disaster; many speak of positive experiences.
2 The difficulties faced by young parents are often linked to wider problems of social disadvantage.
3 Teenage parents dislike being labelled as such and like to highlight their multiple identities, e.g. their status as students, workers, etc.
4 While aware of the stigma associated with single parenthood, many feel well supported by family and friends.
5 There is a lack of evidence suggesting that teenage parenthood leads to social and economic exclusion: many either pursue, or plan to pursue, education, employment and training.

(Alexander et al., 2010)

Some implications for policy

In contemporary contexts, many young people are facing difficulties making a life in circumstances that lack stability and in conditions framed by policies that bear the hallmarks of a past age where journeys were marked by clear normative landmarks. Family life has changed, as have patterns of sociability, leading to situations where learning contexts and support networks have weakened. In a world bearing the scars of recession and where services are threatened by austerity measures, young people are often badly affected. Child poverty is rising in many societies and the types of welfare support once taken for granted are being dismantled. This has strong implications for young people and their future lives.

Linear transitions from dependence to independence, underpinned by policy based on normative assumptions, are changing. Under economic conditions where young people find it difficult to obtain stable and reasonably well-rewarded employment, it can be difficult to establish independent households and, in Northern Europe, North America and Australia, there is a risk that the pattern of prolonged dependency typical of southern Europe will become increasingly prevalent. Indeed, there is a danger that the Russian and Eastern European model, where young families are forced to live with parents will become more common. While non-linear housing transitions have become more common, the danger is that they become chaotic transitions. In modern labour markets young people need to be mobile, but under current economic conditions this has to be facilitated by modern approaches to welfare.

Patterns of family hardship and family breakdown mean that policy assumptions about patterns of parental support may be misguided. Moreover, while peer networks assume a heightened significance in periods of rapid social and economic change, there is evidence that young people are finding it difficult to synchronize their lives with those of their friends. The result can be pressured lives in contexts lacking support. Again there are lessons to be learned from other societies. In Japan and other parts of South East Asia, there is a significant problem relating to extreme social withdrawal; a psychologically damaging situation that must be avoided.

In terms of relationships, sex education is often presented in a context where healthy sexual relations are assumed to be stable and long term, whereas in reality young people often expect to have several lovers and do not necessarily want or expect commitment in all circumstances. While marriage has weakened as an institution and co-habitation has become increasingly popular, legislative change has often lagged behind in ways that provide little protection to long-term co-habitees. There is still an assumption that marriage represents the norm and that other types of relationship are transitory. There is also a strong stigma attached to young mothers, even though very few women become mothers at a young age and, among those that do, some derive clear benefits from their experience.

Summary points

1 The family environment is an important determinant of future life chances, attainment and well-being; however, a significant number of young people grow up in families living below the poverty line.
2 Patterns of peer interaction have changed in ways that place new demands on relationships, but also make it difficult to sustain stable relationships.
3 Young people are experiencing a greater variety of forms of residence which are no longer necessarily linked to other status changes.
4 Leaving home is a process that has become more complex, with end points that are difficult to identify.
5 Family forms and patterns of family formation have changed: families are smaller and single parenthood is more common.
6 While there are often concerns about teenage pregnancy, the numbers involved are small and there are associations with a number of positive outcomes.

Further questions

1 What type of parenting is linked most strongly with positive adjustment? Why is this?
2 Identify a number of social and psychological benefits derived from peer group membership.
3 Have processes of social change strengthened peer networks or made them more difficult to maintain?
4 In what ways can contemporary social change be linked to extreme social withdrawal?
5 Why do people tend to choose friends and lovers who share their own socio-economic backgrounds?
6 Account for variation between groups in the age of leaving home.
7 Should we be concerned about teenage pregnancy?

Further reading

Duncan, S., Edwards, R. and Alexander, C. (eds) (2010) *Teenage Parenthood: What's the Problem?* London: Tufnell Press.

Henderson, S., Holland, J., McGrellis, S., Sharpe, S. and Thomson, R. (2007) *Inventing Adulthoods: A Biographical Approach to Youth Transitions*, London: Sage.

Jones, G., O'Sullivan, A. and Rouse, J. (2006) 'Young adults, partners and parents: individual agency and the problems of support', *Journal of Youth Studies*, 9 (4): 375–92.

Mulder, C. H. (2009) 'Leaving the parental home in young adulthood', in A. Furlong (ed.), *Handbook of Youth and Young Adulthood: New Perspectives and Agendas*, Abingdon: Routledge.

West, A., Lewis, J. and Currie, P. (2009) 'Students' Facebook "friends": public and private spheres', *Journal of Youth Studies*, 12 (6): 615–27.

Internet links

This link will take you to a YouTube clip of a discussion on changing patterns of marriage and co-habitation among young people in the UK:
www.youtube.com/watch?v=C661pmoZiWM

This link will take you to a full downloadable summary report on youth homelessness in the UK:
www.jrf.org.uk/publications/youth-homelessness-uk

chapter 6

Identities

Contents

Perspectives on the development of identity in adolescence

Within the social sciences, there are important differences in the ways in which the development of identity is conceptualized. These differences were most apparent in the past, as modern perspectives have, to a degree, been converging. Essentially, psychologists and sociologists have developed separate approaches to identity and contrast to the extent that they see it as being grounded within the core of the individual rather than being shaped through engagement in an external social world.

Psychologists have a long-standing interest in identity change during youth because they regard the adolescent years as a crucial phase of psycho-social development. In the tradition of Sigmund and Anna Freud and Erik Erikson, psychologists have tended to focus on the psycho-social changes associated with puberty and developing sexualities, the implications of these changes for relationships and the emergence of adult identities. While contemporary psychologists are now much more aware of the 'plasticity' of identity in the years beyond adolescence and the ongoing impact of interactions between an individual and his or her environment (Bronfenbrenner, 1979; Arnett, 2004; Lerner and Steinberg, 2004), much of the classic work took place in a context where adolescence and youth were virtually synonymous, with the physical changes associated with adolescence following a similar chronology to the social changes linked to youth transitions. In the classic tradition, the focus was on *identification*: a process 'through which the child comes to assimilate (or introject) external persons or objects (usually the superego of the parent)' (Plummer, 2006: 281). This process of assimilation was often regarded as characterized by conflict and crises. Indeed, for Jung, adolescence is represented as a psychic birth which requires far-reaching adjustments in family relationships and frequently triggers conflict due to parents feeling threatened by the changes taking place in their offspring (Frankel, 1998).

The idea that the development of an identity is a staged process that begins in childhood and moves through a number of phases before an established adult identity is achieved can be traced back to the work of Sigmund Freud and his daughter Anna. The Freuds placed the development of sexual identity at the core of their theory of personality development. The Freuds outlined five stages in their psychoanalytic theory: oral, anal, phallic, latency and genital. In each of these stages, the individual becomes fixated on a particular erogenous zone. While healthy individuals progress smoothly through these stages, some become stuck, or fixated, within a particular stage until they are able to resolve the conflict that inhibits development. Someone who becomes stuck in the oral stage, for example, may constantly seek gratification though eating or drinking to excess.

> **Oral:** During this stage the infant derives pleasure from oral stimulation primarily through sucking. In this stage the infant is totally dependent on their caregivers and develops a sense of trust. A conflict

youth studies: an introduction

may occur during the weaning process where the infant must become less dependent. Fixation at this stage is seen as leading to an over-dependent personality and to a later tendency to over-eat, smoke or over-use alcohol.

Anal: During this stage the infant learns to control their bowels and bladder and may gain pleasure from toilet activities. But toilet training can be a source of conflict: while successful control may be a source of satisfaction, parents can react negatively and introduce a sense of shame or failure. Where parents are too strict, fixation can lead to a personality obsessed with cleanliness (anally retentive), or, where they are too relaxed about the process, one that is messy (anally expulsive).

Phallic: During this stage the child focuses on deriving pleasure from the genitals and begins to make clear differentiations between the sexes. Freud argued that during this stage of development boys develop an unconscious desire for their mother and begin to regard the father as a rival. The boy's desire to possess his mother and to develop feelings of jealously towards his father is described as the Oedipus Complex; and boys may fear that their father may castrate them as a means of punishment. Partly driven by the unconscious fear of castration, boys eventually come to identify with their fathers, repress sexual feelings towards their mother, and identify as a male. In contrast, it has been suggested that girls develop sexual feelings towards their father and a sense of resentment towards their mother: referred to as the Electra Complex. Freud suggested that girls come to envy their father's penis (penis envy) and blame their mother for their castration. Fixations that develop in the phallic stage can lead to a vain or reckless personality, with Freud also speculating a link with homosexuality.

Latency: The latency stage, which begins at around the age of six and lasts until puberty, is characterized by repression, with boys and girls primarily mixing in same sex groups. Sexual desires are largely dormant in this stage and remain so until the onset of puberty and the awakening of sexual desire. With a focus on same sex relationships, school work and sports, this stage is important for the development of communication and relationship-building skills. Fixation at this stage can result in low self-esteem and low confidence.

> **Genital:** In this stage sexual energies are directed towards the opposite sex and the libido focuses on the genitals. Healthy development will result in a well-balanced personality that is focused not just on individual desires, but on the needs and well-being of others.

Erik Erikson worked with both Sigmund and Anna Freud but came to believe that their emphasis on sexual development was over-played at the expense of personality development. He too subscribed to a staged model of development, with each characterized by a specific type of crisis which could be resolved in a healthy or unhealthy manner. For Erikson, there are eight stages of development: infancy, early childhood, pre-school, school-age, adolescence, young adulthood, mature adulthood and old age. While the stages are biologically determined, crucially he recognized that they are also shaped by environmental factors and by the times in which an individual lives. The crises that characterize each stage are specific to the forms of development taking place. So, for example, the conflict that characterizes infancy is one of trust versus mistrust: through crucial events such as feeding, the infant comes to trust the caregiver when they prove to be reliable and affectionate and may grow mistrustful were care is inconsistent. In early childhood the conflict is between autonomy and shame. Depending on how key events such as toilet training are handled, the child may develop a sense of control and independence or may experience feelings of shame or doubt. In adolescence, the conflict is between identity on the one hand and role confusion on the other.

For young people, dealing successfully with the identity achievement/role confusion conflict provides a foundation for healthy young adulthood and conditions the ability to form relationships with others and negotiate choice in areas such as education and work. Some encounter subjective chaos and confusion and find it difficult to establish a stable sense of self. Others manage to avoid serious crises of identity or manage to resolve conflict relatively quickly to develop a stable adult personality. Many modern social scientists focus on the crisis period referred to as a moratorium. A moratorium is a period of exploration in which a young person may experiment with a range of lifestyles, behaviours and identities until they find a way of being with which they are comfortable. As we have discussed in earlier chapters, youth as a stage of the lifecycle has become more protracted and takes place in contexts that are often complex and unpredictable. As a consequence, the moratorium stage may last longer as young people struggle to locate themselves in a world of uncertainty and

Table 6.1 Erik Erikson's Eight Stages of Development

Stage	Prime conflict	Outcome
Birth to 1 year infancy	Trust vs. mistrust	Through experiencing predictable and reliable care, the infant develops a sense of trust. In the absence of reliable care, the infant becomes mistrustful.
1 to 3 years Early childhood	Autonomy vs. shame and doubt	The child learns to control bodily functions and basic communication skills and through this develops a sense of autonomy. Failure can lead to shame and self-doubt.
3 to 5 years Pre-school	Initiative vs. guilt	Increased control and the ability to translate imagination into actions leads to a sense of initiative and purpose. Awareness of disapproval and a sense of guilt can block action through fear.
6 to 12 years Primary school age	Industry vs. inferiority	Through industry the child develops skills and learns to cope with new demands. Success leads to social recognition and a sense of accomplishment while failure can lead to a sense of inferiority.
12 to 18 years Adolescence	Identity vs. identity confusion	This stage is crucial to the psychological transition to adulthood and the adolescent needs to develop a sense of identity. Failure leads to confusion and a poor sense of self.
18 to 40 years Young adulthood	Intimacy vs. isolation	The young adult must learn to form intimate relationships and learn to commit to others. Failure results in a lack of intimacy and isolation.
40 to 65 years Middle adulthood	Generativity vs. stagnation	The task of middle adulthood is one of caring and contributing to the well-being of others. Failure can result in a sense of self-absorption and uselessness.
65 to death Late adulthood	Integrity vs. despair	In the final stage of life, successfully developed adults can look back at their lives with a sense of fulfilment. Failure can lead to bitterness.

take longer to negotiate the major decisions that underpin an adult identity (Côté and Allahar, 1996).

For psychologists, the development of identity tends to involve both continuity and conflict. Healthy development involves the idea of a core continuity in young people's lives, while conflict and rebellion can characterize movement between stages. The influential adolescent psychiatrist, D. W. Winnicott, suggested that 'adolescence involves the individual in the psychological drama of killing their parents in order to emerge as an independent adult' (Kehily, 2007a: 14). Over time the adolescent matures and the adult personality emerges, although the process can involve trauma and confrontation. Côté and Allahar are particularly critical of the tendency for psychiatrists to pathologize adolescent behaviour and to treat many common experiences as signs of abnormal development. In common with some other psychiatrists, Winnicott is sometimes regarded as having an 'exaggerated tendency to see young people as "afflicted" with the so called condition of adolescence': a 'disorder with various sets of symptoms' (Côté and Allahar, 1996: 8).

The classic sociological approach to identity has its roots in the 1920s and 30s in the symbolic interactionism of George Herbert Mead (1934) and Herbert Blumer (1937) and was developed by Erving Goffman (1959) in the 1950s and 60s. In the symbolic interactionist approach, the self is reflexively created through social interaction and communication. People build identity through social interaction: essentially identity is a social product constructed through interaction and embedded in the various communities we inhabit. Following the work of G. H. Mead, the self is seen as two-dimensional: it involves an 'I' which can be thought of as the source of action, and the 'me' which others react towards. Thought of in this way, the 'me' is the social self that we can only come to know through interaction with others. Described by Cooley (1902) as the 'looking glass self', the 'me' is the side of the self that we see reflected back to us through the reactions of others. 'The "I" is the response of the organism to the attitudes of others; the "me" is the organized set of attitudes of others which one himself assumes' (Mead, 1934: 175).

Building on these perspectives, contemporary youth researchers frequently regard identity as a project which is constructed in a multiplicity of sites and which, in late modernity, can lack a stable grounding. Postmodernists take this a stage further, placing a strong emphasis on the fluidity and instability of identity in contemporary contexts (Rattansi and Phoenix, 1997). The changes that have occurred since the 1970s are frequently linked to a crisis of identity in which individuals find it increasingly difficult to construct and maintain stable identities in contexts where economic life has become unpredictable and where communities have fragmented (Sennett, 1998). Where the core life contexts of the older and younger generations differ significantly, it can be difficult to identify useful role models or to learn through the experiences of an older generation. The fragmentation of experiences also underpins the idea that a process of individualization has taken place, involving increasingly diverse identities and lifestyles. For some, individualization is linked to a strengthening of agency and a weakening of structures such as social classes (e.g. Beck, 1992), while others have argued that late modernity is characterized by an 'epistemological

youth studies: an introduction

fallacy' in which structures become obscure without having diminished in impact (Furlong and Cartmel, 1997).

Identity projects, moratoria and emerging adulthood

Irrespective of whether they are framed within a sociological or psychological perspective, modern ideas about the development of identity in youth and young adulthood share some core assumptions. First, identity developed in a social context is always shaped by the culture within which the individual is embedded and is conditioned in time and place. Second, whether or not they are seen as formally staged or linear, identities can be regarded as life-time projects: few would now argue that a fixed adult identity develops during the later stages of youth or adolescence and some would argue that identity projects are never completed (e.g. Rattansi and Phoenix, 1987). Third, identities develop in multiple sites in ways that can overlap and conflict (Rattansi and Phoenix, 1987). We may simultaneously identify as a member of a particular ethnic group, as a male or female, as a student and an employee, a member of the working class, as gay and as Catholic. Not all of these identities necessarily sit comfortably alongside each other and the individual has considerable scope to develop (or indeed is constrained to develop) a coherent identity script through which these various components are linked. Fourth, there is general agreement that the protraction of the youth phase and the increased complexity of socio-economic contexts have implications for the development of identity, with some highlighting the negative consequences of a moratorium while others identify positive aspects of change. It is the consequences of protraction and the increased scope for individualized identity projects that underpin many debates in youth studies.

Psychologists often use the term moratorium in a negative way to highlight a pause in the process of adolescent development. Coleman, for example, regards a moratorium as underpinned by a lack of commitment to a pathway and involving attempts 'to resolve or avoid the identity work of adolescence' (2011: 69). From a sociological perspective, the Canadian scholar James Côté is one of the most influential writers on the implications of a period of moratorium on the development of identity in youth and young adulthood. While recognizing the potential benefits of 'time-out' (especially for those with the resources to use it constructively), Côté also focuses largely on the negative aspects of the moratorium. He argues that the extended youth phase can be characterized by marginalization and dependence with young people often failing to establish a sense of direction, confused in regard to the choices that may be open to them and being vulnerable to commercial manipulation.

Clearly, many young people from racial and ethnic minorities and the 'lower classes' often cannot afford the 'luxury' of elaborate forms of self-exploration, such as world travel or trying different schools and academic majors. Instead, their identity moratorium can provide neither opportunity nor guidance, especially if it takes place in the same neighbourhood or community in which the person was raised and will live as an adult.

(Côté and Allahar, 2006: 64)

According to Côté, 'the adult community [has] segregated and isolated young people, depriving them of institutionalized supports and ritualized passages into adulthood, the industries of mass culture have moved in, selling young people common sources of ersatz identity and ritual' (2000: 125). In the midst of this 'epidemic of socially produced identity crises' (Côté and Allahar, 1996: xvii), young people have to learn to manage their identities in order to 'continually fit themselves into a community of "strangers"' (Côté, 2000: 123). In late modernity, the identity tasks to be completed are immensely challenging and fraught with risk and young people are forced to make crucial choices in situations where previous norms no longer apply.

It is important here to be aware of the distinction between the late-modernist and postmodernist positions. For writers in the late-modernist tradition, people may have to cope with uncertainty and set-backs and navigate complex pathways without adequate route maps, but they are frequently able to maintain a stable sense of self and have sufficient agency to 'ride out the vicissitudes of late modernity with a sense of continuous self-identity' (Côté, 2009: 377). In contrast, postmodernist writers regard identity as fluid and de-centred because interactions have lost any stability (Côté, 2009).

The key difference between the late-modernist and postmodernist approaches is with the view of agency and the potentials for individuals to direct their own development by anchoring their self- or ego-identity, as opposed to being buffeted about by contradictory 'postmodern' forces with no internal point of reference.

(Côté, 2009: 378)

youth studies: an introduction

The other interpretation of the implications for identity in the protraction of the youth phase is perhaps most closely associated with Manuela du Bois-Reymond (1998, 2009), whose position is much more optimistic. Du Bois-Reymond tends to regard the extension of youth and young adulthood as a period where individuals – those who are free from the restrictions that characterized childhood and yet to be burdened with the obligations of adulthood – can develop alternative lifestyles and experiment with jobs and relationships. In this context it is worth noting that many of the more positive interpretations of identity development can be linked to writers located in the Netherlands and the Scandinavian countries (e.g. Mørch, 1997) where the conditions faced by modern youth are somewhat protected due to youth-friendly policies and economic cushioning. Mørch, for example, has argued that the increased homogeneity of life conditions experienced by young people provides the potential for 'equal conditions of adult life' (1997: 255).

Jeffery Arnett is also relatively positive about the implications of an extended youth phase for the development of identity. In line with classic psychological approaches that lay claim to a staged model of psycho-social development, Arnett (2004) claims that what he refers to as 'emerging adulthood' represents a new stage of development that became established during the latter part of the twentieth century. Emerging adulthood is characterized by a feeling of being 'in-between': a feeling of being adult in some ways, but still an adolescent in others. It is a stage during which young people gradually take control of their lives. During emerging adulthood, young people are self-focused, seeking to establish their identity and, while positive about the range of pathways open to them, they also feel a sense of instability (Arnett, 2004). Like du Bois-Reymond (1998), Arnett regards emerging adulthood as a positive stage: a stage where people are relatively free of obligations, less likely to be regulated by their parents and able to exert some control over their own lives.

Arnett regards emerging adulthood as a time of optimism in which young people look forward to a life filled with possibilities, including the belief that they will be able to create a good life for themselves involving a soulmate and a fulfilling career. Of course these dreams will, at some stage, have to face the test of reality but, 'during emerging adulthood everything seems to be possible, and nearly everyone believes that their dreams will prevail, whatever the perils the world may hold for others' (Arnett, 2004: 228).

The end of emerging adulthood and the start of full-blown adulthood involves the completion of the period of experimentation and the consolidation of identity. It is marked by commitment and responsibility in employment and relationships (Arnett et al., 2011).

Much of the criticism of Arnett's theory has come from sociologists who prefer to regard development as a process rather than a set of distinct stages; he is also criticized for failing to fully acknowledge the diversity of young people's experiences and the extent to which they are structured by factors like social class (Bynner, 2005; Hendry and Kloep, 2010). For Bynner, Arnett 'fails to recognize adequately that the huge diversity of individual experience is constrained by location in the social structure' (2005: 378). Arnett is not unaware of the possibility that social class has an impact on emerging adulthood; however, he argues that empirical work in the US has revealed relatively little impact of diversity on the process. While admitting that the US experience may be atypical, he shows that young people's views about the future display relatively little variation by class, with those from working class families being slightly more optimistic than their middle class peers. He also recognizes that young people from working class families tend to emerge as adults sooner than those from more affluent families; they acquire responsibility more rapidly and regard themselves as adults earlier.

Hendry and Kloep (2010) set out to test Arnett's ideas about emerging adulthood on a small sample of young people in Wales. They concluded that only one sub-group fitted Arnett's model, feeling themselves to be 'in-between' adolescence and adulthood, while others regarded themselves as adults (and had acquired adult responsibilities) at a relatively young age. Significantly, many of these young people lacked a sense of optimism and regarded their future prospects as bleak.

Components of the self-concept

Both sociologists and psychologists recognize the ways in which social contexts can shape identities in diverse ways and acknowledge that the process of adolescent development involves reconciling changing bodily images with a maturing self-concept. There is also a recognition of the ways in which new experiences and evolving expectations on the part of significant others impact of the shape of the self-concept and, frequently, can lead to conflicts with others or personal angst. In the psychological literature, the self-concept involves a number of components. Psychologists differ with regard to the number of dimensions of the self-concept that they see as core. Offer (1969) highlights five core components: the psychological self, which includes body image and emotional health; the sexual self; the social self, which includes attitudes to work and education; the familial self; and the coping self, which includes self-confidence and mental health (quoted in Coleman, 2011).

> Adolescence is a time when an individual struggles to determine the exact nature of his or her self, and to consolidate a series of choices into a coherent whole which makes up the essence of the person, clearly separate from the parents and from other formative influences.
>
> (Coleman, 2011: 58)

In sociological approaches the core components of identity (a term with its roots in Eriksonian psychology and which tends to be preferred over self-concept) are specified rather differently and tend to relate positions in a (divided) society (with key divisions pertaining to class, gender, 'race', etc.) which may or may not involve a subjective identification to membership of an objective group. Identity may also be specified as a variety of forms of identification that lack a linkage to the objective world and may even conflict with other identity-related memberships. A person may identify as being gay, as being religious or as holding strong political views which shape their core beliefs and structure the way they think of themselves in relation to others. Sociologists tend to hold a keen awareness of the real or potential conflicts between identities and regard identities as relatively fluid because they are shaped and revised within changing socio-economic contexts. Vocational identities, for example, are likely to be revised over the life-course and, at various times, one's occupation might be central or very peripheral to one's identity.

Recognizing the potential fluidity of identities, sociologists are cautious about regarding youth transitions as underpinned by the accomplishment of a mature, stable, adult identity. Many core identities are subject to revision throughout young adulthood and, sometimes, throughout the life-course. Indeed, fluid and revisable identities characterize young adulthood in contemporary societies, and youthful identities (in the field of fashion, style and cultural identification, for example) are frequently retained into middle age and beyond (Bennett, forthcoming). In the sociology of youth, discussion of identity is often compartmentalized and tied to the analysis of specific divisions (gender, class, etc.), behaviours and activities. In this book we have already touched on identities in the context of core divisions, and in subsequent chapters will focus on identities in areas such as politics and health and well-being and deviance. In the remainder of this chapter we will focus on the complexities of identity in a number of discrete fields.

Gender and sexual identities

In Chapter 2 we explored gender divisions and highlighted the ways in which they are reinforced subjectively by gendered expectations, and objectively, by processes of exclusion rooted in institutionalized practice in fields like education and employment. In this section we focus on gender scripts and projects that lend shape to sexual identities.

Sexual development and the maturing of sexual identities are often regarded as being at the heart of adolescence. Psychologists like Freud and Erikson regarded sexuality as central to the process of human development and argued that adult mental health was conditioned by the ways in which sexual maturation occurred. For psychologists, adolescence is a stage that begins with the physical onset of puberty and ends with physical, sexual and emotional maturity. During this stage, intimate relationships with others are central to the development of identity including the search for validation through the love of others from outside of the family. From an Eriksonian perspective, the crisis of adolescence is partly resolved through intimate relationships. As Coleman argues, 'an experience of intimacy contributes to the development of identity, and maturity, through opportunities for self-exploration. The intimate relationship enables the young person to hold up a mirror to herself/himself, even if it is a distorted one' (2011: 142).

The development of sexual interests and sexual practice comes into sharp focus in the adolescent stage, although they are likely to have emerged long before the onset of puberty, especially among boys (Savin-Williams and Diamond, 2004). As Savin-Williams and Diamond argue, 'sexuality does not suddenly turn on at puberty but develops over the course of childhood and adolescence through a subtle and gradual intertwining of erotic and social experiences' (2004: 201).

Expressions of sexuality and sexual identity are subject to myriads of rules and conventions that are policed in different contexts from the early years of childhood through to late adolescence and beyond. The social regulation of sexuality takes place within a context of heteronormativity in which boys and girls are expected to focus their sexual interest on members of the opposite sex. Pressure to conform to the heterosexual norm is particularly intense in the school and the peer group where homophobic language is common and where the term 'gay' is frequently used as an abusive label. Research has shown that 'errors' in the ways masculinity and femininity are expressed are quickly 'corrected' in primary school contexts (Davies, 1989) and that school teachers actively discourage affectionate behaviour between boys but are less bothered by such relations between boys and girls (Woodward, 2003).

While socially managed in ways that assume the majority will develop heterosexual identities, psychologists show that in adolescence the boundary between gay and straight has a high degree of plasticity (Savin-Williams and Diamond, 2004). As one young person who identified as transgender put it, 'I've concluded that my identity is as fluid as fuck. Sometimes I feel like a femme fag, sometimes like a butch dyke, sometimes like a cocky

youth studies: an introduction

teenage boy, sometimes like a girly girl' (Regales, 2008). Adolescent girls in particular have greater variety in their desires and expressions of sexual interest and are more likely than boys to experiment with same-sex relationships (Savin-Williams and Diamond, 2004). Estimates of the size of the non-heterosexual population are very difficult to arrive at, especially among young people who may still be coming to terms with sexual interests that may be confused or varied. The highest estimates of same-sex orientations suggest that just under 10 per cent of women and fewer than 9 per cent of men may engage in sexual activities with the same sex (Copas, et al., 2002) while lower estimates put the figure at around 2 per cent (Ford, 1989).

Young people today reach sexual maturity and become sexually active earlier than in the past, and minority sexual practices have become more accepted. The social and cultural environment in which today's young people mature is often regarded as sexually charged, with concerns frequently expressed about commercial and media representations of sex (Buckingham and Bragg, 2004). In this context, parents may worry about the sexual activities of their offspring and might feel ill-equipped to provide information and offer advice. In turn, young people can feel embarrassed by discussion of sexuality in the family and tend to get a lot of their information about sex from peers and the media (Buckingham and Bragg, 2004). Indeed, information provided by schools and from within families often has a negative tone: it can be about avoiding pregnancy and disease rather than about enjoyment.

> Contemporary Western culture considers teenage sexual expression a dangerous activity that should be delayed until greater maturity is achieved, or prevented until marriage, rather than a normative aspect of development with the potential to promote growth and well-being.
>
> (Savin-Williams and Diamond, 2004: 190)

Of course the gendered identities that mature in the adolescent phase have roots that stretch back to infancy. Masculinity and femininity are not innate but are learned identities and, as Foucault (1972) argued, are 'intensively socially organized and managed' and 'produced by institutional and discursive arrangements' (Buckingham and Bragg, 2004: 14). From birth, boys and girls are treated differently and are subject to different sets of expectations regarding dress, demeanour and behaviour: processes that are reinforced in the family, school and peer group and by the media. Parents tend to react differently to boys and girls, rewarding behaviours seen as conforming to beliefs about gender-appropriate ways of being and sanctioning behaviours regarded as inappropriate. Parents often expect boys to be more independent, assertive and competitive while girls may be encouraged to be more passive, sensitive and yielding. Schools and peer groups serve as important secondary sites of socialization, with children and young people often spending time in same-sex clusters learning gendered 'rules' of behaviour and facing a range of sanctions if they fail to conform.

Paechter talks of gender identities being learnt in what she refers to as 'communities of practice'. The 'process of learning to be male or female takes place within loose, overlapping, communities of practice. In these communities, children and young people experience what it is to be treated as male and female, and learn what the expectations of males and females are in the communities of which they are members' (2007: 6). In adolescence, the process of gender identification intensifies, often involving a 'flight to masculinity' for males and a 'flight to femininity' for females; the uptake of outmoded gendered scripts based on roles in bygone eras (Côté and Allahar, 1996).

In the classic tradition, psychologists writing in earlier periods sometimes adopted an essentialist approach in which these gendered 'traits' were regarded as enduring qualities linked to core biological and psychological predispositions. Modern approaches tend not to regard identity as a core biological component but portray gender as a project that is constructed within a social environment.

> A person's masculinity or femininity is not innate, it is not natural, but instead is something that is learned, constantly reworked and reconfigured, and enacted to the self and to others. Masculinity and femininity are active states; they are not just what we are, they are what we do, how we appear, how we think of ourselves, at particular times, and in specific places. It is thus a matter, not of an internal essence or core of our being, but instead of who or what we identify with, and how we demonstrate that identification to ourselves and others.
>
> (Paechter, 2007: 14)

Contemporary social scientists are often keen to show the ways in which gendered identities are the product of ongoing interactions between an individual and the various environments in which they live out their lives. Social class, time and place, for example, represent some of the varied contexts that help shape the variety of ways in which gendered identities are constructed. Moreover within various cultural contexts, there may be deeply entrenched views about the appropriate way to 'do gender'. In working class communities, for example, 'hegemonic masculinity' may involve 'physical "hardness", sporting prowess, "cussing" and hostility to schoolwork' (Frosh et al., 2002, quoted in Robb, 2007a: 121).

To Côté and Allahar, young people are often presented with exaggerated gender identities within school and by the mass media, which they refer to as part of the 'ideology of gender' (2006: 84). They argue that the gendered 'scripts' that are presented tend to be based on old-fashioned and inappropriate stereotypes derived from early industrial divisions of labour under which women tended to be responsible for the domestic sphere while men engaged in manual, male-dominated, work environments. The school offered, and to an extent still offers, a gendered preparation for further education, domestic life and employment, under which certain presentations of the self, aptitudes and possible futures are presented in gendered forms. Certain school subjects, for example, may be regarded as more suited to girls, while careers advice may reinforce tradition. Here Côté and Allahar (2006) argue that small and even non-existent differences in the skill sets associated with different genders are often used to justify widespread inequalities in people's distribution within social and economic life.

In the modern world, the mass media has a significant influence on the development of gendered identities. From their early years, children are exposed to advertisements and television programmes that portray gendered images and stereotypes (Buckingham and Bragg, 2004). The media attempt to promote interpretations of gender linked to specific product ranges, selling lifestyles built on specific constructions of gender. In this context there has often been criticism of the ways in which the media create moral panics about the 'crisis' of masculinity and over-sexualized interpretations of gender are sold to young girls through products such as fashion, cosmetics, music and magazines. 'Playboy' products such as stationary, for example, have recently been criticized by parent groups as inappropriately marketed to children and young people, while parent pressure has forced certain high-street stores to remove products, such as push-up bras and g-strings, which were being sold in child sizes. The UK prime minister, David Cameron, recently revealed that his six-year-old daughter has been banned from listening to music by Lily Allen and 'pledged to clamp down on the inappropriate sexualisation of children' (Mail Online, 2010). In this context, psychologists have argued that the sexualization of girls by the media is detrimental to mental health and healthy sexual development (BBC, 2007).

While families, schools and the media all impact on the shape of gender identities, they do so in socio-economic contexts that are rapidly changing.

Indeed, young people can be encouraged to accept gender scripts that impact negatively on future educational and occupational careers. In a study of white, male, working class youth, McDowell (2003) argued that, as a consequence of changes in the labour market, traditional masculinities can impede progress. With a decline in heavy industry and the growth in service work, employers frequently associate the qualities they desire in employees with traditional femininity: skills that involve empathy, caring and the ability to connect, to pay attention to appearance, and an ability to act as if they cared about providing a personalized, customer-focused, service (McDowell, 2003).

> Idealized versions of masculinity, [...] expectations of particular types of performances in different types of workplace all affect the ways in which young white working class men in Britain today present themselves as masculine as they negotiate the complex transition from school student to adult. [...] Making the best of it for white working class young men involves a complex negotiation between more reckless and hedonistic versions of laddish or protest masculinity and a more dour, serious version of a class-based respectability.
>
> (McDowell, 2003: 222)

Modern gender projects have to be recognized as complex and diverse and deeply enmeshed in the portfolio of identity scripts continuously being negotiated by individuals (Connell, 1987, 1995, 2000; Mac an Ghaill, 1994). Commenting on masculine identities, Connell has argued that across time and within and between cultures, there are a variety of ways of 'enacting manhood' (2000: 10). The same is true of feminine identities. The ways in which a young person constructs his or her masculinity or femininity may be firmly embedded in a class culture, or in an ethnic or sexual identity. With all young people forced to develop identity projects in which gender is but one component part, end products inevitably represent a rich and varied tapestry, and, within peer groups, gender identities are negotiated alongside other (overlapping) identities relating to class, to education and to sub-cultural orientations. Here Paechter (2007) argues that young people divide themselves into highly differentiated 'communities of practice' where, for example, feminine and masculine identities blend with gothic identities or Muslim identities. Within various subcultural contexts, gender identities can be relatively diverse. Mac an Ghaill (1994), for example, identified four typologies of masculinity within a school context.

Connell (1995) has noted that while a plurality of masculinities may exist, one version will always be dominant. She argues that masculine identities are developed within a set of power relations and institutional practices and are framed by reference to women as well as to what she refers to as 'subordinated masculinities' (1987: 183). In an industrial context, for example, the hegemonic masculinity may be one linked to physical strength or sporting ability while subordinated masculinities may be those linked to emotional labour. Another subordinated masculinity might be one linked to minority forms of sexual expression.

Class and identities

Class-based identities, which tend to be strongly conditioned by gender, time and place, have been radically transformed in the post-war period. As late as the 1980s, it was virtually unthinkable for sociologists to overlook the distinct ways in which young people's identities were embedded in class cultures. Yet today many reject the significance of class as a foundation of identity or argue that a process of individualization has all but destroyed cultural distinctions related to class. Changes in the world of work are particularly significant, as social class as a concept has historically been associated with collective relationships in an employment-centred process of production. For Marx, life chances were conditioned by employment relationships which shaped collective relationships and underpinned forms of consciousness.

Outside of the Marxist tradition, social classes have long been seen as linked to employment groups, with occupation impacting on lifestyles and influencing behaviour and opinions and, thus, shaping identity. In the industrial era, the working classes and middle classes were visibly distinct, residentially segregated and characterized by distinct world views. In this era, for young people, class largely determined their educational experiences, and forms of interaction at school and outside the school gates were largely characterized by social apartheid.

As we saw in Chapters 3 and 4, the social exclusivity of educational and employment contexts has been significantly diluted, even though social mobility continues to be seriously restricted. The greater commonality of experience between classes, which can involve working together in the same positions in the same firms, serves to make class less visible and inhibits the development of distinct class-based biographies: the scripts of class have become diverse and often confused. In this context, class has been regarded by some as a concept that has passed its 'sell-by date' and which no longer helps us to understand or explain social and economic divisions in a society where people are reflexively constructing identity scripts in a diverse variety of ways (Beck, 1992). Today social class is often portrayed as a resource or as a form of capital rather than a central component of identity, and there are calls for new approaches to class that capture the ways in which 'class is lived at the individual rather than collective level'

(Hebson, 2009: 29). Such an approach involves asking 'who am I?', rather than 'who are we?' (Hebson, 2009: 30).

Youth style affiliations and fashions were once understood as representations of broader class relations in which middle class and working class subcultures were clearly differentiated. Today the representations of class identities have become much more diverse and obscure. Young people may have greater difficulty identifying with a specific social class, may be reluctant to see the world in terms of class divisions and may even 'borrow' scripts traditionally tied to a class to which they have no objective ties. Thornton (1995), for example, noted the way in which middle class clubbers attempted to pass as working class. Working class identities have even become fashionable in some middle-class-style communities and, today, young people are sometimes regarded as 'creative actors' developing new cultural adaptations that 'waltz around the visible power structures' (Nayak, 2006: 815).

To acknowledge that, for many young people, social class no longer explicitly underpins identities in contemporary societies, is not to accept that class has lost its relevance. The core assumptions of young people, their habitus in Bourdieu's terminology, are still, to a significant degree, shaped by social class. For modern theorists like Giddens (1991), Beck (1992) and Sennett (1998), late modernity is characterized by a weakening of collective identities grounded in employment relationships and manifest in an increased emphasis on cultural and individualized interpretations of social standing. They suggest that many of the changes that have taken place in social and economic life have resulted in a tendency for class positions to become obscure and even meaningless (Beck and Beck-Gernsheim, 2002: 201).

However, research among young adults continues to show that many individuals do have a basic awareness of the ways in which their lives are shaped by unequal opportunity structures and can often link their experiences to a class position (e.g. MacDonald and Marsh, 2005; Furlong and Cartmel, 2009). While the everyday language of class may have declined, surveys continue to show that people are willing to acknowledge the existence of class, to assign themselves to a specific social class (albeit in ambiguous ways) and are able to 'articulate a sense of class' (Savage, 2000: 36). In other words, the scripts of social class may have changed, but class must still be regarded as an important component of young people's identities: identities that are complex, negotiated and multi-faceted.

Racialized identities

Like gender and class identities, 'racial' identities are extremely complex and cannot be portrayed through an essentialist linking of a 'racial' or ethnic identity to someone's skin colour or to the migratory history of their family. Terminology is also contested. Race is a term that may promote essentialist perspectives as it can imply that an unproblematic link can be made to a point of global origin and even to a genetic make-up that may be signalled by skin colour or physical features. Such a perspective has long been discredited as most people's physical and genetic background is the product of centuries of migration and inter-group marriage. The commonly used alternative – ethnic minority – is equally problematic because it carries the assumption that there are easily identifiable cultural expressions that can be linked to geographical origin and also, through the term minority, it implies a subordination to an unproblematic majority group. Here, Miles (1989) proposes that we use the term 'race' in inverted commas to signal the view that it is a socially constructed category rather than something that has an objective base.

> Customary categories such as 'Black', 'Asian', 'White', 'Other', and more recently, 'Mixed', hardly do justice to either the diversity within these categories or the influx of new migrants and their children. Similarly, customary descriptions of a white majority and ethnic minorities in some urban areas seem increasingly outmoded in new complexions of inter- and intra-ethnic group relations in western societies.
>
> (Webster, 2009: 67)

Sociologists have tended to focus on the complexity of racialized identities and the ways that they develop in conjunction with other identities such as class and gender. The themes of power and racism underpin much of the literature, with identities linked to patterns of exclusion via a process of Othering. Psychological perspectives have focused more sharply on 'developmental needs, stages and outcomes' (Deutsch, 2008: 82). Processes of self-definition for minority groups are seen as more problematic, as they involve positioning themselves in relation to a visible majority in ways that promote cognitive health and positive self-images (Deutsch, 2008). For some psychologists, developmental trajectories among minority groups can be quite distinct. For Hébert (2001), for example, racialized identities develop through a series of stages, beginning with an initial awareness in early childhood, moving through stages of conflict in adolescence and concluding in adulthood with resolution and acceptance. However, we must approach the idea that cognitive stages of development have a distinctly 'racial' dimension with caution. In many advanced countries certain racialized minorities are recorded as having relatively high rates of psychosis and hospitalization (in the UK, for example, in comparison to the population average, those of Afro-Caribbean origin are 44 per cent more likely to be detained under the Mental Health Act), but it has been argued that 'culturally appropriate and acceptable behaviour has been wrongly construed as a symptom of abnormality and aggression' (Black Mental Health UK, 2008).

As with other identity scripts, young people develop and hold 'racial' identities in conjunction with other identities. In particular, social class and gender both cross-cut 'racial' identities in powerful ways. Through colonial and migratory history and through direct discrimination, groups from different global locations are often drawn into low-skill employment and residence in poor, stigmatized, neighbourhoods, even when they have advanced skills (see Chapter 2). For young people of colour, many of whom have been brought up in advanced Western societies, there tends to be a strong association between 'race', poverty and criminalization. Transitions to employment can be difficult, partly because of a concentration in deprived, job-poor neighbourhoods, but also due to a stigma associated with residential location and direct and indirect discrimination on the basis of colour.

Racialized identities are essentially linked to a process of 'Othering' in which visible (e.g. skin colour) or cultural characteristics (e.g. Gypsy travellers) are used in a way that puts distance between one group and the more powerful majority. This is a two-way process which, in a negative sense, can involve racist practices through which a majority group labels a minority as subordinate; while in a positive sense, a racialized identity is embraced on the part of a minority as a way of celebrating and protecting aspects of a shared history. Identity work that involves the subjective association with a racialized group and thus a rejection of stigma associated with being a part of the Other, can have positive benefits for mental health (Ali, 2003), although may lead to negative reactions on the part of a majority who interpret cultural association as a sign of a refusal to 'assimilate'.

Here we have something of a 'Catch-22'. In the UK, Conservative concerns over a lack of assimilation (sometimes related to trivial behaviours such as supporting the Pakistani over the English cricket team) led to the introduction of citizenship tests and ceremonies for new immigrants. Better assimilation was seen as the way forward for stronger community relations. On the other hand, in a more liberal tradition, recent fostering and adoption policy has explicitly favoured placing young people of colour with adoptive parents who are regarded as sharing a cultural background as a way of building positive ethnic identities.

Religious identities

For some young people religion is a core part of their identity, shaping the way they live their lives and impacting on their beliefs and priorities. Young people may be brought up in families that strictly follow a particular religion, may be sent to faith schools and may be expected to curtail their activities in line with religious strictures. While profoundly important to some, in mainstream youth studies religion can be treated as something of an abnormality and as something that may prevent young people from participating in the rich and varied activities that underpin youth life; particularly in terms of the normalization of sex, alcohol and drugs. Indeed, Collins-Mayo has argued that 'religion has attracted only sporadic attention from youth studies scholars, even though religion – and more broadly spirituality – can be a core dimension of personhood, an important source of values, life purpose and communal belonging, and a vehicle for marking the transition from adolescence to adulthood' (2010: 1).

While young people may be willing to acknowledge affiliation to a specific religious community, membership of a religion does not necessarily imply that they hold a set of inspired beliefs that form an important part of their overall identity. Indeed, religions are often cultural communities as well as communities of belief and people may even attend religious services or participate in religious rituals without necessarily subscribing to the core tenets of their church. Catholics may attend mass regularly, for example, while neither accepting the infallibility of the Pope or even believing in a God. Similarly, people may believe in a higher being without feeling the need to affiliate to an organized religion, and membership of a faith community does not necessarily impact on social behaviour: there are Muslims who drink alcohol, for example, and Catholics who use contraceptives.

In the UK, one of the largest surveys of religious values among teenagers reported that around four in ten 13–15 year-olds believed in God, while nearly one in two never attended a religious service (Robbins and Francis, 2010). In contrast to northern European societies which are often perceived as secular and even as characterized by 'militant atheism' (Hoare, 2009), the US is frequently portrayed as a society where religious affiliation is high and where extreme forms of fundamentalist Christianity are rife. The evidence from surveys of young people does not always match this image. While 65 per cent of 18–29 year-olds in the US described themselves as Christian, around two thirds rarely or never attend religious services or read the Bible or other sacred texts (Grossman, 2010). Indeed, it has been argued that young Americans are less likely than the older generation to identify with a religious group, while almost three quarters of 18–29 year-olds agree that they are more spiritual than religious (Grossman, 2010). In Europe, research into the attitudes and beliefs of people recorded before and after confirmation preparation courses in Protestant churches in a number of countries showed that even after completing the course, belief in some of the central tenets of Christianity were relatively low. In Norway, Denmark and Finland, less than one in two confirmands thought that God created the world, while less than six in ten believed in life after death (Christensen *et al.*, 2010).

Religious characteristics of generation Y

1 They believe religion to be a choice and not an obligation.
2 Religious labels, including denominational identifications, are relatively unimportant to them.
3 They are typically tolerant of other people's beliefs and, in fact, enjoy the variety of different religious practices they see on campus.
4 Religious authority is internal rather than located in some external source, such as the hierarchy of a church.
5 They see more value in religious experience than in a codified set of beliefs.
6 They affirm the idea of being on a religious journey rather than embracing a static set of beliefs and practices.
7 If they join a religious group, they are more interested in the authenticity of the people – their honesty, openness, and humility – than they are in an authoritarian presentation of the truth.
8 They have no problem being eclectic in their religious taste, which sometimes includes creating their own hybrid religious identities.
9 They want to make a difference in the world and therefore believe that religion should address issues of justice and equality.

Source: Flory and Miller, 2010: 10–11

Religious identities are increasingly articulated in different ways among the younger generation compared to their parents' generation, providing greater opportunity for interpretation and allowing the possibility for blending aspects of a religion that they value with other core parts of their identity (Flory and Miller, 2010). Religion can be a lifestyle identity constructed reflexively as part of an overall biographical project (Giddens, 1991; Collins-Mayo, 2010).

Of course office holders in many established religions are hostile to the idea of people (young or old) taking a 'pick and mix' approach to their doctrine, regarding this as a challenge to their authority and even an affront to their God. Yet it would be seriously misleading to regard young people as part of a liberal vanguard facing up to the conservatism of an older generation. Young people sometimes represent the fundamentalist opposition to the perceived liberalism of the older generation. In the Christian world, 'straightedge' youth cultures are opposed to the practices, morality and sexual mores of their contemporaries (Wood, 2006) while among Western Muslims, an Islamic revival may involve the adoption of traditional forms of dress rejected by some of their parents' generation. Indeed, the growth of Islamophobia in post 9/11 may, in the face of racism and hostility by their Western peers, encourage Muslim youth to embrace an Islamic identity.

Some implications for policy

In a policy context, an explicit focus on identity is often centred on psychological pathology and is concerned with damage to the individual that arises from maladjustments that can be linked to traumatic experiences in childhood or adolescence. While often implicit, the concern with the 'healthy' development of identity underpins thinking on transitions. A common assumption underpinning policy is the idea of identity development as linear and as involving staged movement towards the stable identity of adulthood. Yet research suggests that the process of identity development is more accurately portrayed as a process that is characterized by a high degree of fluidity, often involving a moratorium. In policy terms this moratorium is often regarded with suspicion as an unconstructive phase impeding 'normal' progression and development. While it is true that moratoria can have negative consequences, especially when young people find themselves struggling to find a sense of coherence in their lives, time out can be used constructively in ways that allow individuals to develop plans and make sense of the complexity of life in late modern contexts.

Along with assumptions pertaining linear development, in a range of contexts pressure is put on young people to accept identity scripts relating to traditional interpretations of gender, class and 'race'. In terms of gender, these scripts are underpinned by tradition and heteronormative values which can discourage experimentation and lead to the repression of identities that fall outside of a narrow frame of reference. Gender roles that are promoted can also be rooted in an industrial past that often entailed a clear separation between masculine and feminine roles.

In the context of social class and 'race', young people can also be pigeonholed in policy terms in ways that bear little relation to how they live out and construct identities. In terms of social class, lines have become increasingly blurred and class scripts are interpreted in a diverse range of ways. At the same time, how individuals interpret and live out class-based identities can help frame aspirations and impact on patterns of mobility.

'Race' can also be a confused category that often rests on the idea that factors like country or origin and skin colour are key to understanding social difference when, for many, 'racial' identity usually confirms one aspect of a complex mosaic of cultural identity. To be effective, it is necessary to underpin policy with a more complex and nuanced image of modern youth in which negotiated identities are not seen as mapped onto visible traits in an unproblematic way.

Summary points

1 In the psychological tradition there has been a long-standing tendency to present identity as a staged process in which a series of crises mark out potentially traumatic adjustments from one stage to the next.

2 The development of sexual identities are central to the adolescent experience, often underpinned by pressure to conform to dominant heterosexual norms.

3 Sociologists tend to regard development as a process, placing a strong emphasis on the ways in which the self is reflexively constructed through interaction with others in societies marked by division.

4 Contemporary youth researchers often present identity as an ongoing project shaped by experiences in a multitude of sites.

5 Individuals hold a variety of identities, which may conflict. Some identities are more fluid than others, with some associated with youth while others will be retained well beyond young adulthood.

6 With transitions having become protracted, a number of researchers have argued that young people face a 'moratorium' in which development may be put 'on hold'. From a negative perspective this may be marked by a period of confusion in which people have to make important choices in situations marked by instability and unpredictability. A more positive interpretation presents this moratorium as a stage where people are free to experiment with alternative lifestyles, jobs or relationships.

7 Many of the bedrocks of identity in the industrial era have been re-shaped in contemporary contexts in ways that challenge classic perspectives. Social class, for example, is often re-interpreted in ways that lack a clear and stable link to employment relationships and may involve contradictions in the ways collective identities are expressed.

Further questions

1 Describe some of the ways in which conflict can mark out stages of development and how failure to address conflict can impede successful development.
2 What is meant by the term 'moratorium'? On balance, do you think it has negative or positive consequences?
3 In what ways can the development of identity be thought of as a project?
4 Does the idea of emerging adulthood help us understand the implications of protracted transitions?
5 What are the key differences between sociological and psychological approaches to identity?
6 How do intimate relationships contribute to the development of identity?
7 What is meant by the term 'heteronormativity'? What are the implications for identity development?
8 Can social class still be regarded as an important component of identity? How have class identities changed?

Further reading

Côté, J. (2000) *Arrested Adulthood: The Changing Nature of Maturity and Identity*, New York: New York University Press.
du Bois-Reymond, M. (2009) 'Models of navigation and life management', in A. Furlong (ed.), *Handbook of Youth and Young Adulthood*, Abingdon: Routledge.
Holland, J. (2009) 'Understanding the sexual lives of young people', in A. Furlong (ed.), *Handbook of Youth and Young Adulthood*, Abingdon: Routledge.
Kroger, J. (2004) *Identity in Adolescence*, 3rd edn, Abingdon: Routledge.

Internet links

YouTube clip illustrating Freud's stages of development:
www.youtube.com/watch?v=gFNU-RHTMOo&feature=related

YouTube clip illustrating Erikson's stages of development:

www.youtube.com/watch?v=dGFKAfixHJs

Alternative YouTube clip illustrating Erikson's stages of development:
www.youtube.com/watch?v=bdPPXGadRAU&feature=fvw

BBC article on the way sexualization of young girls impacts and harms development:
BBC News, 20 February 2007, http://news.bbc.co.uk/1/hi/health/6376421.stm

Article on the mental health of black people in the UK:
www.blackmentalhealth.org.uk/index.php?option=com-content&task=view&id=154&Itemid=139

Youth cultures and lifestyles

Bringing in culture

While there has been a strong and fruitful research tradition in the area of youth cultures and lifestyles, there has been a long-standing separation, and sometimes hostility, between what might loosely be referred to as the 'cultural' and the 'transitional' perspectives in youth studies which are manifest most strongly in discussions of lifestyles. Whereas those who identify with the 'cultural tradition' have focused on fashion, style and cultural responses and representations in youth, those working in the 'transitions tradition' have focused on patterns of economic socialization, linkages between education and work, processes of incorporation into employment and studies of social reproduction. This 'false binary' (Furlong *et al.*, 2011) partly stems from differences in methodologies (those working within the 'cultural tradition' have tended to use qualitative approaches, while those in the 'transitions tradition' have been more likely to use quantitative methods), but is also linked to a confusion of the ways each of the traditions contributes to a holistic understanding of youth in modern societies. While early work within the 'cultural tradition' (particularly the work of Stuart Hall and Tony Jefferson (1976) and Paul Willis (1977)) had a core concern with understanding the dynamics of processes of social reproduction through cultural resistance by young people, all too often contemporary work on cultural dimensions of young people's lives has focused on 'spectacular', deviant or risky expressions while sidestepping core sociological concerns relating to the ways in which inequalities are reproduced across generations. Part of the problem here relates to the broader theoretical trends of social science under which explanations that are linked to people's locations within social structures, such as class, have become unfashionable. The other issue relates to the weakening of class-based identities and the fuzziness of the link between social class and youth cultures and lifestyles.

If we maintain that, in contemporary societies, youth identities tend to lack strong and clear links to social class (see Chapter 6), then it is important to explore new understandings of processes of social reproduction in youth and young adulthood and of the role of cultural dynamics in the process. In this context, it is more important than ever to bridge the gulf between the cultural and transitions perspectives. Andy Bennett (2011) offers a fruitful way forward by arguing that we need to consider structural experience as reflexively managed through the creative appropriation of cultural resources. In particular, he acknowledges the need to develop new understandings of the ways structured inequalities are negotiated through cultural practices and present culture as a process within which people are active in shaping their social milieu.

In this chapter we explore changes in young people's leisure and lifestyles and patterns of consumption. These are areas of analysis that triggered much of the early interest in the study of young people's lives. The study of young people's leisure and lifestyles highlights a range of conflicts between young people and adults, ranging from concerns about 'hanging around' through to worries about the ways they use drink and drugs: it also illustrates change in the dynamics of class and patterns of sociability.

Young people and leisure

The ways in which young people use their leisure time and spend their resources has been a long-standing source of conflict between themselves, their families and the state. While parents and social commentators may have clear ideas of what constitutes 'healthy' and 'constructive' use of leisure (participating in youth groups, sport and hobbies, etc.), young people frequently spend a large part of their free time 'hanging around' with friends, watching TV, playing computerised games or hooked up to social networking sites. Conflicts and misunderstandings about the way young people use their leisure are also evident in policy documents that continue to reflect a 'devil finds work for idle hands' philosophy. These concerns (and even fears about unoccupied youth) are reflected in discussions about compulsory youth 'volunteer' programmes, in curfews to prevent young people hanging around the streets in the evening and in the emphasis on 'good, clean, constructive fun' – priorities that underpin organizations such as the Scouts and resolutions passed by bodies like the UN. The following quote is taken from the text of a government-committed resolution as part of the world programme of action for youth on leisure time activities; it highlights the belief that activities such as sports and community service are key to tackling deviant behaviour.

> The importance of leisure-time activities in the psychological, cognitive and physical development of young people is recognized in all societies. Leisure-time activities include games, sports, cultural events, entertainment and community service. Appropriate leisure programmes for youth are elements of any measure aimed at fighting social ills such as drug abuse, juvenile delinquency and other deviant behaviour.
>
> (United Nations, 1995)

Contrary to popular images of youth engaged in risky and anti-social behaviour, the leisure lifestyles of many young people are fairly traditional and even mundane, and the activities and lifestyles of the young in all Western societies show a great deal of similarity. Across the developed world, young people enjoy the same sorts of activities and participate in a globalized consumer culture, although of course the level at which young people are able to consume and indulge their tastes for leisure lifestyles are constrained both by income and by local availability. In England, more than eight in ten 16–24 year-olds spend part of their free time watching television (82 per cent), listening to music (83 per cent) and spending time with friends and family (83 per cent). Shopping is also a very popular activity (69 per cent), as is going to the cinema (64 per cent) and going to pubs, bars and clubs (60 per cent) and taking part in sport or exercise (59 per cent) (Hughes, 2010). Many of these activities are equally popular with other age groups, although 16–24 year-olds are more likely than older people to spend time listening to music, and going to the cinema and bars and clubs. Young people are less likely than those in older age groups to spend time reading, eating out in restaurants and gardening (Hughes, 2010). In terms of active citizenship, four in ten 16–24 year-olds in England participated in volunteering activities informally at least once a month in 2010: a higher rate of participation than any other age group (DCMS, 2011).

Trends in leisure patterns over time show a decline in active outdoor pursuits (such as sports) among young people and an increase in indoor, sedentary activities such as computer games (Abbott-Chapman and Robinson, 2009). These changes not only have health implications, but they also impact on forms of social engagement more generally. Sport for youth has long been promoted by governments on the grounds of building a population fit for work and national defence. But sport is also regarded as a means of promoting teamwork, conformity and a citizenry that respect rules (Furlong and Cartmel, 2007; Kehily, 2007). Sport has a long history as a set of activities that help to entrench class and gender inequalities. There has been a long-standing tendency to prevent competition between men and women, ostensibly to ensure people compete on equal terms, but in practice framing a belief that women have inferior sporting abilities and preventing a situation arising where men are publicly defeated by women on a regular basis. Class divisions in sporting activities also help prevent sporting humiliation of the upper classes by the working classes. This is achieved partly through the establishment of separate leagues whereby private schools compete with other private schools and universities compete in a university league, but also through a class-based segmentation of sporting interests (Roberts, 2004). As Roberts argues,

> the higher-socio-economic strata are the most likely to play sports that involve the use of 'sticks' (golf, tennis, squash, skiing and so on) plus large ostentatious outlays of money (as in horse riding and yachting, for example). The lower strata dominate in some solitary sports (angling and cycling, for instance) and in sports that require body contact such as boxing and karate.
>
> (Roberts, 2004: 85)

Although young people like to spend time hanging out with friends, adults can be suspicious, or even hostile, of young people engaged in unstructured leisure activities, especially when these take place in public spaces

youth studies: an introduction

(Waiton, 2001). When groups of young people congregate on streets, in parks or in shopping malls, adults can feel threatened and may assume that they are engaged in violent and illegal behaviours. An electronic device, known as the mosquito, which emits a high-pitched, uncomfortable sound only picked up by the ears of under-25 year-olds, has even been marketed and widely used to deter young people from loitering in public areas. The mosquito has been described by Shami Chakraborti, director of the human rights organization Liberty, as a 'low level sonic weapon' used on children (*The Times*, 2008).

Liberty's concerns about the mosquito

The mosquito targets any young person in the area, including very young children and babies.

It affects law-abiding children in the same way as those who are committing offences, which is degrading and discriminatory.

It assumes young people will behave badly, and doesn't affect adult law-breakers at all.

It is a disproportionate and unfair reaction to the bad behaviour of some children, often creating no-go areas for young people in their own towns.

It alienates young people from the community, which could prove counter-productive.

It exposes young people to extreme discomfort, and little is known about the long-term effects on people's hearing.

www.liberty-human-rights.org.uk/human-rights/discrimination/young-people/the-mosquito/index.php

Most young people do tend to spend significant periods of time hanging around and 'doing nothing', and this may be interpreted negatively as unconstructive or as 'wasted time' (Abbott-Chapman and Robinson, 2009). This is a misunderstanding, as 'doing nothing' is in itself an important part of youth life. Young people need to reflect, to make sense of experiences and to withdraw, at times, from communal life. Teenagers 'need space to retreat from the things or people that "bother them" and, to develop independence and a sense of self, they need privacy and psychological "space" away from the surveillance of parents and other adults' (Abbott-Chapman and Robinson, 2009: 246).

In the face of negative public attitudes and unwelcome attention by the police, those who are too young to spend time in pubs and bars and who lack the resources to spend much time in commercial forms of leisure, often seek alternative spaces. Youth clubs have long provided a safe space for young people to socialize and engage in both structured and unstructured activities. Youth clubs also provide informal education and youth workers tend to see themselves as helping empower young people. However, youth club membership, which tends to peak in the early teenage years, tends to fall sharply with age and is often more attractive to young people from middle class families whose parents may discourage 'hanging around' and promote more structured activities (Furlong *et al.*, 1997). Youth work and youth clubs are discussed in Chapter 12.

While young people in Western societies spend their leisure time in broadly similar ways, there are quite strong contrasts between the West and Eastern Europe and the former Soviet Union (Roberts, 2009), where rates of participation in out of home activities are relatively low. In part, differences between the East and West are due to resources, but they are also shaped by tradition and patterns of availability. Under communist regimes, commercial leisure provision was almost non-existent, but young people were well provided for with state-sponsored youth organizations and high-quality sports and cultural facilities (Roberts, 2009). Comparing leisure patterns among young people in neighbouring regions of Finland and Russia, Puuronen and colleagues (2000) found that the Finns spent more time in bars and cafes, drinking alcohol and taking drugs, while the Russians spent more time at home, reading books, listening to music and watching videos.

The advance of information technologies has had a profound impact on the leisure lifestyles of young people in all developed societies. By 2000, mobile phone use among young people was almost ubiquitous, texting friends had become a constant feature of young people's lives and access to the internet at home was spreading fast, bringing with it new forms of sociability among youth (Henderson *et al.*, 2007). Information communication technologies (ICT) intensified communication between peers and between families and led to a blurring of the relationship between the public and private spheres (Henderson *et al.*, 2007). In contemporary contexts, new technologies make it even more difficult to separate public and private space or compartmentalize time among what Abbott-Chapman and Robertson (2009) have referred to as the 'always on' generation. Digital communications mean that young people may be socializing via text or email while working or studying, and computer games may be played as a freely undertaken leisure pursuit or as part of an educational activity. ICT can smooth direct communications between peers and allows young people to avoid direct parental scrutiny of their social contacts. Here Henderson and colleagues (2007) offer the example of a young woman from a British/Turkish family who was able to use ICT to communicate with her boyfriend in ways that would not normally have been possible and of a gay male whose 'coming out' was facilitated via chat rooms. On the negative side, ICT can become a catalyst for cyber bullying (Collin and Burn, 2009).

The rapid spread of ICT has also helped close the digital divide: mobile phones and computers are no longer the preserve of the affluent. Indeed, in a study of street youth in Canada, Karabanow and Naylor (2010) found that the vast majority were not only competent users of ICT, but they managed to incorporate use into their daily lives, gaining access through homeless drop-in centres and libraries. These homeless young people reported that use of ICT helped them feel more connected, provided a way of passing the time and allowed them to disengage from their street identities.

Subcultures and lifestyles

Differences in the ways in which people use their free time and engage in processes of consumption in areas as diverse as fashion, drink, drugs and music have been conceptualized in a variety of ways. Early work that focused on differences in style and taste between young people and adults often spoke of youth cultures or youth subcultures; later work has tended to refer to youth lifestyles. These changes reflect underlying theoretical trends in social science and draw attention to a shift from structural analysis to theoretical perspectives that emphasize fluidity.

The focus on youth as a group who developed distinct styles and engaged in patterns of consumption that set them apart from the adult population took off in the post-war period, particularly from the 1950s onwards. However, historians have shown that the emergence of distinct youth cultures and fashions can be traced back much further. Well-defined youth fashions were evident in Britain as far back as the late-nineteenth century at which time concerns were expressed about the leisure habits of young people who lacked responsibilities and had access to relatively high disposable incomes (Thompson, 1975; Osgerby, 1998).

Modern sociological research work on youth cultures really emerged in the late 1950s, developing significantly in the 1960s to reflect the growing visibility of youth and media-generated moral panics about the activities of the younger generation. In the US, the popularity of rock'n'roll led to the emergence of new youth styles that were imported and interpreted in other Westernized countries. In the UK the Teddy boys adopted distinct dress styles, often involving Edwardian drape jackets with velvet collars and drainpipe trousers while the girls (known as Judies) wore pencil skirts and ponytails. The leisure lifestyles of the Teds centred around rock'n'roll, dance halls and coffee bars.

During the post-war era the growth of participation in visible youth cultures was made possible by the high levels of disposable income among young people as a result of labour shortages and demand for young unskilled workers. Osgerby (1998) also highlights the impact of the baby boom in increasing the visibility of youth, the expansion of education and the preferences of some young people to take high-paid unskilled jobs rather than lower paid forms of employment involving training. In Abrams' (1959) extremely influential study of teenage consumption in the UK, it was argued that discretionary spending among young people had doubled since the pre-war era with 44 per cent of their income being spent on records and record players (Osgerby, 1998).

It is important to remember that youth cultures in the 1950s and early 60s were effectively dominated by the working classes, as it was they – not their middle class counterparts – who had high disposable incomes from unskilled forms of employment. Among the middle classes deferred gratification was the norm, involving long periods in training positions on low wages. As Osgerby put it, 'with less disposable income than their working peers, and often alienated from the subcultural world of groups such as the Teddy boys, middle-class youth did not make its cultural presence felt in Britain's youth "spectacle" until the rise of the counter-culture during the mid-sixties' (1998: 82). Despite being active participants in youth subcultures in the 1950s and 60s, females too, often had a low visibility in youth research. Youth cultures were arenas where gender roles were rehearsed and challenged, and in the 1950s and 60s male and female roles within youth cultures where often differentiated, involving a physical separation of activities. A hegemonic masculinity prevailed in which boys were prepared for a future in male-dominated workplaces while females anticipated future roles as wives and mothers. Yet while gender roles within early youth subcultures were largely conservative, youth cultures often tend to contain some seeds of change, implicit challenges to the existing order and an element of sexual rebellion (Kehily, 2007a).

The use of the term 'subculture' is often employed to draw attention to the ways in which youth cultures can be regarded as a sub-set of a broader class culture. Early youth cultures, such as the mods and rockers, Teds, hippies and skinheads represented arenas in which young people played out class and gendered identities in ways that were intertwined with a critique of existing conditions (Cohen, 1972; Clarke et al., 1976; Hall and Jefferson, 1976). These class-based identities may be represented among young people in ways that emphasize certain traits, such as toughness, a penchant for expensive clothes, or cultural sophistication which can vary over time and may result in contrasting expressions among groups of young people from similar class backgrounds: in Britain in the 1960s, for example, the mods can be seen as highlighting working class affluence while the rockers emphasized working class tradition.

The mods, many of whom came from the housing estates of East and South London, were emblematic of a working class in transition. The mods' neat image of cool sophistication reflected the upwardly mobile character of post-war working-class life and contrasted sharply with the more class-bound qualities of their contemporary adversaries, the rockers. Tending to have lower paid, less skilled occupations, the rockers represented an affirmation of 'traditional' working-class lifestyles. With their motorbikes, leather jackets, jeans and boots the rockers rejected the 'effeminacy' of conspicuous consumption and instead cultivated an image of sturdy masculinity.

(Osgerby, 1998: 42)

In the UK, middle class youth subcultures did not emerge until the mid-1960s, triggered by an increase in educational participation and increased affluence. The subcultural styles adopted by the middle classes in this era, such as hippies, were often juxtaposed with 'anti-establishment' standpoints. Osgerby refers to these positions as 'counter-cultural', while acknowledging heterogeneous positions and arguing that 'the post-war counter-culture is better seen as a diverse range of loosely related anti-establishment, non-conformist and bohemian factions' (1998: 82).

From the mid-1960s, youth subcultures not only involved interpretation of a parent class culture, but also articulated political standpoints and class-based oppositions. The hippies and the punks often supported movements like Campaign for Nuclear Disarmament (CND), as well as other environmentalist, anarchist, and anti-racist pursuits, while skinheads supported anti-immigration policies and far-right political groups like the National Front. Glam rock posed a challenge to sexual norms, while punk provided 'a musical and stylistic commentary on both the pretentiousness of the hippie era and the rapid socio-economic decline of Britain and other Western nations from the 1970s onwards' (Bennett, 2009: 264). Similarly, ethnic minority groups developed styles that aligned musical preference, such as reggae and rap, with broader sets of values, such as Rastafarianism and a political critique of the racism of Western societies. Music, fashion and politics were being expressed in diverse ways within subcultures, sometimes re-affirming class-based perspectives while at other times clashing with the views of an older generation.

Beginning in the 1980s, but intensifying from the 1990s, the links between social class and youth cultures underwent a process of diversification. In part, this was due to an increased obscurity of class-based identities in Westernized societies, but was also linked to an individual-ization of lifestyles more generally, promoted by the consumer industries. Steve Miles refers to the growth of a 'supermarket of style' and the aban-donment of 'lifelong stylistic and ideological commitment' (2000: 102), while Polhemus speaks of a new world 'where no one "uniform" would become a straightjacket [sic]' (1994: 132). In the late-modern world, youth cultures were no longer represented as sub-sets of a parent class culture, but as a potpourri of styles picked up and put down by young people with-out involving broader commitments to a perspective or position. In this context it has been argued that the active diversity of the culture industries help block stable bounded subcultures (Muggleton, 1977).

The changes highlighted by writers like Muggleton are most visible in rave cultures that reached a peak of popularity in the 1990s. For Thornton, ravers were 'Thatcher's children': 'their cultural heroes came in the form of radical young entrepreneurs, starting up clubs and record labels, rather than politicians and poets of yesteryear' (1995: 166). Rave culture involves what has been referred to as 'the perfect post-modern experience' (Smith and Maughan, 1998: 218): here both music and the experience were created and transformed in unique ways that existed at one point in time, never to be reproduced. The embrace of postmodern perspectives was reflected in the rejection of the idea of subculture with its structural connotations and the introduction of the term post-subculture or club culture (Redhead, 1997).

The rave scene facilitated a mix of hedonism, escapism and con-sumerism which provided a valued escape from the mundanity of day-to-day life. Identities grounded in work and education were temporarily cast aside, opening up a space where young people felt that they were in the driving seat. Rave represented an individualization of style; as Wilson notes, 'simply put, rave is whatever you want it to be. It is, in fact, a com-plete escape from any and all establishments' (2006: 147). Here Miles argues that 'rave represents a misguided effort on the part of young peo-ple to take control. They cannot control anything else, so they take control of their bodies' (2000: 98). In this context, the rave also represents what Furlong and Cartmel (1997) have referred to as an epistemological fallacy: a process in which a disjuncture between subjective and objective life con-texts misleads people into thinking that they have control over a situation when in reality their control is superficial. Indeed, Reynolds (1997) has argued that while the rave scene is often portrayed as fluid, within it clear divisions can be identified relating to class, 'race', region and so on.

In youth studies, the diversification of youth cultures and the weaken-ing of links to class cultures resulted in a challenge to the use of the term subculture, especially among researchers whose main interest was music rather than youth. As David Hesmondhalgh points out, music studies and

youth studies: an introduction

youth studies do share a common history (early studies of popular music drew on youth studies in the Centre for Contemporary Cultural Studies (CCCS) tradition), but have 'grown apart' and should be 'free to go their own ways in an amicable separation' (2005: 38). Literature on youth cultures and on popular music tends to display a strong overlap, but this obscures a difference of emphasis and carries an assumption that youth and music have a special affinity (young people may have been the prime consumers of music in the 1950s and 60s, but today youth form a relatively small market segment of the industry).

Confusing concepts

Youth culture: This is a broad term used to make a distinction between the cultural orientations, interests and affiliations of young people as compared to adults. Used in this way, it implies a degree of homogeneity among young people and clear age-related cleavages.

Subculture: A term used extensively in the 1960s and 70s, it implies that youth cultures are a sub-set of broader class cultures and can only be fully understood in the context of the dynamics of class.

Post-subculture: Associated with the 'cultural turn' in social science and the rejection of structural perspectives, this term is linked to the idea that there are a variety of fluid and overlapping youth cultures which cannot be understood through class-based analysis.

Lifestyle: This is a term most frequently used to highlight shared patterns of consumption and the ways in which young people express identity through consumer purchases.

Scene: Usually used in relation to groups of people whose lifestyles revolve around musical styles, either as producers or consumers.

Tribe: Associated with Maffesoli (1995), this is another term used to signify a rejection of subcultural perspectives and used to highlight the temporary and unstable nature of youthful affiliations.

Some of the key changes in the terminology that has been used to describe young peoples' cultural affiliations have been taken from researchers whose core interest is in popular music, and not all of them are entirely appropriate to use in a broader sense. The term 'scene', for example, is widely used in the literature on popular music to denote collective musical identities, while the term 'tribe' (or neo-tribe), with its origins in

youth cultures and lifestyles

the work of Maffesoli (1995), has been popularized by Bennett (1999) who wishes to highlight the unstable and temporary nature of youthful affiliations. Here Bennett wishes to make a break with the subcultural tradition and its links to structural understandings so as to highlight mix-and-match musical styles and flexible affiliations to style groups. While Bennett is right to highlight the increased fluidity of associations and consumer fads that characterize late modernity, there is also a danger of exaggeration. Hodkinson (2002), for example, points out that some style groups, such as the goths, are in fact highly committed group members who display a 'consistent distinctiveness' (2002: 28).

While much of the critique of the idea of subculture has arisen from the music-oriented youth literature, in the broader field of youth studies, especially in the field of consumption, the term 'lifestyle' tends to predominate. Again this is a terminology introduced to avoid the perceived rigidities of subculture and its link to class, while highlighting the importance of agency and a more fluid relationship between identity work and stylistic choices. Here young people's lifestyles are portrayed as important expressions of identity that link, in a variety of ways, to social status and resources (Miles, 2000). In youth as in adulthood, 'lifestyle enclaves' (Bellah et al., 1985) are an important expression of status, culture and taste. Lifestyles are related to, although not determined by, social status with the link between social class, education, gender, ethnicity, sexuality and so on seen as having weakened significantly over time. As Miles argues, 'lifestyles are, in effect, lived cultures in which individuals actively express their identities but do so in direct relation to their position as regards the dominant culture' (2000: 26).

> A lifestyle enclave is formed by people who share some feature of private life. Members of a lifestyle enclave express their identity through shared patterns of appearance, consumption, and leisure activities, which often serve to differentiate them sharply from those with other lifestyles'.
>
> (Bellah et al., 1985: 355, quoted in Miles, 2000: 24)

Consumption and leisure industries

Young people's changing lifestyles and leisure pursuits are, of course, heavily influenced by the consumption industries, but there is usually an interplay between the creativity of young people and the industries in which a youth-generated style or product is adopted, developed and sold back as a commodity of mass consumption (punk fashion is a classic example of a situation where a DIY style was developed and marketed by the fashion industries). While big business plays a significant role, young people are often the initiators of style: subcultural entrepreneurs who both develop and market fashions. Hodkinson (2002), for example, describes how goths play entrepreneurial roles within their own subculture and shows how consumers create styles through mixing purchases from both mainstream and subcultural retailers. Indeed, there are numerous examples of young subcultural entrepreneurs who were associated with specific scenes, but who later made a transition from niche to mainstream trade: Mary Quant, Vivienne Westwood and Richard Branson are all good examples.

The influence of the consumer industries relative to that of young consumers is a topic that has provoked much discussion. On the one hand, the culture industries undoubtedly make serious, and often successful, attempts to engineer demand for their products and exploit markets. Marketing departments keep abreast of cultural trends, manufacture demand and actively seek out ways of exploiting new markets. The culture industries clearly recognize that, for all consumers, patterns of consumption are highly symbolic and help to establish and signal group affiliations. In the case of young people, marketers may play on insecurities and provide props for emerging identities. In this context, Horkheimer and Adorno (1972) and others belonging to the Marxist-oriented Frankfurt School regard the culture industries as engaged in ideological manipulation: they are a repressive force that helps produce committed and compliant workers who know their position. In terms of gender oppression, for example, Best (2009) has argued that advertisers exploit concerns held by teenage girls about appearance and social acceptance and, in doing so, promote the adoption of 'traditional' feminine stereotypes and heterosexual romance.

There is much disagreement among academics about the level of control exerted by the leisure industries and of the ability of consumers to shape products. It would be somewhat misleading to argue that young people simply respond to the manipulative forces of the culture industries: there is evidence showing that young people are culturally creative and frequently resist attempts to be sold packaged consumer identities. One position is to propose an interplay between industries and consumers: Best, for example, argues that 'youth identity, youth experience, and youth culture are produced out of the resources offered by cultural industries, but not determined by them' (2009: 259). In opposition, Hodkinson is sceptical about any tendency to put young consumers in the driving seat:

> The ongoing diversification of the cultural industries arguably makes it increasingly unlikely that new styles or subcultures could simply emerge purely on the basis of youth spontaneity. Through the

employment of 'cool hunters', among other tactics, commercial organizations seek to latch onto, publicize and exploit new styles before they have even been fully conceived.

(Hodkinson 2009: 280)

Music is big business and historically young people have been significant players in the consumption and production of musical products: from records, CDs and digital downloads to photographic equipment and iPods. While young people have recently been displaced as the prime consumers of music (due to a decline in relative disposable income, a tendency to consume illegal digital downloads and a continued interest in popular music by middle-aged adults), the consumption of music-related merchandise remains part of a set of identity packages sold to young people. From trainers to T-shirts, jewellery and hairstyles, the consumption industries do not only rely on the youth market, they also depend on the endorsement of the youth demographic in order to sell a prized eternal youthfulness to an older age group who place a high value on a feeling and appearance of youth.

For young people, shopping is an important leisure activity: it provides an opportunity to spend time with friends and to explore ways of presenting an identity through fashion. Moreover, shopping is not simply about being sold pre-packaged identities by the consumption industries, it can also be seen as a subcultural activity. For young people, a sense of belonging in a cultural context is established through a process of consumption. As Hodkinson argues, 'obtaining and displaying the right commodities was, more than anything, the key to subcultural capital, and hence to identity' (2002: 150). Hodkinson also highlights the ways that goth identities are affirmed through hanging out in specialist shops and argues that shopping can be regarded as a subcultural activity in its own right, providing young people with a wide range of scene-related information. Best (2009) also notes some of the contradictions inherent in the process of consumption: people spend in ways that enable them to highlight their individuality, but in doing so also make claims to be recognized as the member of a group.

Youth are increasingly drawn into the consumer market and into a culture of spending to forge their identities as individuals as much as to gain membership in specific groups. Their consumption of cultural forms and cultural experiences are as much about being individuals, distinguishing oneself *from* the group as they are about keeping up *with* the group.

(Best, 2009: 261, original italics)

youth studies: an introduction

Much of the consumer spend of young people occurs within what Hollands (2002) refers to as the night-time economy: a space that has been significantly re-shaped in recent years by the leisure industries. While 'nightscapes' vary within and between countries, the places that young people congregate and consume in the evening and at night have been heavily shaped by commercial concerns, often leading to the exclusion of groups with limited spending power (Hollands, 2009).

In the UK, in the 1950s and 60s, the pub with its traditional atmosphere and mixed age clientele was not always attractive to young people who gravitated towards coffee bars, often with jukeboxes. While pubs were subsequently modernized in order to try to attract a younger clientele, they often failed to attract subcultural groups who preferred highs other than alcohol (especially in the rave era). Today city centre pubs and bars are fashioned to appeal to a range of style communities and to women who were not attracted to traditional pubs in the past. The new venues tend to have an upmarket, corporate atmosphere, although the product tends to be heavily branded and standardized – described by one of Hollands' respondents as 'McDonalds with a marble bar' (2009: 252). In the corporate 'nightscapes' of the modern city, there is little room for those without the means (or desire) to enter these corporate palaces of consumption. The poor and the industrial working classes are increasingly excluded and pushed back into the peripheral areas now inhabited by

> the unemployed, welfare dependent and criminalized, which represent the other city of dirt, poverty, dereliction, violence and crime, in contrast to the stylish gentrifying mainstream. More connected to the city's industrial past, residual spaces are now surplus to requirements in the newly emerging post-industrial corporate landscape, replete with its themed fantasy world and expanding consumer power.
>
> (Hollands, 2009: 252)

Drink, drugs and leisure

Whether it takes place openly in the stylized environments of bars and clubs, in the family home or covertly in parks or on the streets, in Westernized societies young people are no strangers to alcohol. Most young people will have their first encounters with alcohol in their early teens and by their late teens will be established consumers. Drinking alcohol and learning to become accomplished drinkers is a normal part of growing up and a key activity in many social events involving young people. While establishing a relationship with alcohol is an important part of the transition to adulthood, for parents and policy makers it is often an area of great concern. There are worries that young people will be unable to control their drinking, that they will put themselves into risky situations and engage in activities that they might avoid if sober.

One of the key issues is that young people are often legally barred from drinking, often until the age of 18, but in some places, like the US, until 21. The legal position, however, has little impact on young people's behaviour: by the time they reach the age of legal consumption, most will have tried alcohol, many will have experienced a state of intoxication and a high proportion will have become regular consumers, often gaining under-age access to licensed premises. As with Prohibition in the US in the 1930s, a legal ban does not mean that behaviour will necessarily be curtailed, and the determined consumer will find ways of satisfying their desires. Prohibition means that many young people will learn to drink in the company of other novices and will be denied the opportunity to consume in safe environments.

While drinking alcohol is an important part of young people's leisure lifestyles and while most consume alcohol safely, moral panics about heavy drinking among young people have a long history. For Stan Cohen (1972), this involved the attention of government, amplified by the media, in ways that demonize young people as 'folk devils'. Contemporary moral panics relating to young people and alcohol have centred on heavy drinking among teenage girls (the 'ladette' culture), on the practice of targeting high alcohol content drinks towards the youth market (the so called 'alcopops'), and on cheaply available alcohol sometimes sold as a 'loss leader' by major supermarket chains (leading to calls in the UK for a legally enforceable minimum 'price per unit' for alcoholic drinks).

Despite the health risks associated with heavy use of alcohol (see Chapter 8), drinking alcohol in many countries is such a normal part of youth life that those who fail to participate risk social rejection (Nairn *et al.*, 2006; Järvinen and Gundelach, 2007). In a study of drinking practices among Danish youth, Järvinen and Gundelach present drinking skills as a form of symbolic capital, even arguing that 'experience with drinking/partying is decisive for teenagers' position and prestige in the peer group' (2007: 55). Drinking skills signal maturity and as young people move from 'childish' forms of alcohol practice (such as regular sickness or passing out) to more mature practices (such as drinking heavily without becoming sick) they gain respect from their friends and an enhanced social status (Järvinen and Gundelach, 2007). Being able to 'take your drink' is perceived as a sign of adulthood.

> [H]eavy drinking, frequent partying, drinking Friday-Saturday and daily smoking or party smoking – in other words, the lifestyle of the experienced drinkers – are behaviours accepted or even idealised among a broad section of teenagers.
>
> (Järvinen and Gundelach, 2007: 67)

The importance of alcohol in peer groups presents difficulties for those who, for whatever reason, prefer not to partake. Indeed, Nairn and colleagues (2006) highlight the problems faced by non-drinkers and describe some of the strategies they use to try and 'pass' as drinkers so as to keep face in social contexts. Some young people attempted to justify their position as non-drinkers by presenting themselves as 'healthy sporty types', thus avoiding being labelled as 'uncool'. Others used a range of strategies to pretend they were drinking through keeping an alcoholic drink (or something that looked like an alcoholic drink) in their hands. As one of their respondents put it, 'If I've got a drink in my hand, even if it's not really alcohol, people just kind of think "oh yeah, she's drinking, she's all good", kind of thing' (Nairn et al., 2006).

As with alcohol, accurate figures on patterns of drug usage are difficult to come by due to a combination of under-reporting and exaggerated use as well as patterns of response bias to surveys that lead to an under-representation of vulnerable groups. In terms of prevalence, it is clear that cannabis is the number one drug by a large margin (Figure 7.1). In England, among 16–24 year-olds, almost one in five have used cannabis during the previous 12 months, with the next most popular drugs (amyl nitrates, amphetamines, cocaine and ecstasy) all used by a relatively small minority. Aside from cocaine, drugs commonly referred to as 'hard drugs', such as heroin, have been used by less than one in a hundred young people in the last year. In the UK in 2006/07, around one in four 16–24 year-olds reported that they had used some sort of illicit drug during the past 12 months; down from almost three in ten a decade earlier. For most young people who experiment with drugs, first use usually occurs in the mid-to-late teens, peaking in the early twenties and falling off quite sharply thereafter (Shiner, 2009). There is evidence suggesting that the greater protraction of transitions has led to prolonged patterns of drug use (Shiner, 2009).

International comparisons show that use of cannabis in the UK is broadly in line with countries like Canada, Switzerland, Spain, the US and France, but well above low-use countries such as Finland, Sweden, Greece and Romania (Currie et al., 2008). The UK tends to come top, or close to the top of European league tables, but falls someway behind the two largest consuming non-European countries: the US and Australia (Newcombe, 2007).

> Britain has slightly lower rates of drug use compared with the world 'leaders', the USA and Australia, but still ranks among those countries with the highest levels of both illicit drug use and problem drug use in Europe, along with such countries as Ireland, France, Spain and the Czech Republic.
>
> (Newcombe, 2007: 31)

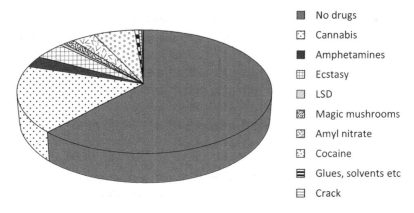

Figure 7.1 Use of specific drugs among young adults in the last 12 months (%).
Source: derived from Shiner (2009) and the British Crime Survey.

Trends in drug use in the UK show both an overall decline in most drugs, but a rise in cocaine as its popularity as a party drug has increased. Indeed Shiner (2009) shows that while there was once a strong association between the use of heroin and cocaine, cocaine is now more strongly associated with the use of ecstasy. Ecstasy itself has seen a drop in popularity that corresponds with the decline in the rave scene with which it was strongly associated.

> Ecstasy was important in shifting people's ideas about what constitutes a good night out and its arrival revitalised the nightlife of this country. It facilitated the change into an alternate social and sensual experience of the night in opposition to the booze-fuelled sociality that preceded it. That shift defined the model of what a club should feel like for punters and made them more intense spaces. This model has shifted as fashions and drugs changed. Ecstasy is only one drug amongst many that now plays a role in generating the party.
>
> (Jackson, 2004: 85)

Although the use of drugs among young people still triggers moral panic, especially when stories of drug-related deaths of moderate middle class users hit the headlines (Blackman, 2009), there is a degree of acceptance about the use of soft drugs, particularly cannabis, which once enjoyed fairly widespread use among now middle-aged politicians. Indeed, there is widespread concern that the use of illegal drugs has increased to a level at which it has become 'normalized'. The 'normalization thesis' is most closely linked to the work of Parker and colleagues (1995, 1998) who argued that drug use among young people had become so common that 'over the next few years, and certainly in urban areas, non drug-trying adolescents will be a minority group. In one sense they will be the deviants' (1995: 26). The idea of normalization was not just linked to a growth in the prevalence of drug use, it also highlights changes in the relationship between class, gender and 'race' and drug use. Parker and colleagues (1998) also suggested that normalization was not about majority or minority experiences, but about widespread acceptance of drug use within youth cultures alongside other accepted 'deviant' activities such as binge drinking and causal sex.

In many countries, drug use is now equally likely to be found among middle class and working class youth, among white population and black minority populations and among young men and women: women, it is argued, 'have achieved the (dubious) equality of consuming as many illegal mind-changing substances as the next man' (Henderson, 1999: 36, quoted in Shiner, 2009: 76).

The 'normalization thesis', however, is not without its critics. In the UK, Michael Shiner has used national surveys to highlight what he describes as 'the limited and transient nature of most young adults' involvement with illicit drug use' (2009: 47). Drug use among young people is fairly common, but it is certainly not unusual for someone not to have tried illegal drugs. While there may be problems in trying to apply the 'normalization thesis' to whole populations, there is greater support for the idea of subcultural normalization, signifying the commonality (and sometimes near ubiquity) in the association between certain drugs and membership of specific subcultures (such as the association between cannabis and LSD and the hippies, for example, or the use of ecstasy among ravers). Here the term 'differentiated normalization' has been used to highlight the ways in which 'different types of drugs and different types of drug use may be normalized for different groups of young people' (Shildrick, 2002: 36).

It is also important to note that the 'normalization thesis' should not simply be assessed by reference to large-scale statistics; it also has a subjective dimension (Shildrick, 2002). As Blackman (2007) argues, the thesis encourages us to recognize that those who consume recreational drugs are just as normal as those who don't and suggests that Parker and colleagues (1995, 1998) raise the thesis as a way of challenging the dichotomy between normal and deviant behaviour. With an awareness of the dangers of harder drugs, consumption of soft drugs is driven by 'fun, the pleasures and joys that come from the use of recreational drugs in leisure contexts' (MacDonald et al., 2007: 169).

Some implications for policy

Young people's leisure and lifestyles are shaped more by fashion than by policy. Nevertheless, young people are affected, often adversely, by attempts to shape and control their behaviour in ways that governments regard as appropriate. Suspicion of youth and fear about their preferred activities is long-standing and is not confined to any one generation or spatial location. Conflicts partly revolve around the use of public space, with adults suspicious about young people hanging around the streets or in parks or shopping malls, and policies and practice can be framed in ways aimed to reduce the 'problem' of young people on the streets, thus leading to alienation and resentment. Officially sanctioned forms of leisure, such as participation in sports and youth clubs, are not necessarily activates that appeal to a majority – and even sporty and clubbable youth like to spend time on unstructured activities. The challenge to policy is to provide safe and accessible spaces for young people, without impinging on their rights to use public space as they see fit.

Reactions to youth cultures and to patterns of consumption among youth have often been shaped by moral panics, especially in the fields of drug and alcohol use, and legislation to address perceived problems is not always helpful. The criminalization of recreational drug users, for example, may impede young people's career progress, and criminalizing a behaviour that is a normal, if fleeting, part of growing up is somewhat pointless. Similar over-reactions can be seen in the field of alcohol. While the recreational use of many drugs is declining, some young people do drink to excess and there are well-founded concerns about the health and social consequences of heavy alcohol use. At the same time, we live in a wet culture and policy focusing on safe drinking needs to work with the grain of youth cultures, not against it.

Summary points

1 There are often concerns about the ways in which young people use their free time, with a particular suspicion about time spent hanging around in public places. Yet most young people spend a lot of their time engaged in traditional leisure pursuits and benefit from time apparently spent 'doing nothing'.

2 The spread of digital technologies has impacted on patterns of communication among young people, allowing the blurring of public and private dimensions of life as well as helping young people to avoid parental scrutiny of their contacts.

youth studies: an introduction

3 Early youth subcultures had clear links to social class and often involved a political stance. More recently styles have become more individualized and membership is often more fluid.
4 Youth lifestyles are big business and the interplay between youthful creativity and the leisure and consumption industries can be difficult to disentangle.
5 Activities like shopping, musical style and participation in the night-time economy highlight some of the ways in which young people's identities are shaped and a sense of belonging is established.
6 Although often involving moral panics, for many young people, the use of alcohol and illicit drink and drugs is a central part of the experience of being young. At the same time, in relation to drugs, the term normalization can be misleading as some young people do not consume while for many the experience is fleeting.

Further questions

1 Explain why the term 'lifestyle' is preferred by some over the term 'subculture'.
2 How can youth lifestyles or subcultures provide insights into the dynamics of social class and social change?
3 How would you describe the relationship between young people's lifestyles and the consumer and leisure industries?
4 Can shopping be regarded as a subcultural activity?
5 Does the term 'binge drinking' suggest a moral panic?
6 Has drug use among young people become normalized?

Further reading

Bennett, A. (2009) 'Spectacular soundtracks: youth and music', in A. Furlong (ed.), *Handbook of Youth and Young Adulthood*, Abingdon: Routledge.
Best, A. L. (2009) 'Young people and consumption', in A. Furlong (ed.), *Handbook of Youth and Young Adulthood*, Abingdon: Routledge.

Hesmondhalgh, D. (2005) 'Subcultures, scenes or tribes? None of the above', *Journal of Youth Studies*, 8 (1): 21–40.

Hollands, R. (2009) 'Young adults and the night-time economy', in A. Furlong (ed.), *Handbook of Youth and Young Adulthood*, Abingdon: Routledge.

Miles, S. (2000) *Youth Lifestyles in a Changing World*, Buckingham: Open University Press.

Simpson, M., Shildrick, T. and MacDonald, R. (2007) *Drugs in Britain: Supply, Consumption and Control*, Basingstoke: Palgrave Macmillan.

Internet links

An illustration and short descriptions relating to ten different youth cultural styles from dandies and flappers in the 1920s to ravers:
www.guardian.co.uk/culture/gallery/2011/jul/10/10-best-british-youth-cultures#/?picture=376607410&index=5

Three useful fact sheets on young people and alcohol and drugs from the Institute of Alcohol Studies. They include some up-to-date statistics:
www.ias.org.uk/resources/factsheets/adolescents.pdf
www.ias.org.uk/resources/factsheets/adolescents_problems.pdf
www.ias.org.uk/resources/factsheets/comparisons.pdf

chapter 8

Health and well-being

Contents

A healthy generation?

Young people are often thought of as being in the peak of health. Fitness, energy and strength are terms used to define youth and young adulthood; the demographic is seen as being in their prime. It is young people who are seen as most able to fight for their countries and young women most suited to cope with the strains of childbirth and childrearing. The slow deteriorations of health associated with adulthood have yet to take hold, and childhood illnesses and vulnerabilities have been left behind. Youth and young adulthood marks a stage where individuals begin to take responsibility for their own bodies, to be aware of their own health needs, to prepare for a healthy life and learn to avoid or minimize exposure to behaviours that carry health risks.

In the developed countries high standards of living, developed public health systems and accessible medical facilities mean that youth and young adulthood are not associated with high levels of morbidity. Relatively few young people die or have to face major illness, and when young lives are lost they tend to be linked to accident or to deliberate harm at the hands of themselves or others. While youth is a time of life characterized by low health risks, young people do behave in ways that have implications for health in later life: eating and drinking habits established in the youth period may cause damage long beyond youth. In this context there are concerns that the health-related behaviours of contemporary youth may, in the long-run, lead to an overall rise in premature deaths. Poor eating habits leading to obesity, and excessive use of alcohol resulting in liver damage may mean that the current generation of young people have shorter lives than their parents' generation. To add to these potential problems, there are concerns that modern living conditions have helped trigger a range of mental health problems that can affect levels of happiness and well-being, impact on relationships and trigger physical conditions.

Concern about deteriorating health and the emergence of an unhealthy generation is widely expressed. Policy makers have youth firmly in their sights and there is little dissent from the view that there are a range of (physical and mental) health risks facing youth that need careful management if we are to avoid serious long-term damage with expensive consequences. In the media, the chef Jamie Oliver has conducted a long-running high-profile campaign centred on the poor diets of school children in a number of developed countries. Oliver is concerned that we spend too little on food for young people, that we over-expose them to foods that are high in sugars and saturated fats and that, as adults, we provide a poor example, partly due to our lack of culinary skills.

Of course health is strongly conditioned by social class: material resources are linked to health in a way that our position in a socio-economic hierarchy links, incrementally, to health. Wilkinson and Pickett have made it quite clear that 'health disparities are not simply a contrast between the ill-health of the poor and the better health of everybody else. Instead, they run across society so that even the reasonably well-off have shorter lives than the very rich' (2010: 84). The prime targets of Jamie Oliver's campaigns were working class families and the schools that their children and young people attended: primarily those serving poor neighbourhoods. In all countries the health profiles of populations are powerfully

youth studies: an introduction

affected by social class. It is not simply that there is a threshold below which families are poorly nourished and above which health needs are adequately met: health is distributed incrementally and people's position in a socio-economic hierarchy has a significant bearing on their health (West, 2009a). Interestingly though, Patrick West has argued that while health inequalities are clearly linked to social class in childhood and adulthood, youth is a time of relative equality (West, 1997). While this may well be true, many health-related behaviours present in youth are affected by social class and these will have a direct bearing on the class-related health gradients present in later life.

Physical health

While young people may be at the peak of their physical health, significant numbers have to cope with impairments and long-standing conditions that impact on their activities. In the UK, around one in five young people have a long-standing illness or disability, with around one in ten reporting an illness or disability that has some limiting affect on their activities. With strong variations in the extent to which activities are curtailed, at the severe end of the spectrum around 2 per cent are deemed to have a disability (West, 2009a). Figures from Australia are broadly comparable (Australian Institute of Health and Welfare, 2007).

Although a little dated, one of the best sources of comparative data on young people's health comes from the HBSC Inequalities in Young People's Health project (Currie et al., 2008). The survey covers more than 200,000 11, 13 and 15 year-olds in 41 countries in Europe and North America and was last conducted in 2005/2006 (the seventh survey in a series going back to 1983/1984). In terms of self-reported health among 15 year-olds (self-reported health is a good predictor of health-related conditions in adulthood), almost one in four females (23 per cent) and just over one in ten males (13 per cent) rated their health as either fair or poor (on a four point scale from poor to excellent). Countries where self-reported health among 15 year-olds was relatively poor included Ukraine, Russia, Hungary and Great Britain; at the other end of the scale more positive health was reported in Greece, Israel, Spain and Switzerland (Currie et al., 2008).

It is widely believed that the health of young people has deteriorated over time. [...] On the positive side, mortality in youth, particularly from accidents, has declined substantially in virtually all developed societies, and health status (as indicated by disease/disability) has not markedly altered. Indeed, the secular trend in height (taller with each successive generation) can be seen as an indicator of increasing health potential, anticipating increased life expectancy. However, the evidence in relation to the 'obesity epidemic' complicates this picture hugely, suggesting the possibility that for the first time in more than a century, life expectancy may fall. Less well understood, but of potentially greater significance for youth when symptoms may be most marked, is evidence of increasing rates of allergic disorders, notably asthma. [...] Explanations include the so-called 'hygiene hypothesis', which postulates that reduced exposure to infectious diseases in childhood reduces the body's immunity to allergens, and it is also possible that it may in part be attributable to increased medical surveillance and, hence, diagnosis.

(West, 2009a: 336)

One of the health conditions often presented as having the most serious long-term health consequences for young people is obesity, which has been described as a 'global epidemic' (West, 2009a). Here it is argued that in many affluent countries a 'junk food' diet which is high in saturated fats and sugars, combined with a sedentary lifestyle have resulted in a generation of young people who are seriously overweight. Obesity in young people is associated with cardiovascular problems, hypertension, diabetes, psychological problems, some cancers and with premature mortality. It has been estimated that in North America around one in three children and young adults are overweight or obese, compared to around one in five in Europe (West, 2009a). In the 41 countries covered by the latest HBSC surveys, among 15 year-olds, 17 per cent of females and 10 per cent of males were obese: countries with high levels of obesity include the US and Canada (one third of males and a quarter of females in the US were obese), while countries with low levels of obesity centre on parts of Eastern Europe, Russia and former Soviet states such as Lithuania and Latvia (Currie *et al.*, 2008).

While in most countries boys are more likely to be overweight than girls, it is females who are more likely to regard themselves as being too fat and to embark on diets (Currie *et al.*, 2008). As a result of media images that equate slimness with attractiveness and success, females may face greater pressure to conform to gender stereotypes and may hold a negative bodily image if they perceive themselves to be overweight. Interestingly, the

youth studies: an introduction

number of young people who report that they are too fat do not conform to objective measures of obesity. Among 15 year-olds responding to the HBSC survey, males and females in the US were close to the 41-country average in a ranking of countries where young people reported feeling too fat (despite being close to the top of the league for actual obesity): countries at the top of the league table included Germany, Austria and Luxembourg (Currie et al., 2008).

While eating habits are clearly associated with high levels of obesity, there is also a widely held view that contemporary youth have become sedentary, spending more time watching television and playing computer games and less time engaged in healthy outdoor pursuits such as sports. While it is undoubtedly true that young people are spending significant amounts of time playing electronic games and watching television, there is not the evidence to support the view that they are getting less exercise. Indeed, Coleman (2011) argues that there is no strong evidence suggesting a decrease in physical activity among young people. At the same time, relatively few young people meet recommended guidelines relating to exercise which suggests that young people should engage in moderate to vigorous activity for at least 60 minutes a day: in the HBSC survey, among 15 year-olds, just 20 per cent of boys and 12 per cent of girls met these guidelines (Currie et al., 2008) (however there is no suggestion that a majority of young people in advanced societies have *ever* engaged in this level of activity). While it has long been true that engagement with sport decreases with age (especially among females), there is no evidence of a reduction in the numbers getting regular physical exercise (Coleman, 2011).

Emotional well-being and psycho-social disorders

Problems relating to mental disorders and poor levels of well-being among young people are the areas of health that cause much concern. Bluntly, mental health among young people has been deteriorating for a number of years and has reached levels where it is argued that mental health is the most important health issue facing young people (Wyn, 2009b). Rates of psychological ill-health among young people are shockingly high, and are higher among the 18–24 age group than among any other demographic. In Australia, which is well in line with other developed countries, almost three in ten (27 per cent) 18–24 year-olds will have experienced mental health problems in the previous year while four in ten (40 per cent) display low levels of social and emotional well-being (Eckersley, 2009). Young women also suffer more than young men. Using figures relating to psychological distress among young people in Scotland as measured on the General Health Questionnaire (GHQ), West (2009a) shows that 42 per cent of females and 33 per cent of males displayed clinically significant levels of depression and anxiety. West concludes that 'mental health problems, particularly of an emotional nature, characterize the lives of a significant minority of young people' (2009a: 335).

Evidence from a number of countries suggests that psycho-social disorders among young people have been increasing for some time; certainly since the 1970s and perhaps since the end of the Second World War. The causes of the decline in mental health and emotional well-being are complex and can be linked in a variety of ways to the conditions of late modernity. Rutter and Smith (1995) point towards changes in family structures and material circumstances as well as to changing experiences of education and transitions. Family breakdown does seem to have an impact on the mental health of young people, with rates of psycho-social disorders being higher among young people living in single parent or reconstituted families, although the net effect is not large (West, 2009a). With education playing a more significant role in young people's lives, expectations and pressures to perform have increased. Young people are aware of the importance of education for their future lives and careers and are under pressure from parents and teachers to do well: school can be a significant source of stress (West, 2009a).

The impact of changing transitional experiences on mental health is partly linked to protracted participation in education and to the 'tightening bond' between educational qualifications and labour market outcomes. It also relates to difficulties in predicting labour market outcomes and navigating the 'sea of uncertainty' (Evans and Furlong, 1997) that characterizes modern transitions. In late-modern contexts, young people are forced to negotiate sets of insecurities that were not part of the life of previous generations. Whereas the transitions experienced by their parents' generation were generally characterized as collective, modern transitions have become individualized with young people being forced to interpret diverse sets of experiences in ways that allow them to represent fragmented experiences as coherent. Uncertainty results in an 'ontological insecurity' (Giddens, 1991) that can result in self-doubt, anxiety and depression. As Furlong and Cartmel argue, in the late-modern world, 'individuals are forced to assume greater responsibility for their, increasingly fragmented, experiences in the labour market and to assess constantly the implications of their actions and experiences' (2007: 35): a process that is associated with stress and anxiety.

> The costs of individualism relate to a loss of social support and personal control, both of which are important to resilience and wellbeing. These include: a heightened sense of risk, uncertainty

youth studies: an introduction

and insecurity; a lack of clear frames of reference; a rise in personal expectations, coupled with an expectation that the onus of success lies with the individual, despite the continuing importance of social disadvantage and privilege.

(Eckersley, 2009: 358)

Aside from the well-documented effects of recent social changes on standard measures of mental health among young people, there is also evidence that, in some countries, the intensity of social pressures has been associated with a process of social withdrawal. In Japan, young people referred to as *hikikomori* withdraw from all social life for protracted periods of time, sometimes for several years (see Chapter 5). It has been suggested that the *hikikomori* phenomenon can be linked to changing transitional experiences in Japan and other parts of South East Asia and it is clearly a phenomenon that suggests that there are negative psychological consequences associated with patterns of change in late modernity.

Another factor that has been linked to a declining sense of well-being, anxiety and deteriorating mental health among young people relates to a growth in materialism (Eckersley, 2009). Eckersley uses the term 'cultural fraud' (2009: 358) to refer to a process in which lifestyles are promoted for the benefits they bring in terms of economic growth while overlooking the psychological consequences. As Eckersley argues, 'materialism (the pursuit of money and possessions) breeds, not happiness, but dissatisfaction, depression, anxiety, anger, isolation and alienation' and that 'the goal of marketing becomes not only to make people dissatisfied with what they have, but also with who they are' (2009: 357).

Dissatisfaction with bodily image, which can also be linked to a materialist culture, has consequences both for the mental and physical health of young people. For young people the presentation of self is integrally tied to bodily image and to forms of adornment. The juxtaposition of the idea of immaculate bodies and perfect lifestyles makes personal fulfilment dependent on the resources to indulge in consumer cultures, and can result in the exclusion of the less affluent. One of the consequences of the link between resources, body-work and identity is that young people who lack the resources to consume at the same level as their peers suffer a range of harmful psychological consequences (Frost, 2003). As Wyn argues, 'the requirement to be recognized in order to become somebody and at the same time the impossibility of achieving the "perfection" young people are encouraged to aspire to has been seen by many researchers as leading to insecurity around identity' (2009b: 81).

Young people, especially females, are often very concerned about body size and appearance, and where expectations in relation to these seem to fall short of an idealized image they can be a source of anxiety and psychological distress which may become associated with eating disorders. The media play a significant role in the development of bodily dissatisfaction among young people, bombarding them with unrealistic images. Research has shown that young people's exposure to the media has a significant impact on levels of satisfaction with their own bodies. Tiggemann and Pickering (1996), for example, found a correlation between the levels of exposure girls had to soap operas and music videos and bodily dissatisfaction while Field and colleagues (1999) found that those who read fashion magazines at least twice a week had lower levels of satisfaction with their bodies. Indeed, for Roberts and colleagues, 'the media's pervasive and largely unattainable standards of weight and beauty tend to complicate adolescents' task of developing and maintaining a positive body image' (2004: 502).

Of course many young people maintain positive levels of well-being and, despite exposure to a range of potentially damaging experiences, fail to develop symptoms of psychological malaise. In explaining why some people manage to cope with adverse events and experiences, psychologists have suggested that some people are more resilient than others. Resilience should not be thought of as some kind of innate psychological characteristic, but is best thought of as a 'positive adaptation in the presence of risk' that can be linked to an interplay between individual and environmental factors (Compas, 2004: 266).

The focus on resilience has encouraged researchers to try to identify factors associated with healthy psychological development. This approach can be seen as involving a 'strengths-based model' as opposed to the more common 'deficit model' that focuses on problematic forms of development (Coleman, 2011). By putting the spotlight on resilience an emphasis is placed on identifying 'the building blocks that underlie healthy development' (Coleman, 2011: 210). Examples of these positive building blocks include establishing positive and supportive relationships with others (Wyn, 2009b), good communication skills and a sense of humour (Mental Health Foundation, 1999). Resilience is not simply about personal qualities, but is about networks, environments, community connectivity and emotional literacy (Mental Health Foundation, 1999; Robb, 2007b). In this context, the idea of resilience can be linked to the development of the life management skills that have come to be regarded as central to the effective navigation of transitions in late modernity (Giddens, 1991; Robb, 2007b).

Suicide and self-harm

Globally, one million people successfully end their lives each year (WHO, 2004), with unmarried males being especially vulnerable. Suicide is one of the leading causes of death among young people while self-harm is also highly prevalent in many societies: among 10–24 year-olds suicide is typically the second leading cause of death[1] while it has been estimated that there are 20 attempted suicides for every successful suicide (World Health Organization, 2006). It is important to put these figures into context: compared to older age groups, relatively few young people take their own lives and suicide only figures among the leading causes of death because so few young people die of causes other than accidents.

While levels of suicide and trends vary, in many countries youth suicide rates rose between the early 1970s and late 1990s and since then have been in decline. In the UK, for example, suicides among 15–24 year-olds began to decline from 1999, while in Australia the peak was reached in 1997 (Hughes, 2010; Australian Bureau of Statistics, 2008). Compared to Western societies, suicide rates among young people are particularly high in parts of South East Asia such as Japan, South Korea and Taiwan (World Health Organization, 2006), a trend that is sometimes explained by reference to conflicts between traditional and modern values and family pressure to succeed academically in a highly competitive environment (Lee, 2010).

Suicide is far more prevalent among males, often by a factor of three or four. Causal factors are wide ranging, but frequently involve mental illness, especially depression: it has been argued that around nine in ten people who commit suicide have a psychiatric disorder while the risk of suicide is 15 times higher among those who suffer from depression (Mind, 2011). Up to 15 per cent of people with schizophrenia will commit suicide while those who have been psychiatric patients see their suicide risk increase by a factor of ten (Hawton, 1987; Goldacre et al., 1993; Platt 2000). Other factors include a family history of suicide, alcohol and drugs, physical and sexual abuse, a history of self-harm and incarceration (Platt, 2000).

> Suicidal behaviour has a large number of complex underlying causes, including poverty, unemployment, loss of loved ones, arguments, breakdown in relationships and legal or work-related problems. A family history of suicide, as well as alcohol and drug abuse, and childhood abuse, social isolation and some mental disorders including depression and schizophrenia, also play a central role in a large number of suicides. Physical illness and disabling pain can also increase suicide risks.
>
> (World Health Authority, 2004)

Suicide among young people is relatively rare, but it is far more common for them to attempt suicide, to have suicidal thoughts or to self-harm. While suicidal thoughts may not result in any action, they are considered to be an important warning signal. Although more males commit suicide than females, females are far more likely to attempt or consider suicide or to deliberately harm themselves (Marcenko *et al.*, 1999). Estimates of the numbers of young people who have suicidal thoughts or who attempt suicide vary wildly, especially across countries. In a review of the literature, Diekstra and colleagues (1995) reckoned that, in any year, around one in five young people will think about suicide or commit an act of serious self-harm. One study of American college students suggested that over the course of a year around one in ten had serious suicidal thoughts (American College Association, 2001). Self-harm is somewhat different: while it signals distress it may not be associated with a desire to end life.

While there are undoubtedly psychiatric triggers that help explain why people take, or consider taking, their own lives, it is important not to lose sight of the salience of social factors. In one of the classic studies in sociology, Emile Durkheim (1952) argued that it was important to think of suicide as a social phenomenon which had clear patterns relating to factors such as religion, marital status, economic conditions and so on. In modern societies, Durkheim stressed the importance of social integration and the risks associated with excessive individualization and the breakdown of social norms. For Durkheim, 'suicide varies inversely with the degree of integration of social groups of which the individual forms a part' (1952: 209).

Adopting a sociological perspective on suicide does not mean that we have to reject psychological explanations (which can help predict which individuals will kill themselves), but does mean that the primary focus must be on changing rates of suicide and the socio-economic factors that impact on patterns. In explaining changing suicide rates among young people, it is necessary to focus on significant changes that directly affect young people. Rates of unemployment, for example, impact on social integration, well-being, a sense of having a future and, among all age groups, are clearly linked to rates of suicide (Platt, 1994; Gallie and Russell, 1998). In this context, the rise in suicide among young people in the 1980s and 90s, and the decline from the late 1990s broadly reflects trends in unemployment in the Western world. Logic would suggest that the recent rise in unemployment following the recession from about 2008 would be accompanied by a rise in suicide among young people.

Less-visible changes that can impact on suicidality among young people relate to rises in uncertainty linked to the state of the economy and its impact on the quality of opportunities. Indirectly, processes of individualization leading to the need for greater self-determination in contexts where collective links have weakened can lead to stress and discontent and may challenge mental health. In this context, Eckersley and Dear (2002) argue that suicide represents the 'tip of an iceberg of suffering' and conclude that 'increased youth suicide reflects a failure of Western societies to provide appropriate sites or sources of social identity and attachment, and, conversely, a tendency to promote unrealistic or inappropriate expectations of individual freedom and autonomy' (2002: 1891). In a different vein, the so-called 'Easterlin effect' is a hypothesis developed by a demographer who holds that the relative size of a birth cohort impacts on a range of outcomes, including suicide, by creating additional competition for scarce resources, leading to frustration and social disruption (Easterlin, 1980).

Health challenging behaviours

Some of the key challenges to young people's health and well-being stem from behaviours that may involve some form of risk or damage. Classic examples of such behaviours include the use of mind-altering drugs, heavy exposure to alcohol, smoking, unsafe driving practices and unprotected sex. While sometimes described as risk behaviours, Coleman (2011) rightly makes a distinction between risky behaviours and experimentation. For Coleman, the term risk has negative connotations and is applied to forms of behaviour that adults perceive as in some way threatening. Yet the label is frequently applied to behaviours that are entirely normal: getting drunk, trying illegal drugs or having sex (especially if this happens whilst under the influence of drink or drugs). Certainly activities such as these carry risks – the risk of alcohol poisoning or road accidents, the risk of overdose, the risk of sexually transmitted infection or unwanted pregnancy – but most young people engage in these sorts of activities and the vast majority do so without harming themselves or others.

In most Westernized countries, learning to drink alcohol is an important rite of passage and young people are socialized into a culture where moderate use of alcohol in social settings is expected. In some Western cultures, especially wine drinking cultures like France and Italy, the family is an important arena for developing drinking skills and it is customary for children and young people to be offered alcohol with meals. Other countries have more of a puritan (and frequently hypocritical) attitude towards alcohol, regarding use as largely inappropriate for young people (although regarding adult intoxication as entirely normal and acceptable).

Despite legal prohibitions that in many countries prevent the sale of alcohol to young people, many will begin to experiment with alcohol in their early teens and many will be experienced drinkers by the time they reach the legal drinking age. Young men tend to drink alcohol more regularly than females and are more likely to be intoxicated on a regular basis:

figures from Scotland show that by the age of 18, 80 per cent of males and 70 per cent of females will be regular drinkers while almost one in four males and nearly three in ten females will regularly drink in excess of recommended limits (West, 2009b). Nevertheless, in the UK, a country often portrayed as occupying a high position in international league tables for 'binge drinking' and drunkenness among young people (Blackman, 2009), the most reliable statistics show that, among 16–24 year-olds (in 2008), nearly four in ten young men and nearly one in two young women drank no alcohol in the past week (Hughes, 2010). At the higher end, three in ten young men and one in four young women drank more than eight units in the last week (in the UK for men the recommended safe limit is 21 units per week and for women 14 units). It has been estimated that, in Britain, no more than one in five young people exceed the recommended weekly limits for alcohol consumption and probably around half of that number are frequent 'binge drinkers' (Shiner, 2009).

The best comparative statistics on young people's use of alcohol come from the HBSC Inequalities in Young People's Health project (Currie et al., 2008). This shows that around 5 per cent of young people drink alcohol once a week at age 11, rising to 11 per cent at 13 and 26 per cent at 15. The highest levels of weekly alcohol consumption among 15 year-olds is found in countries like Ukraine, Malta, Wales and England (in Ukraine, 59 per cent of males and 47 per cent of females drink at least one a week) while the Scandinavian countries (not including Denmark) have relatively low levels of consumption (in Finland, just 12 per cent of 15 year-old males and 8 per cent of females drink alcohol once weekly) (Currie et al., 2008). At age 15, 37 per cent of males and 30 per cent of females in the 42 countries covered by the HBSC surveys had been drunk at least twice (at the top of the league table, in Denmark 59 per cent of males and 56 per cent of females had been drunk at least twice) (Currie et al., 2008).

While young people tend to drink for enjoyment in social contexts, concerns are often expressed about so-called 'binge drinking'. Binge drinking refers to excessive levels of consumption in a single session, although is often defined in policy discussions as drinking more than half the recommended weekly allowance in a single session. To put this in the context of UK recommendations, this relates to 7 units for women or 10 for men, which translates into around four pints of lager for men and about three for women. Many young people (and adults) would not regard a night out involving three or four drinks as in any way excessive.

While health promotion agencies try to promote a message of moderate, safe drinking, competing messages in the media promote a very different set of values. In the UK it has been shown that eight in ten popular TV programmes make some reference to alcohol with an alcohol-related reference being made every six minutes (Pendleton et al., 1991). In a study of 18th birthday cards on sale in Ireland, Loughran (2010) noted that 46 per cent of cards had some level of reference to alcohol, while 26 per cent made reference to 'excessive' consumption. Messages on birthday cards highlight gender stereotypes in drinking cultures, but both male and female versions often highlight the normality of intoxication with the typical message being that the 'best sort of birthday [is] one you'll have trouble remembering' (Loughran, 2010: 639). Some messages indicate the number of drinks that might be involved in a 'good' celebration: 'Happy Birthday to someone who likes nothing better than a quiet drink on her Birthday. . .followed by 15 loud ones' (2010: 639). Others even provided humorous guides to drinking that implicitly rejected 'official' advice: '(1) don't eat anything before drinking – it just takes up valuable space; (2) why stick to one drink all night when there is such a selection; (3) if the room starts spinning just spin in the opposite direction to cancel it out; (4) try to keep your willy in your trousers and; (5) if you feel sick do not put your hand over your mouth' (2010: 640).

> Cards did convey the notion that celebration of an 18th birthday is not just about having a drink but is about consuming amounts of alcohol that are designed to intoxicate, often to the level of being sick, having blackouts or even collapsing and perhaps losing consciousness. This creates the danger of normalising or desensitising attitudes to risky drinking and links aspirations such as the desire for independence, central to this life stage transition and to this drinking message.
>
> (Loughran, 2010: 640)

Despite widespread knowledge of the health risks associated with tobacco – and determined attempts by governments in many countries to restrict smoking by limiting the places where tobacco can be consumed, imposing heavy taxes, restricting advertising and insisting on prominent health risk messages on packaging – smoking, like drinking, remains widespread among young people. In the countries covered by the HBSC survey, more than six in ten young people had tried smoking by the age of 15 with almost one in five being regular smokers (Currie et al., 2008). There is strong variation between countries with smoking being particularly prevalent in Austria and Bulgaria but much less common in the US and Canada (Currie et al., 2008). Smoking is a classic example of youthful experimentation: most who try tobacco do so between the ages of 11 and 15, with males starting smoking before females. By the age of 15 it is common for more females than males to smoke. Smoking trends among young people are showing a decline, although not as steep as among adults (Coleman, 2011).

Like alcohol and the use of tobacco, experimentation with illicit drugs (especially 'soft' drugs) is extremely common among young people, although most consumption involves cannabis (see Chapter 7). As Shiner argues, 'It is far from unusual for young adults to have used illicit drugs at some point in their lives, but much of this use remains hesitant, tentative and short-lived' (2009: 55). While there is some evidence linking extensive use of cannabis to schizophrenia, moderate use among young people probably carries few health risks. In some countries, an appreciation that cannabis is relatively harmless in health terms is reflected in legislation. In some countries, possession of small quantities for personal use is either legal or largely overlooked (e.g. the Netherlands); in others use is illegal with penalties ranging from small fines in a legal context where use is decriminalized (e.g. Germany), to places where the full force of the criminal law (including the use of imprisonment) may be brought to bear on those apprehended (e.g. Japan and the UK). One of the dilemmas facing governments stems from the recognition that cannabis use is widespread and that its use is unlikely to be prevented by the imposition of legal sanctions: where laws are breached on a regular basis by large sections of the population, there is the risk of bringing the law in general into disrepute. Other issues relate to the fact that leading politicians often admit to having used cannabis in their youth and to the acknowledgement that legal drugs such as alcohol or tobacco carry much greater health risks.

The debate about cannabis is further complicated by the activities of powerful groups lobbying on behalf of the alcohol and tobacco industries and the health professionals. Recent changes and policy U-turns in England and Wales illustrate these issues nicely. In 2004 cannabis was reclassified from a Class B to a Class C drug, meaning that maximum penalties for possession were lowered from five years imprisonment to two years (although prior to 2004 first offences for small quantities were likely to result in a fine or a caution). In 2008 cannabis was reclassified from Class C to Class B, a move largely justified due to fears about the impact of potent strains of cannabis, such as 'skunk', on young people's long-term mental health. The change led to a conflict between the government and its 'independent' Advisory Council on the Misuse of Drugs: the chairman of the Council, Professor David Nutt, was sacked by the Home Secretary, Alan Johnson, for publicly arguing that cannabis was less harmful than alcohol and tobacco and suggesting that it should be decriminalized. He also argued that the reclassification was a political decision and ran counter to health-related advice given by experts. Five other members of the Council subsequently resigned over what they regarded as political interference. Nutt not only favoured decriminalization; he argued that young people

youth studies: an introduction

should be able to access cannabis in a safe and controlled environment using a model similar to the Dutch coffee shops where customers can legally purchase and use small quantities of the drug.

> *Extract from an open letter to the British prime minister, signed by a number of prominent individuals including three former chief constables and an ex-drugs minister, urging a shift from criminal justice approaches to drugs to a health-focused approach.*
>
> We, the signatories of this letter, call on the Coalition Government to undertake a swift and transparent review of the effectiveness of current drug policies. Should such a review of the evidence demonstrate the failure of the current position we would call for the decriminalisation of drug possession.
>
> This week marks the 40th anniversary of the Misuse of Drugs Act 1971. In the past forty years use of illicit drugs in the UK has grown rapidly. It is clear that the present system of applying the criminal law to personal use and possession of drugs has failed in its aim. Conversely, the harms caused by pursuing this approach to drug use have been significant.
>
> In the last year alone nearly 80,000 people in the UK were found guilty or cautioned for possession of an illegal drug – most were young, black or poor. This policy is costly for taxpayers and damaging for communities. Criminalising people who use drugs leads to greater social exclusion and stigmatisation making it much more difficult for them to gain employment and to play a productive role in society. It creates a society full of wasted resources.
>
> In 2010 the Vienna Declaration was launched at the International AIDS conference, the Declaration called for a more evidence based health focused approach to drug policy and for the decriminalisation of drug possession. To date the Declaration has been signed by over 20,000 people worldwide including former presidents of several South American countries, Nobel Prize winners in the field of science and literature, members of the judiciary and senior law enforcement officials.
>
> In 2001 Portugal decriminalised the possession of all drugs and, despite sensationalist predictions to the contrary, this has led to a decrease in the number of young people using illicit drugs, an overall reduction in the number of young people using drugs

One of the other arguments used by prohibitionists is that cannabis can be regarded as a 'gateway drug', used as a first drug experience but paving the way for a subsequent journey into 'hard' drugs, although this is seriously undermined by figures that highlight a trickle through from cannabis to 'hard' drugs rather than a flood (Blackman, 2009). Indeed, there is evidence that young people make very clear distinctions between cannabis and other drugs and are as likely as adults to regard drugs such as heroin, cocaine and ecstasy as harmful to their health: as Shiner argues, 'young people who use any other drug than cannabis do so in a general context in which the vast majority of their peers, as well as their elders, are thoroughly convinced of the potential harmfulness of their actions' (2009: 39).

Sexual health

Sexual experimentation and the initiation of sexual relationships is a normal part of a healthy adolescence but, like many activities that engage young people, fun and enjoyment is accompanied by the potential for harm. In many countries, there has been a long-standing tendency to focus on the risks associated with sex while focusing attention away from the pleasurable dimensions, perhaps because sex education and public health are issues that tend to be conflated. Moreover, there is a widespread reluctance to acknowledge young people as sexual beings and a fear that promoting sexual awareness equates to the promotion of sexual activity. As Levine has argued, 'it is nearly impossible to publish a book that says children and teenagers can have sexual pleasure and be safe too' (2002: xix). For young people, as for adults, the two prime risks associated with sexual activity relate to unwanted pregnancy and sexually transmitted infections: both being outcomes that impact on a small minority of young people, while sexual pleasure is an issue that concerns all young people.

> Adolescent sexual activity is commonly associated with a host of negative by-products, including pregnancy, sexually transmitted diseases (STDs), abortions, substance abuse, delinquency, AIDS, and bad grades. Scare tactics are widespread, with the expressed purpose of convincing adolescents to avoid sex.
>
> (Savin-Williams and Diamond, 2004: 189)

Young people tend to engage in first sex during the mid-to-late teenage years. However, accurate information on sexual activities is not always easy to come by as survey respondents may exaggerate experience or conceal activities. In a survey of 29,623 listeners carried out by *BBC* Radio 1 in the UK, a third of respondents said that they lost their virginity before the age of 16, while 43 per cent of 16–24 year-olds had had five or more partners (*BBC*, 2006b). In a US study (Davis and Friel, 2001) the average age of first sex was reported as being 14.3 for boys and 14.9 for girls, although there was strong variation by social class and 'race'. While boys tend to have first sex earlier than girls, the gap is closing (Currie *et al.*, 2008). The HBSC Inequalities in Health Survey show that first experience of inter-course varies significantly between countries: the numbers of 15 year-olds who were sexually experienced ranged from 5 per cent for girls in Macedo-nia to 66 per cent for girls in Greenland, with the vast majority of countries clustering around the 20 to 30 per cent mark (Currie *et al.*, 2008).

Most young people who are sexually active use some methods of contra-ception, although a significant number do not or, more commonly, fail to do so on occasions. In the UK, 57 per cent of 16–19 year-olds use contracep-tion, a figure that has been rising (Children and Young People Now, 2009). However, *BBC* Radio 1 found that almost four in ten young people did not always use a condom with new partners, usually because they were too drunk (*BBC*, 2006b). Use of contraceptives is highest among the middle classes and varies strongly between countries. Use of the contraceptive pill tends to be highest in Northern Europe and Canada while use of condoms is more popular in southern Europe (Currie *et al.*, 2008).

While the contraceptive pill protects against unwanted pregnancy, only barrier methods, such as condoms, block the spread of sexually transmit-ted infections (STIs). In the post-war period disease profiles have changed, generally involving a fall in syphilis and gonorrhoea and a rise in chlamydia, genital warts and HIV. In the UK, as in many other countries, young people (especially those under 20) are most vulnerable to STIs, partly because they engage in sex with a greater number of people, but also because they are less likely to use condoms (Hughes, 2010). Since reaching a peak in the UK in 2004, rates of HIV infection have been falling and the most common infections among young people are chlamydia and genital warts (Hughes, 2010).

Teenage pregnancy was discussed in Chapter 5 where it was argued that, despite regular moral panics, many young mothers highlighted the positive side of the experience, with pregnancies frequently being planned. As we noted, teenage pregnancies have been declining in many countries, partly due to the increased emphasis placed on educational success. In countries where terminations are legal and freely available, unwanted pregnancies frequently lead to abortion, which may carry health risks, especially in terms of future fertility. In the UK, nearly half of all pregnancies of under-18 year-olds result in a termination, as do around 60 per cent of those involving under-16s (Hughes, 2010). In the US, around a third of teenage pregnancies end in abortion, although rates have been declining, partly due to changes in public opinion which has been turning against abortion on demand (a poll for *CBS News* (2006) found that a majority of Americans (55 per cent) oppose abortion in virtually all circumstances).

Some implications for policy

Although youth is a time of relatively good health, it is also a time when the positive habits that will ensure a long and healthy adulthood must be laid down. Learning to drink sensibly, to be aware of the risks of drug abuse, to avoid becoming a regular smoker, to establish good eating habits and to engage in safe sex are lessons learnt by many people during their youth and young adulthood. Of course, like most learning experiences, it is very common to get it wrong on occasions, but to learn through mistakes.

Health policy often focuses on avoidance and on moderation rather than being framed in terms of inevitable experimentation. The consequence of such an approach is that health-related messages lack credibility. Most young people will get drunk, experiment with drugs and smoke; health policy has to work with the grain in trying to ensure smooth transitions to healthy behaviours. Campaigns that ask people to 'just say no' to drugs or which describe levels of alcohol use that will be considered moderate by many young people as 'binge drinking' are simply off target. Similarly, criminalizing 'normal' behaviour is not only counter-productive, it is often harmful and damages young people's long-term prospects.

One of the key areas where there are profound and growing health risks relates to the psycho-social consequences of the new modernity: and here policy action is somewhat thin on the ground. In late modernity young people have to deal with a range of insecurities that were not a central part of the lives of the previous generation. The stresses that impact on the lives of young people are often exacerbated through policy and through lack of action on the part of government. In education, for example, there is a tendency to make people jump more hurdles and to create more pressured regimes. Little is done to curtail the activities of the media who play on young people's insecurities as a way of selling their products. Finally, as much as it is a capacity, resilience is a skill that is learnt: building the development of resilience into youth policy should be seen as a priority.

Summary points

1 There is evidence that poor diet and sedentary lifestyles have resulted in an obesity epidemic in many developed countries.
2 Although there are clear links between social class and health inequalities, there is evidence to suggest that youth is a time of relative equality for health.
3 Poor levels of well-being and mental health problems are seen as a significant and growing problem among young people. There is evidence that this can be linked to the conditions of late modernity.
4 Materialist culture and the media can lead to dissatisfaction with aspects of the self, leading to insecurity and psychological distress.
5 Young people tend to experiment with a range of behaviours that have potential consequences for their health, especially in the consumption of tobacco, alcohol and illicit drugs. At the same time, there is a tendency to overstate harm done by alcohol and drugs.
6 Sexual experimentation is an importance part of a healthy adolescence. While there are associated risks relating to sexually transmitted infections and unwanted pregnancy, in Westernized countries these risks are small.

Further questions

1 What does Eckersley mean by 'cultural fraud' and how might this impact on well-being?

2 What is resilience? Explain some of the ways that social and environmental factors can help build resilience among young people.
3 How is it that the conditions of late modernity have a negative impact on well-being?
4 Why is it that the current generation may have shorter lives than their parents?
5 In what ways can the media be seen as triggering anxieties and psychological distress in young people?
6 Should we be concerned about the long-term health consequences of young people's behaviours?

Further reading

Eckersley, R. (2009) 'Progress, culture and young people's wellbeing', in A. Furlong (ed.), *Handbook of Youth and Young Adulthood*, Abingdon: Routledge.

Shildrick, T. (2002) 'Young people, illicit drug use and the question of normalization', *Journal of Youth Studies*, 5 (1): 35–48.

West, P. (2009) 'Health in youth: changing times and changing influences', in A. Furlong (ed.), *Handbook of Youth and Young Adulthood*, Abingdon: Routledge.

Wyn, J. (2009) *Youth Health and Welfare: The Cultural Politics of Education and Wellbeing*, Melbourne: Oxford University Press.

Internet links

The following report provides a good overview of health inequalities among young people in Europe. It can be viewed via the link below:

Currie, C., Gabhainn, S. N., Godeau, E., Roberts, C., Smith, R., Currie, D., Picket, W., Richter, M., Morgan, A. and Barnekow, V. (2008) *Inequalities in Young People's Health: HBSC International Report from the 2005/2006 Survey*, Edinburgh: Child and Adult Health Research Unit, www.euro.who.int/-data/assets/pdf-file/0005/53852/E91416.pdf

The following link provides some statistics on young people and mental health:

www.youngminds.org.uk/training-services/policy/mental-health-statistics

chapter 9

Crime and justice

Contents

Young people and crime

Young people are widely perceived as being unruly, anti-social and prone to participate in illegal activities. Indeed, while teenage lawlessness has long been the staple of the tabloid media, the study of youth has always had a strong focus on crime and deviance. Politicians are also keen to be regarded as tough on crime, particularly when it involves young offenders. While it is important to note that perceptions of crime frequently bear little relation to the underlying reality, there are a number of reasons why the terms youth and crime are often juxtaposed. It is true young people are responsible for a high proportion of recorded crimes, although this is partly because illegal activities that involve large numbers of young people are both visible and targeted by the police. There has also been a long-standing tendency for the media to construct moral panics relating to youthful behaviour, often resulting in the reframing of criminal justice policy so as to capture and criminalize young people's activities.

There is no getting away from the fact that the newspapers and television news programmes are often filled with youth crime, often violent, sometimes involving vulnerable victims and frequently focused on visible minorities and those from lower working class housing estates. Gun crime is particularly newsworthy, especially when it involves black gunmen with gang affiliations and innocent victims who are caught in crossfire. Column inches can also be filled focusing on extreme consequences of anti-social behaviour: in the UK several cases have been heavily profiled by the press where groups of teenagers have harassed vulnerable adults to the point where the victim has committed suicide. Such cases are extremes. In countries where gun access is strictly controlled, very few young people either use guns or are victims of gun crime (events in Norway in 2011 being an extreme aberration). In the UK, gun crime increased between 1998 and 2006, although has since begun to fall, but most of these crimes do not involve young people and many relate to the use of imitation weapons (Casciani, 2008). Similarly, while many adults find the behaviour of teenagers annoying, there are rarely tangible consequences for the so-called victim.

Discussions about youth and crime often overlook one important fact: young people are, overwhelmingly, the victims of crime. However, many of the illegal activities that engage young people can be described as 'victimless' crimes in that while breaching a statute (such as consuming alcohol before the legal minimum age or using illicit drugs) no direct harm is caused to a third party. It is worth noting from the outset that the majority of illegal activities committed by young people are petty, opportunistic and hedonistic. Moreover, where young people do commit more serious acts over a prolonged period, in the absence of intervention from the agents of the criminal justice system, they will usually desist as they take on adult responsibilities (Graham and Bowling, 1995). Ironically, it can be argued that criminal justice interventions may actually help prolong offending behaviour (McAra and McVie, 2007a).

The 'problem' of youth crime

So how serious is the problem of young people and criminal behaviour? The answer to that question partly depends on whose statistics you turn to

youth studies: an introduction

and the extent to which, in different jurisdictions, a crime will be reported by a victim, recorded by the police, taken to court by prosecutors and result in a guilty verdict by a judge. At each of these stages there is attrition, with certain crimes (such as rape and sexual assault) being far less likely to result in a successful prosecution than others (such as theft or burglary). With official criminal statistics being limited to cases involving some police activity, many criminologists argue that statistics garnered through population surveys are much more reliable (although some groups such as homeless and transient populations will be under-represented in surveys). The problem though, is that different sets of statistics can tell divergent stories: one source suggesting a rise in certain types of crime, for example, while another suggests a fall.

In terms of recorded crime, in England and Wales more than seven in ten recorded offences committed by young people fall into five categories: theft and handling (19.7 per cent), violence against the person (19.4 per cent), criminal damage (13.8 per cent), motoring offences (9.4 per cent) and public order offences (8.6 per cent) (Institute for the Study of Civil Society, 2010). While nearly a fifth of offences committed by young people are classed as violent crimes, it is worth noting that the vast majority of these are minor assaults (Casciani, 2008). It is also important to recognize that most serious crime is committed by adults who are far more likely to commit both violent offences and sexual offences (Muncie, 2009).

In Australia the overall picture is very similar: in Western Australia, for example, the top offences attributable to young people were, in order of offence counts, theft and burglary, good order offences, offences against the person and motor vehicle offences (Fernandez et al., 2006). In the US, around half of the recorded crimes involving young people fall into five categories: theft, simple assault, drug abuse, disorderly conduct and curfew violation (Office of Juvenile Justice and Delinquency Prevention, 2011). In Japan, a country with relatively low levels of recorded crime, around nine in ten crimes committed by young people involved theft or traffic offences (Nakanishi, 2003).

Crime surveys tend to paint a slightly different picture, as a high proportion of offences (especially those relating to the consumption of drugs and alcohol, minor assaults between young people, petty theft and so on) will never come to the attention of the police. Survey statistics highlight just how petty most of the illegal activities committed by young people actually are. In a survey of 11–16 year-olds carried out for the Youth Justice Board of England and Wales (MORI, 2008), the most commonly reported offences were: fare dodging (53 per cent), stealing from shops (45 per cent), hurting someone who did not require medical help (42 per cent), damage to property (39 per cent), graffiti (33 per cent) and stealing items from school (33 per cent). Use of illicit drugs is also common: in the UK nearly a third of 15 year-olds had used illegal drugs (mainly cannabis), although use has been declining (Omole, 2011). In terms of more serious offending, in the UK, national crime surveys show that around one in four young people admit to having committed an indictable offence within the previous 12 months (Phillips and Chamberlain, 2006), although only one in ten had committed a serious crime in the last year, such as burglary or assault causing injury (Institute for the Study of Civil Society, 2010).

Trends in youth crime follow a broadly similar pattern irrespective of whether survey data or official statistics are used. In the UK, youth crime increased through the 1980s and peaked in the first half of the 1990s. Survey data then shows a continual fall until around 2005, followed by a plateau. Official statistics suggest that youth crime fell throughout the second half of the 1990s, followed by a rise during the early 2000s (which was probably attributable to changes in the ways in which crime was reported), falling again from the mid-2000s (Halsey and White, 2009). Trends in Australia also show a decline in a wide range of crimes (e.g. theft, property crime and sexual assault), but a steady increase in the number of assaults (Australian Institute of Criminology, 2011). In the US, there is a common perception that crime among young people, especially violent crime, has been increasing. In fact victim reports show that violent crime in schools has been decreasing since 1994, as has the number of young people carrying weapons (US Department of Justice, 2007).

In all advanced societies, young people who are convicted of crimes tend to come from deprived backgrounds: they tend to come from low-income families, have often experienced poor parenting or broken homes, have low educational attainments and have been suspended or excluded from school (Farrington, 2007; McAra and McVie, 2007b). In many Western countries black youth are over-represented as perpetrators of crime and are more likely to be apprehended and convicted (Panel on Juvenile Crime, 2001; Muncie, 2009). Crime statistics also have strong local variations: some neighbourhoods are far more likely to be affected by crime than others, partly because of the ways in which they are affected by factors like unemployment and poverty, but also because poor areas tend to be the focus of intense policing. There is also evidence suggesting that those from poor neighbourhoods, members of certain minority groups and those whose circumstances are challenging tend to face harsher sentences. In a study of young people apprehended for involvement in drug sales in Baltimore, black youth were 100 times more likely than white youths to be arrested, even though patterns of use were similar (The Leadership Conference on Civil and Human Rights, 2000).

In Australia, indigenous youth are 28 times more likely than non-indigenous youth to be detained (ABC News, 2011), while in the US black and Hispanic youth face harsher treatment at each stage in the criminal

youth studies: an introduction

justice system (The Leadership Conference on Civil and Human Rights, 2000). While black youth represent 15 per cent and Hispanic youth 19 per cent of the juvenile population in the US, respectively they account for 45 per cent and 25 per cent of the incarcerated youth population (Saavedra, 2010).

Criminal careers

One of the key concerns about young people and crime is that while many of the illegal behaviours that they engage in are petty, and while accepting that most young people will desist from criminal activity as they mature, there is a hard-core criminal class in the making who can be identified early so as to prevent the establishment of long-term criminal careers. Within criminology there has been a long-standing interest in identifying those 'risk factors' that predict long-term and serious patterns of criminality and using these associations as a way of setting priorities for policing (Pitts, 2001; Muncie, 2009). Farrington and Welsh (2007) have gone so far as to argue that we have sufficient knowledge about the salience of various risk factors to be able to predict serious future offenders by the age of 10. The problem with this approach is that cause and effect are easily confused and there is a grave danger of causally associating patterns of criminality that arise from policing strategies with assumed characteristics of a target population (Pitts, 2001). There is also a risk of stigmatizing vulnerable populations on the basis of statistical probabilities: as many as half of those who are considered high risk using Farrington and Welsh's criteria will never offend (Webster et al., 2006). This can be a particular problem for young people of colour whose street-based lifestyles, dress and demeanour lead them to be targeted by the police (Gunter, 2010).

Involvement in crime peaks in the late teenage years; it varies within and between countries, but the statistical spikes occur at around age 18 for males and about 15 for females, with the vast majority of offenders being male (Muncie, 2009) by a ratio of as much as 4:1 (Coleman, 2011). A wide range of other 'risk factors' have also been identified to highlight which young people are most likely to be involved in criminal behaviour (or, thought of another way, which young people are more likely to be caught in the criminal net as a result of targeted policing strategies). Many of the 'risk factors' involve contextual factors, such as deprived neighbourhoods, the schools that serve them, and weak labour markets. Individual and family-based 'risk factors' commonly highlighted include family poverty and worklessness, family criminality, low educational attainment, having friends who have been in trouble with the police, family turbulence, dysfunctionality and poor parental supervision (Farrington, 1996; Pitts, 2001; Muncie, 2009). With a tendency to regard criminality as a problem of maladjustment (France, 2007), various psycho-social disorders are frequently seen as significant, especially impulsiveness, attention deficit disorders, low intelligence and school truancy (Farrington and Welsh, 2007).

Longitudinal research has been used extensively to study pathways in and out of crime and to highlight the significance of factors that predict long-term involvement in crime or engagement in serious offences, although the tendency to think of criminal careers as liner pathways has been criticized by those who regard movement as much more fluid (France, 2007). Here Matza (1964) has argued that many young people 'drift' between delinquent and non-delinquent behaviour. In a study of black youth in East London, Gunter also argues that some of his respondents 'drift' in and out of 'badness', they 'flirt with badness', but are not 'career criminals who have created lifestyles around deviance' (2010: 137–8).

In England, the study led by Farrington (often referred to as the Cambridge Study) (West and Farrington, 1977; Farrington and Welsh, 2007) followed a group of over 400 working class boys from London primary schools at regular intervals from age 8 to 48. Some of the most illuminating studies have been able to use a combination of self-report data alongside information on individuals collected by the police or have used mixed methods. In Scotland, the Edinburgh Study of Youth Transitions and Crime followed a cohort of around 4,000 through secondary school and was able to supplement survey data with school, social work, police and court records. In the US, Sampson and Laub (1995) undertook secondary analysis of a sample of 1,000 men born during the Great Depression (500 offenders and 500 non-offenders), supplementing analysis of survey data with 50 biographical interviews (Sampson and Laub, 2003).

While the Cambridge Study has been used to highlight the strength of the association between individual and social factors in childhood and subsequent offending behaviour, other longitudinal studies have been more sceptical about this link, either arguing that it simply captures policing strategy or that longer term evidence shows that patterns of behaviour that are evident in childhood and youth are frequently abandoned as responsibilities are acquired. Sampson and Laub (2003) use the term 'age-graded life-course theory' to show the way that behaviour is mediated by contexts over time with patterns of criminality decreasing through bonds to relationships and employment. Indeed, Sampson and Laub (2003) argue that (aside from violent behaviour in males) childhood characteristics and family background are relatively poor predictors of criminal careers in the long term.

The idea that offending behaviour in youth is usually a transient phase is clearly born out by statistics that show a peak in criminality in the mid-to-late teenage years. However, concerns have been expressed that

youth studies: an introduction

changes in the timing of youth transitions have effectively prolonged young people's involvement in crime (Graham and Bowling, 1995). Delays in entering the labour market, extended involvement in education and the later onset of stable sexual relationships are all factors that defer responsibilities and prolong hedonistic tendencies. Although it goes against the grain politically, the evidence suggests that interventions by the apparatus of the criminal justice system do more harm than good: where young people are subject to criminal justice, they are more likely to continue to offend as adults (McAra and McVie, 2007a), suggesting that resources are most effective when they are used to support troubled young people and divert from sanctions.

Imagined crime and incivility

Criminal justice agendas are frequently driven by perceptions of patterns of criminality that bear no firm link to the reality of the situation. Such perceptions are frequently generated by media-driven moral panics and by the opportunistic activities of a political class motivated by political philosophy and the need to win votes by appearing to be in tune with the concerns of the electorate. Young people, who are most often involved in visible, street based, forms of offending are frequently the scapegoats who are seen as representing much of what is perceived as wrong in contemporary societies. As shown earlier, there is little evidence to suggest that there has been a rise in youth crime in recent years (in fact many countries have witnessed a decline in youthful offending since the mid-2000s), yet public perceptions of crime have been very different, as have responses within the criminal justice system. Indeed, it has been argued that activities that were once interpreted as 'immature' or 'adolescent' are increasingly interpreted as potentially linked to future criminality (Waiton, 2001).

The British Crime Survey includes a question that asks respondents about their perceptions of changing crime levels over the last two years. A majority of respondents thought that, nationally, knife crime, bank and credit card fraud, gun crime and the numbers of people getting beaten up had increased a great deal (Hughes, 2010) (Figure 9.1). More than four in ten thought that muggings, street robberies and vandalism had significantly increased – perceptions that are not supported by crime statistics. Interestingly, very few thought that these crimes had increased in their local area, suggesting that their 'evidence' is drawn from national media rather than from first-hand local experience.

Media-driven moral panics often focus on the activities of young people, with stories framed in ways that suggest generational contrasts and a breakdown in the moral fabric of society. As I write this (summer 2011),

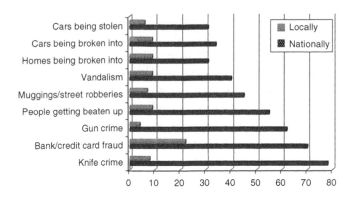

Figure 9.1 Respondents who thought that various crimes had increased a lot over the last two years at local and national levels, England and Wales, 2008/09 (%).

Source: British Crime Survey, derived from figures presented by Hughes (2010).

London has just seen the third night of street disorders involving running battles with police, looting and arson. The news media have tended to frame this as an issue involving young people (frequently male and black) with the *Daily Telegraph*, for example, reporting that hundreds of youths were running riot across the capital. Yet footage shown on television news clearly shows that, while young people are well represented, older people are also participating. Figures compiled by the *Guardian* newspaper from court records show that just 26 per cent of those accused were under 18 (*Guardian*, 2011c). Research has also shown that people significantly over-estimate the proportion of crime that is committed by young people, especially when it comes to crimes involving violence (Mattinson and Mirrlees-Black, 2000; Ipsos MORI, 2006). Hough and Roberts (2004) found that at a time when crime rates were falling, three in four people thought that levels of offending by young people had increased.

The tendency to focus on youth is long-standing: Cohen (1972) used the idea of moral panics as part of a study focused on mods and rockers in the 1960s, showing how media amplification led to a fight between two groups in a seaside town being described as a major riot and a threat to the social order. Other moral panics have related to football hooliganism and the use of party drugs. Here it is recognized that patterns of reporting shape public perceptions of crime, with the overall effect being to present young people as a population with little respect for the law (Hough and Roberts, 2004).

Perceptions of crime, even when they bear little relation to reality, can have a huge impact on policy and practice. One of the perceptions that

youth studies: an introduction

have had a big impact on the criminal justice agenda in the UK relates to anti-social behaviour. Here there is a belief that there has been a significant increase in minor but annoying forms of misbehaviour and incivilities that signal a lack of respect for the community. Some forms of anti-social behaviour are illegal (such as graffiti), while others are not (such as hanging around on the streets and playing loud music), and, while it evades precise definition, it is claimed that most of us will recognize anti-social behaviour when we see it (France, 2009). In legal terms, anti-social behaviour has been defined as 'acting in a manner that caused or was likely to cause harassment, alarm or distress, to one or more persons' (Home Office, 1998). While nearly one in five people in the UK believe that there are high levels of anti-social behaviour in their area, statistics on a range of indicators (such as vandalism, excessive litter, public drunkenness) show little change over the decade to 2008/09 (Hughes, 2010). Indeed, the UK Independent Commission on Youth Crime and Antisocial Behaviour concluded that 'we have found no overall indication that antisocial behaviour, whether it involves children, young people or adults, is any more common than a decade ago' (2010: 21).

Anti-social behaviour

Low level behaviour that can cause nuisance, alarm, harassment or distress to local communities as well as individual residents. [It includes] criminal offences such as drug dealing, street prostitution, vandalism and 'joyriding'. But it also includes non-criminal acts such as rowdy behaviour, playing loud music and skateboarding or playing ball games in restricted areas.

(Independent Commission on Youth Crime and Antisocial Behaviour, 2009)

The focus on anti-social behaviour has its roots in the US and can be linked to what is often referred to as the 'broken window thesis', which holds that tolerating low-level crime such as graffiti, litter, drinking in public and so on is symbolic of a lack of care and respect and encourages more serious patterns of offending (France, 2009). While the empirical evidence underpinning the idea of a causal connection is weak (France, 2009), it gives rise to a 'zero tolerance' policy under which all offending and nuisance behaviour, no matter how trivial, should be tackled.

In the UK, tackling anti-social behaviour was adopted as one of the key priorities of the Labour Government under Tony Blair. It was not suggested that anti-social behaviour was solely a characteristic of a youthful population, although clearly young people were regarded as a major part of the problem. The recognition that much behaviour that could be regarded as anti-social was not actually illegal, posed a problem. The solution agreed on was to introduce a new class of offence that was peripheral to the criminal justice system, but which could invoke criminal law where an order was breached. Anti-Social Behaviour Orders (widely referred to by their acronym, ASBOs), which were introduced in 1998, could be imposed on individuals by the police or local authority officials[1] if they thought those individuals were 'causing alarm, distress or harassment' (France, 2009: 433). An order was to last for a minimum of two years and was imposed through a civil, rather than criminal, procedure and did not require the level of proof that would be required in a court of law (France, 2009). ASBOs were to be preceded by a formal warning and the voluntary signing of Acceptable Behaviour Contracts.

While ASBOs were civil orders, the twist was that breaching an order was a criminal offence that could lead to up to five years' imprisonment. Some 40 per cent of ASBOs were issued to young people under the age of 18 (Macdonald and Telford, 2007), with fears expressed that boisterous youthful behaviour and high jinks were leading to the imposition of ASBOs (*BBC*, 2006a), followed by criminal sanctions. Figures suggest that around a third of ABSOs are breached, with around two-thirds of these resulting in the imposition of jail sentences (France, 2009), leading to fears that low-level anti-social behaviour is being criminalized with young people provided with a rapid route into the criminal justice system (France, 2009). The counter-argument is that many of those imprisoned for breaking an ASBO have a long history of offending.

The internet is full of examples of ASBOs issued for seemingly trivial behaviour. A 60 year-old woman was threatened with an ASBO for feeding birds in her garden, although the threat was dropped when she agreed to restrict feeding. There are a number of cases where young people have been served ASBOs to prevent them from wearing 'hoodies' where they are seen as a means of masking identity, while in Bedfordshire, officials wanted to ban an 18 year-old from wearing his trousers so low that people could see his underwear: the case was dropped when the magistrate accepted the argument that a ban would contravene his human rights.

Gangs

Youth gangs are an emotive topic and represent another area where public perceptions are often out of sync with street-based realities. The stereotypical gang draws on images from the shanty towns of Africa and Latin America where young people (usually young men) may be armed and have a heavy involvement in organized crime, including drug running (Hagedorn, 2009). These stereotypes are often used as an inappropriate model through which people come to think about gangs in urban environments such as North American cities. Drawing on an American perspective, and with a research tradition going back to the Chicago School in the 1920s, gangs are often presented as mafia-like organized groups with a clear hierarchy and leadership, engaged in criminal activities, such as dealing in narcotics, and usually centred on a specific locality and carrying visible forms of adornment as markers of membership.

> Territorial, hierarchical and incredibly violent, the gangs are mostly composed of young boys, mainly from dysfunctional homes. They earn money through crime, particularly drugs, and are bound together by an imposed loyalty to an authoritarian gang leader.
>
> Prime Minister David Cameron describing the nature of the gangs he regarded as being at the centre of the urban disturbances in British cities in August 2011.
>
> (*Guardian*, 2011b)

The classic study of gangs is Frederic Thresher's (1927) book, *The Gang: A Study of 1313 Gangs in Chicago*. In Thrasher's view, gangs were regarded as an entirely normal art of life for young people growing up in poor inner city areas in the US. Moreover, gangs were not seen as 'inherently evil' (1927: 51) or as necessarily centred on criminal activities. Here, the gang has a positive function; they are sites of secondary socialization, an arena for learning, developing identities and of mutual support. Indeed, Hagedorn (2008) regards gangs as being central to culture and cohesion in poor neighbourhoods and, with links to politics and music, can be linked to change in a positive way. Similarly, Batchelor (2009) argued that involvement in girl gangs has positive as well as negative consequences for members and can promote feelings of empowerment and belonging.

If we try to see beyond the classic stereotype of a gang as integrated through crime and conflict, we are faced with the thorny problem of defining what a gang is (and even gang researchers argue about this). One of the leading gang researchers, John Hagedorn (2008), argues that there are huge difficulties in distinguishing a gang from run-of-the-mill neighbourhood-based peer groups, who may engage in anti-social or illegal activities, without either having any clear identity as gang members, any organizational hierarchy or any involvement in organized crime. Hagedorn supports the definition proposed by Moore:

> Gangs are unsupervised peer groups who are socialized by the streets rather than by conventional institutions. They define themselves as a gang or 'set' or some such term, and have the capacity to reproduce themselves, usually within a neighborhood.
>
> (Moore, 1998: 67)

Is a group of young people hanging out together a gang? What if this group is hanging outside a convenience store talking loud and acting proud? What if this group creates a name for itself, starts identifying members with specific clothing, and uses secret hand signals and handshakes and intimidating nicknames such as 'killer' and 'assassin'? But the group just described could actually be a sports team! Add to this description the commission of a number of deviant acts and fraternities and sororities would also fit this profile.

(Delaney, 2005: 6)

Confusion about what constitutes a gang can fuel moral panics and can lead to misjudged youth crime strategies on the part of the police. A report by the BBC (2007) suggests that the police had identified 169 gangs in London who were responsible for around a fifth of all youth crime, with more than half involved in murders. In Scotland, Strathclyde Police (who are responsible for the Greater Glasgow area – a much smaller area than London), have apparently identified 170 gangs, although they use a very loose definition of gangs and base their information on 'soft' intelligence (Fraser, 2010). Gangs are often portrayed as masculine arenas, perhaps with females granted associate membership. However, while many classic studies have reinforced the view of gangs as a masculine phenomenon (e.g. Thresher, 1927), there is an increasing awareness of female gangs which, among younger teens, can be just as prevalent as male gangs (Batchelor, 2009).

Clearly, groups of young people in a neighbourhood can often take on the label of a gang, without necessarily matching any of the usual stereotypes. The UK Independent Commission on Youth Crime and Antisocial Behaviour (2010) found that one in ten 10–19 year-olds thought of themselves as members of a gang, although for many this did not entail criminal activity (although those who regarded themselves as gang members were more likely than non-members to commit offences or carry weapons). If the more emotive label of gang is substituted for the more neutral label of group, more than eight in ten young people in the UK regard themselves as a member of a group, some of which give themselves a name, wear approved forms of dress, have rules or are associated with a territory (MORI, 2008).

Confusion of what constitutes a gang and about when the activities of a group of young people should concern law enforcement officials can lead to a focus on visible groups who adopt street-based lifestyles and common forms of dress. The young black males in East London studied by Gunter (2010) presented an image that outsiders often perceived as threatening and which was frequently associated with criminality. Yet many of these young people were not involved in criminal activities or engaged in these activities on an infrequent basis; indeed, criminal behaviour was often viewed in negative terms. Gunter describes the ways these young males present themselves on the streets:

> The road culture style and fashion [...] is very much influenced by the hyper-masculine and style conscious attitudes and personas of the 'rude boys'. Therefore the majority of young males involved in road life will tend to walk around in small groups, wearing designer sportswear [...]. When walking these young black males will tend to 'hog the pavement' by walking in small groups oblivious to other pavement users' needs. They also will adopt a 'screw face' in order to warn potential male foes that they are 'not to be messed with'. In short these young males are putting out a message that they are not victims (weak or 'pussies'), rather they are the victimizers.
>
> (2010: 99–100)

As Gunter notes, the problem is that dress and demeanour makes it almost impossible for outsiders to distinguish ordinary young black males engaged in harmless forms of behaviour from the gangs that may inhabit the same social space. However, street presentation can enhance reputation and respect and can help prevent victimization.

Drawing on a study of gangs in Glasgow, Fraser argues that gangs play a symbolic role in young people's lives without necessarily having a link to crime or violence and that they often exist as 'more of an idea than a reality' (2010: 11). Fraser portrays gang membership as fluid and as part of the experience of growing up in poor neighbourhoods. Gang identities can help create bonds between young people in a neighbourhood and can create a sense of belonging. Indeed, some of the rituals of membership that are seen as signalling integration and commitment can come across as juvenile, even comical. In his Glasgow study, Fraser (2010) asks a gang member how someone would go about joining their gang: the reply was that they simply had to 'hang about' with them, although they may be required to do 'a challenge' – which turned out to be pulling down their trousers and running down the street.

Punishment

The ways in which young people are punished for offending is an inherently political act that is rarely underpinned by research on effectiveness or informed by the experience of those who work with young people. Governments on the left and the right tend to have different attitudes towards systems of punishment, although all are sensitive to media criticism that they are 'soft' on crime. Indeed, although offending by young people is not rising, in many countries punishment has become more severe.

Approaches to punishment vary strongly by country. The age at which young people may be held criminally responsible for their actions ranges from 7 in Switzerland and India to 18 in Columbia and Luxembourg: the most common age of criminal responsibility is 14, although in England and Australia it is 10 (Hazel, 2008). There are also significant differences in the maximum sentences that can be imposed on young people: two years in Spain and Switzerland, but not subject to limits in England and Wales, Japan and Italy (Hazel, 2008) (Table 9.1). The different approaches used tend to reflect philosophical principles adopted, at a basic level involving a division between welfare and justice approaches. Hazel (2008) argues that the welfare approach (adopted in countries like Sweden, France and Japan) focuses on the conditions that impact on the offender and makes welfare-based interventions a form of redress. In contrast, justice approaches (used in the US) hold the offender responsible and punish accordingly. In most countries a distinction is made between adult and juvenile justice systems, with the latter tending to focus on protection and diversion rather than retribution.

In countries that use welfare-based interventions, custodial sentences tend to be used as a strategy of last resort, reserved for particularly serious offences, such as murder or extreme violence, or used when all other approaches have failed. The focus tends to be on community-based punishments and supervision orders, with the aim of rehabilitating and

Table 9.1 Maximum custodial sentences for juveniles

Duration (years)	Countries
2	Australia (ACT, NSW, TAS), Lebanon, Senegal, Spain, Switzerland, Togo
3	Australia (Vic), Columbia, Malaysia, Slovenia
4	Australia (SA), Ecuador
5	Brunei
8	Estonia
10	Australia (QLD), Azerbaijan, Bahrain, Egypt, Germany, Libya, Qatar, Slovakia
15	Austria, Finland, Mongolia, Korea
25	Israel
Unlimited	Argentina, Armenia, Australia (WA), Chile, China, England and Wales, Italy, Japan, Kazakhstan, Kuwait, Mauritius, Panama, Poland, Saudi Arabia, Syria, Trinidad and Tobago, Zambia

preventing further contact with the criminal justice system. There are a wide variety of approaches that come under this umbrella, including restorative approaches aimed to reconcile and repair damage, community service orders and referral to programmes that will address offending behaviour or factors seen as influencing offending, such as drug and alcohol programmes, official warnings, good behaviour contracts, family supervision orders or placement with foster parents. Approaches based on the principles of restorative justice were promoted on the basis of a criticism of the formal criminal justice system as at best ineffective, at worst as exacerbating problems (Pitts, 2001).

Restorative justice aims to offer offenders 'opportunities and encouragement to understand the harm they have caused to victims and the community and to develop plans for taking appropriate responsibility' (Pitts, 2001: 68). The Scottish Children's Hearings Panel is an example of a welfare-based system built on restorative principles. Young people under the age of 16 (18 in certain circumstances) who offend or who are in need of protection are dealt with under the one system, with the needs of the young person being paramount. The panel, which is made up of voluntary, trained, lay people, make decisions about the best way to ensure the welfare of the young person. Disputed facts can be decided by a court where necessary, but decisions about treatment rest with the panel.

While the UN Convention on the Rights of the Child promotes welfare-based approaches to youth justice, punitive approaches have become increasingly common in the face of a (largely imagined) rise in youth crime. In England and Wales, welfarist approaches have been diluted with young people increasingly regarded as responsible and treated more like adults, with the imposition of tougher penalties and greater use of custodial sentences. More secure units for young people have been built and courts have been granted greater powers to lock up children and young people.

> n a context where politicians were promising to 'get tough' with people convicted for offences during the recent urban disorders in England, courts have been passing down sentences based on retribution rather than restoration. A first-time young offender found with a stolen violin was sentenced to four months' imprisonment, while a young adult who stole a £3.50 case of water was jailed for 6 months. A young man who admitted purchasing stolen goods was committed to Crown Court for a probable prison sentence. Meanwhile, some newspapers were carrying reports that the police were unhappy about the leniency of sentences handed down to 'rioters'.

The US has tended to shun welfarist approaches and is one of the countries which treats young offenders most harshly. Legislation allows prosecution of juveniles in adult courts where cases are judged to be particularly serious and, despite evidence that the approach is counterproductive, the number referred to adult courts have been increasing (Kupchick, 2006). In the US, the death penalty for those under the age of 18 was only abolished in 2005, although there are a number of people on death row who committed a capital crime before the age of 18. Of the 38 states that retain the death penalty, 23 allow the execution of offenders who committed a capital offence before they reached the age of 18. Only three states prohibit courts from sentencing those under the age of 16 to life without parole (Coordinating Council on Juvenile Justice and Delinquency Prevention, 2000). Compared to most other advanced societies, young offenders in the US are much more likely to face jail sentences, although rates of incarceration have been increasing in many countries, including the UK and Australia. In contexts where young people's involvement in crime is falling and where signatories[2] to the UN Convention on the Rights of the Child (by which means those under the age of 18) oblige national governments to prioritize community-based sanctions for young offenders and to use custodial sentences only as a last resort, current trends are worrying.

Custodial sentences are both costly and counter-productive: in the UK, it has been estimated that it costs nearly £100,000 a year to keep a young offender in custody, with further costs to the state of around £40,000

youth studies: an introduction

incurred over a lifetime through the impact of incarceration on subsequent life chances (such as higher rates of unemployment and lower income employment) (Institute for the Study of Civil Society, 2010). Around seven in ten young people who receive a custodial sentence will be reconvicted within a year (Institute for the Study of Civil Society, 2010). Economists in the US have argued that with half of the prison population having dropped out of high school, investment in education is one of the most effective strategies to reduce crime (Levin *et al.*, 2007).

Victims

The media can be enthusiastic reporters of youth crime and active campaigners for harsher sentences for lawless young people. What is frequently overlooked is the extent to which young people are victims of crime, especially violent crime. In the UK it is estimated that around one in two young people have been a victim of an offence in the last 12 months (MORI, 2008). In a survey of 11–16 year-olds in England and Wales, nearly three in ten had been the victim of bullying and a similar number reported having been threatened, while around one in five had been physically attacked (Anderson *et al.*, 2010) (Figure 9.2).

In the British Crime Survey, the group who were most likely to have been the victim of a violent crime in the preceding 12 months were young men between the ages of 16 and 24, followed by people who had visited a nightclub or disco once a week or more in the last month, and full-time students. Men aged 16–24 were more than four times as likely as all-aged adults to have been a victim of a violent crime (Hughes, 2010). Young people are more likely to be victims of certain types of crime, such as theft or assault, but far less likely to be a victim of crimes such as burglary and car theft.

Figure 9.2 Offences experienced by 11–16 year-olds in England and Wales in the last 12 months (%).

Source: derived from Anderson *et al.* (2010), *Youth Survey 2009*, London: Youth Justice Board © Crown copyright.

crime and justice

In Australia, around a third of young people reported that they had been the victim of a crime in the last 12 months – mainly theft and threats of violence (Smart *et al.*, 2005), with those in the 15–24 age group most likely to be victims of assault, and young women most likely to be victims of sexual assault (Australian Institute for Family Studies, n.d.). Members of visible minority groups are particularly vulnerable and may be victims of hate crimes (Anderson *et al.*, 2010). Most young people who have been victims have been offended against at school, although those who have been victims of knife and gun crime are more likely to have been attacked in their local community (Anderson *et al.*, 2010).

Although bullying by other young people is often treated as a minor transgression and even as a normal part of growing up, bullying is prevalent in schools and can be extremely damaging. There is also evidence that cyber bullying (typically using email and text messaging) is a growing problem. Figures from a range of sources suggest that perhaps one in six young people have been bullied at some stage (Sullivan *et al.*, 2004), with figures for cyber bullying as high as one in four (Wade and Beran, 2011). Bullying has been linked to self-harm and even suicide among victims, while a culture of bullying has been seen by some as a trigger for the school shootings at Columbine High (Corliss, 2011).

With young people who live in poor neighbourhoods and those whose leisure lifestyles regularly involve street-based activities being particularly vulnerable to crime, it is not unusual for people to be both offenders and victims at different points in time. The idea that people can be neatly divided into offender and victim categories is a gross simplification, as many offenders are victims on occasion while many victims also offend. In England and Wales, nearly seven in ten 11–16 year-olds who had reported committing an offence had also been victims, compared to around one in two of those who had not committed an office (Anderson *et al.*, 2010).

> Survey data have consistently revealed that young people are more likely to be victimized than older people; the economically marginalized more than the wealthy; ethnic minorities more than white populations; and men more than women (at least in regard to street crime). In reality it is young working class males who are the 'typical victims' but they are least liable to be identified as vulnerable to victimization.
>
> (Muncie, 2009: 164–5)

Part of the closeness in the relationship between offending and victimization has been illustrated very effectively in studies of offending groups, prisons and poor neighbourhoods (e.g. Batchelor, 2005; Gunter, 2010). Avoiding victimization in 'hard' communities can be difficult and it may be necessary to offend in order to avoid victimization. In Batchelor's (2005) study of female prisoners in Scotland, the common refrain was 'better a sair face than a red face':[3] in other words, it was preferable to fight (even if they came out worst) than to lose respect by backing down. To avoid victimization it was important to come across as tough, even aggressive, and to be known as someone who would stand up for themself. Maintaining self-respect and status in the community was seen as crucial. Similarly, among the black youths in East London studied by Gunter (2010), dipping in and out of 'badness' could enhance reputations and help ensure that they were not regarded as a 'pussy'.

In poor communities, respect may also involve defending a territory, and breaches of territoriality may involve violence or threats of violence against the perpetrator. Young people may feel safe in their own community, even when it has a high rate of offending, but fear becoming victims if they stray into a neighbouring territory. As one of Gunter's respondents put it, 'if you put yourself in a room full of thieves, but you actually know the thieves and you grew up with them then you're not in any danger? But if your [sic] a person whose just come in the area and you don't know the thieves, you don't know the muggers, you don't know the whatever else, then to you it's dangerous' (2010: 120). In a study of mobile phone theft, it was argued that young people's phones could be taken as a way of establishing territorial control (referred to by the perpetrators as 'taxing') (Harrington and Mayhew, 2001).

Territoriality and the fear of crime can seriously constrain social and economic horizons and even limit the search area for jobs and education. Like gang membership, coming together to defend a community can be a source of solidarity and friendship and can build personal respect; it can also be about personal safety. As Holligan and Deuchar (2009) discovered in their study of young people in Glasgow, participation in neighbourhood territoriality may build individual and community social capital, social support, belonging and solidarity. In certain neighbourhoods, defence of the territory has been described as a 'cultural expectation': something that is passed down the generations; it could involve recreational violence, but equally it could be about promoting community safety (Kintrea et al., 2008).

Many young people also have offences committed against them in the home, domestic violence is all too common and each year many children and young people are placed on child abuse registers. The statistics tend not to make a distinction between children and young people and while much domestic violence goes unreported, UNICEF reports that worldwide up to 275 million children are exposed to violence in the home (UNICEF, 2006). Sexual harassment also tends to go unreported, yet it has been argued that, in the UK, one in two young women have experienced sexual harassment by adults including indecent exposure and sexual pestering (Anderson *et al.*, 1994).

Some implications for policy

The ways in which we report and respond to criminal behaviour by young people are rarely informed by evidence or acted upon in ways that are focused on a long-term reduction in criminality. Most young people are law-abiding or occasionally take part in petty, hedonistic forms of offending, frequently without there being a victim involved. Where young people do become involved in crime, even relatively serious crime, they will grow out of it as they mature and acquire adult responsibilities. Where we intervene, especially when interventions invoke a criminal justice system rather than welfare agencies, criminal careers are often prolonged rather than averted.

Some of the recent trends in patterns of policing and criminal justice systems are likely to have a detrimental affect on young people. Zero tolerance policies capture non-malicious youthful behaviour while the focus on anti-social behaviour treats the normal behaviour of young people as problematic, sometimes as criminal. There is no evidence to suggest that criminal behaviour among young people is becoming more prevalent, yet punishments seem to be getting harsher. The most obvious example here is the ridiculously harsh punishments meted out even to first-time offenders in the aftermath of the recent civil disorders in UK cities. Another indicator of a growing intolerance is the growing tendency to treat young offenders as adults, even among countries that have signed up to the UN Convention on the Rights of the Child.

Young people who spend considerable time on the streets have long been targeted by the police, yet street-based youth cultures can be creative and can provide peer support and solidarity. Labelled as gangs who are involved in illegal, often violent, behaviour, groups of young people who are engaged in harmless leisure can be subject to scrutiny and harassment by law enforcement agencies. Young people are just as entitled as any other age group to use public space and do so without being victimized and subject to intolerant forms of policing.

youth studies: an introduction

Summary points

1 The statistics on young people's involvement in crime are problematic and vary according to whether they are collected through police or court records or through population surveys. Statistics on recorded crimes overlook the large number of crimes that are unreported or unrecorded.

2 Many crimes committed by young people are trivial and many involve no victims.

3 While certain groups of young people (such as those from poor neighbourhoods) are over-represented in the crime statistics, this partly reflects patterns of policing.

4 Involvement in criminal activities tends to peak in the late teenage years and falls off thereafter as people take on responsibilities and 'grow out' of crime. Interventions by the criminal justice system can prolong involvement in crime.

5 Perceptions of patterns of criminality often have little grounding in reality and can be amplified by the ways that the media report crime. Groundless perceptions can impact on policy and practice.

6 While gangs are often seen as firmly linked to criminal activity, not all gang members participate in illegal acts and membership can reinforce neighbourhood solidarity.

7 The focus on young people as perpetrators of crime detracts from the extent to which they are over-represented among victims of crime.

Further questions

1 Why is it that patterns of crime recorded in official statistics and through surveys differ? What are the relative advantages of different statistics?

2 Why do patterns of criminality tend to fall from the late teenage years onwards? What are the factors that prolong criminal careers?

3 Describe some of the ways that youth-focused moral panics have led to the perception that youth crime is increasing.

4 Outline the 'broken windows thesis' and explain why it promotes a zero tolerance approach to policing.
5 What is a gang and in what ways can it be seen as a positive force?
6 Describe the differences between 'welfare' and 'justice' approaches to offending behaviour.

Further reading

Farrington, D. (1996) *Understanding and Preventing Youth Crime*, York: Joseph Rowntree Foundation.

France, A. (2009) 'Young people and anti-social behaviour', in A. Furlong (ed.), *Handbook of Youth and Young Adulthood*, Abingdon: Routledge.

Gunter, A. (2010) *Growing Up Bad: Black Youth, Road Culture and Badness in an East London Neighbourhood*, London: Tufnell Press.

Hagedorn, J. M. (2009) 'Youth in a world of gangs', in A. Furlong (ed.), *Handbook of Youth and Young Adulthood*, Abingdon: Routledge.

Muncie, J. (2009) *Youth and Crime*, 3rd edn, London: Sage.

Internet links

Greene, J. and Pranis, K. (2007) 'Gang wars: the failure of enforcement tactics and the need for effective public safety strategies', Washington, DC: Justice Policy Institute, www.homeysf.org/images/gangwars.pdf

Independent Commission on Youth Crime and Antisocial Behaviour (2010) *The Case for a Fresh Start: The Report of the Independent Commission*, London: Nuffield Foundation, www.youthcrimecommission. org.uk/attachments/076-FreshStart.pdf

Institute for the Study of Civil Society (2010) *Factsheet: Youth Crime in England and Wales*, Institute for the Study of Civil Society, London, www.civitas.org.uk/crime/factsheet-YouthOffending.pdf

chapter 10

Citizenship and political engagement

Contents

What is citizenship?

Formally, a citizen can be regarded as a naturalized member of a nation state who is entitled to a package of rights by virtue of their citizenship. In democratic societies, the classic citizenship right involves the entitlement to have a say in who governs at local and national levels. More broadly, in advanced societies, citizenship brings with it an entitlement to a raft of benefits ranging from the right to protection and representation to the right to state support if living standards are in danger of falling below an agreed threshold. The rights of citizenship tend to be accompanied by a series of responsibilities under which various 'entitlements' are deliverable conditionally in the event that the citizen meets a defined set of obligations. The right to income support in a period of unemployment, for example, is often conditional on providing proof of job search activity. Similarly, the right to vote in general elections may be removed from those who have been incarcerated for committing certain crimes.

Not all residents of a country are entitled to citizenship rights: refugees and asylum seekers as well as long-term visitors from other countries may be formally denied certain rights and, in these cases, the state may limit entitlements or make them conditional upon a range of criteria that are more strict than those available to its own citizens. While young people may be naturalized citizens, entitled to live in a particular jurisdiction and, in certain circumstances, to expect protection, their position is highly ambiguous. All advanced societies are happy to pass legislation to exclude young people from a range of rights granted to the rest of the population and to oblige them to participate in activities, such as education, that are voluntary engagements for full citizens. As we noted in Chapter 1, young people are granted the rights normally accorded to citizens in a piecemeal fashion, and while the age at which voting rights are bestowed usually represents an important landmark, an additional package of rights are frequently held back until a later stage. The overall impression given as a result of the piecemeal handover of citizenship rights is that young people are not to be trusted as full-blown citizens: they can be taxed without representation and allowed to vote before they are allowed to drive certain categories of vehicle.

Young people may be regarded as restricted citizens by the state, granted limited rights and subject to unique obligations, but the paradox is that, in turn, they are expected to be active citizens who, within these constraints, participate in their communities and learn to embrace the principles of equal opportunities and respect for the rights of others. In such circumstances, it is perhaps little wonder that young people develop their own interpretations of citizenship and frequently adopt a cynical approach to the contradictory values of adult society.

Active citizenship involving an awareness of rights and responsibilities and engagement in the life of the community is currently in vogue in a number of countries. The emphasis on responsibilities, which was once clearly associated with a New Right agenda has increasingly been embraced by the social democratic mainstream and, in some countries,

youth studies: an introduction

citizenship education has found its way into the school curriculum. In the UK, the 1997 Labour Government, concerned about low voter turnout among young people, set up an advisory group under Bernard Crick to consider the introduction of citizenship education in schools. The group's terms of reference were 'to provide advice on effective education for citizenship education in schools – to include the nature and practices of participation in democracy; the duties, responsibilities and rights of individuals as citizens; and the value to individuals and society of community activity' (Crick, 2002). For Aristotle, citizenship in ancient Greece involved an expectation that citizens should be active in public life, able to anticipate in political debate and to contribute to the common good. The modern translation of citizenship tends to be somewhat less ambitious.

In terms of Crick's recommendations, citizenship education has three main strands: learning 'socially and morally responsible behaviour' (Crick, 1998: 11) towards fellow citizens and to those occupying positions of power; learning the value of community involvement, particularly through voluntary activities in the community; and developing political literacy and becoming engaged in the political process (Crick, 1998). In Australia a similar exercise was undertaken, leading to the establishment of a set of principles relating to the components of a programme of citizenship education. These included a commitment and understanding of Australian democratic traditions, underpinning values and of the meaning of responsible citizenship (Farthing, 2010). One of the problems is that citizenship education has been seen as placing rather more emphasis on 'apolitical forms of citizenship' while failing to promote 'political activism and the development of political agency' (Biesta, 2009).

> We aim at no less than a change in the political culture of this country: for people to think of themselves as active citizens, willing, able and equipped to have an influence in public life and with the critical capacities to weigh evidence before speaking and acting; to build on and radically extend to young people the best in existing traditions of volunteering and public service, and to make them individually confident in finding new forms among themselves.
>
> Statement by the Advisory Group on
> Citizenship Education (Crick, 2002)

The social theorist T. H. Marshall conceptualized social citizenship more broadly in a way that was much more concerned with the rights to be accorded to the citizen than with obligations or with forms of political engagement. Citizenship rights for Marshall extended 'from the right to a modicum of economic welfare and security to the right to share to the full in the social heritage and to live the life of a civilized being according to the standards prevailing in the society' (1963: 74). In this context some commentators have argued that recent political trends have led to the dismantlement of the 'post-war settlement based on social rights and have moved towards conditional welfare' (Powell, 2000: 6). In this interpretation, 'social citizenship is a non-economic, unconditional status, like the political citizenship of voting' (Powell, 2000: 6).

In many advanced societies, including those based on strong welfare regimes such as Scandinavia, an entitlements-based model of citizenship was an early casualty of the swing to the right during the 1980s. Young people, who already had restricted citizenship rights, were an early target of the welfare reforms that increasingly made benefits conditional. The spread of workfare policies in several countries, for example, made eligibility for social assistance dependent on demonstrating active job search strategies and participation on training schemes and work experience programmes. Jones (2009) argues that whereas the policy trend in the 1960s and 70s involved an increased tendency to treat young people as independent citizens deserving of welfare support as an entitlement, the New Right backlash of the 1980s removed rights in areas such as housing, student support and unemployment benefits and started to regard young people as dependents of their parents with limited citizenship rights. In this respect, the trend towards greater protraction of transitions that we noted in earlier chapters has been accompanied by a move to delay the granting of full citizenship rights and enforce a prolonged period of dependency. As Jones notes, 'young people who are economically dependent cannot be full citizens' (2009: 145) because, without direct access to resources they are denied a position in society.

Involved and responsible citizens

While having restricted citizenship in society at large, young people learn the skills associated with being an involved member of a broader social circle in a range of different institutional contexts. School and university are crucial contexts for learning citizenship skills, as are non-academic institutions such as sports clubs, voluntary organizations or church groups. Such organizations not only provide opportunities to learn to interact with others in either flat or hierarchical settings, they also help young people to develop the skills to interact with others in structured environments and provide them with an awareness of the functions of rights and responsibilities. Historically, an awareness of the ways in which youth organizations help young people to develop citizenship skills underpinned the emergence of groups like the Scouts and the Girl Guides, although such movements placed a strong emphasis on duty and conformity in a hierarchically structured society where social harmony was often linked to 'knowing one's place' in the class structure.

> In the context of their membership in local groups, institutions and organizations, youth practice citizenship. In such contexts they learn what it means to be a member of a group, to exercise rights, to have a say in the group's affairs, and learn to be accountable to fellow members and to the mission of the organization.
>
> (Flanagan, 2009: 293)

Young people's involvement in institutions and organizations also brings them into contact with other people who may have contrasting opinions or points of view. For Flanagan (2009), these new exposures have an impact on the construction of identity as well as promoting reflection about political issues in the broadest sense. Here Flanagan draws attention to colleges as contexts where students are encouraged to join a number of associations and as settings in which they may encounter views of staff and other students that contrast with those previously encountered in the home and in the less socially diverse contexts of the neighbourhood. Highlighting a study of students at a US college in the 1930s, Flanagan describes how their views became more left wing as they interacted with lecturers and began to challenge the more right wing views of their parents. College provided them with an opportunity to engage in political reflection and draw considered opinions and helped them construct viewpoints that were relatively stable across the lifecycle.

Opportunities to become engaged and reflective citizens arise in a wide range of contexts, some of which offer clear connections to conventional political themes and agendas. At work, for example, trade unions can provide a form of political socialization under which the idea of oppositions of interests between employers and employees is projected to new members. In communities there are often a range of organizations that aim to promote a set of local priorities, ranging from social clubs promoting neighbourly association, to those established to put pressure on local officials to improve specific facilities and to those that have a strong political agenda linked to improving the living conditions of a disadvantaged group.

There is a strong association between civic engagement in youth and subsequent involvement in political activities in adulthood, partly because 'joiners in youth become joiners in adulthood', but also because one organization may become a recruiting ground for another, related, organization (Flanagan, 2009: 297). In this context, Putnam (1995) has raised concerns about a decline in organized social interaction and its impact on civic engagement as a result of an individualization of leisure activities. Putnam uses the example of bowling among Americans: as an activity it has become more popular, but people are increasingly bowling alone or in family groups rather than in organized leagues. As a result, people have lost an important opportunity for social interaction and political discussion on a wider social stage. For Putnam, this decline in community connection has a negative impact on social capital, weakens the social fabric and leads to more widespread disengagement from public participation and political participation.

Organizations that are oriented specifically towards young people – the Scouts and Guides, youth clubs and youth sports clubs, drama and dance groups, the Boys Brigade and so on – all provide valuable opportunities for civic engagement, but many such groups are ill-suited to the conditions of late modernity. In particular, many of these groups hold most appeal for those in the early teenage years, with membership rates and perceived relevance declining with age (Furlong et al., 1997). In a sense many of the traditional youth groups that emerged during the industrial era were designed to meet the needs of young teens in an age when many young people entered the adult world of work by their mid-teens (Jeffs, 1979). Participation in sports clubs also falls sharply with age, especially for girls (Hendry et al., 1993). The protraction of youth has occurred without any significant move to design a new set of organizations which would capture the interests and meet the needs of young people from their mid-to-late teens into their early to mid-twenties. This gap in the provision of organizations relevant to older youth may be linked to a decline in collective orientations and the fall in participation in conventional politics.

Involvement in conventional politics

Political scientists have repeatedly shown that young people in all advanced countries are under-represented in conventional politics. Voter turnout among young people tends to be low, relatively few belong to political parties and, in surveys, they tend to express a low level of interest in national politics (Henn et al., 2002, 2005; Park, 2004; Sloam, 2007). At the same time, it can be argued that conventional politics largely disregards young people as voters and sidelines political issues that are important to younger voters. Politicians tend to pay lip service to the idea that parliamentary democracies should fully represent the diverse pop-ulations they serve and, in this context, most will accept the premise that efforts should be made to increase the presence of groups currently under-represented, such as women and members of certain ethnic minor-ity groups. Few such calls are made with respect to young people and many oppose the suggestion that the franchise should be extended to those below the age of 18. The Scottish government is currently proposing that in a forthcoming vote on independence, 16 and 17 year-olds should be granted the right to vote: a proposal vigorously rejected by the government in Westminster.

In many senses, the approaches of older and younger people towards the political system can be regarded as reciprocal: older people marginalize the views of the young and younger people have little time for the conven-tional politics of the older generation. Indeed, older voters often place a relatively low priority on issues that are of core concern to young people, such as unemployment (Furlong and Cartmel, 2012). It is wrong, however, to suggest that young people are apathetic or alienated politically: they are simply involved in different ways (Marsh *et al.*, 2007). In particular, it has been argued that young people are engaged politically and construe many of their day-to-day activities as broadly political, yet fail to see the relevance of conventional party politics (Furlong and Cartmel, 2007; Marsh *et al.*, 2007).

In political circles there has been a long-standing concern about the lack of involvement in conventional politics among young people and, in many countries, leading politicians have tried to reach out to young people either by highlighting an issue that is believed to be of interest to the younger voter, or, perhaps more patronizingly, through association with youthful celebrities. Back in the 1960s, Prime Minister Harold Wilson attempted to woo the youth vote through appearing on television with the Beatles and making the first ever nomination of pop musicians for the award of MBEs. Tony Blair tried to pull off a similar stunt by inviting contemporary pop stars to 10 Downing Street and by issuing a campaign text message aimed at young voters promoting his proposal to liberalize drinking laws with a text that read 'cdnt give a XXXX 4 lst ordrs?' In Israel, prime ministerial candidate Tzipi Livni appeared in a trendy Tel Aviv dance club while, in the US, the Democrats paid for an advert within an Xbox 360 car race game in which roadside placards urged players to vote for Obama.

One of the problems with enlisting the support of celebrities to help capture the youth vote is that the strategy can backfire if a celebrity publicly loses faith with a politician or a party. Farthing refers to the process of enlisting the services of a celebrity to promote policies as 'cool hunting' (2010: 184), arguing that 'cool hunting is at best an inauthentic exercise that runs the high risk of being counterproductive as young people become even more cynical about the value of their "culture" and opinions. "Cool" musicians are there to build a political brand, not to voice the concerns of a generation or to have any real opinion' (2010: 184). Over a number of years members of the Beatles made a public show of returning their MBEs to the Queen in order to register strong disapproval with a particular policy. Noel Gallagher subsequently turned on Tony Blair, arguing that he was acting like a president and was tainted by the Iraq war. Gallagher also suggested that the failure of governments to listen to the electorate meant that it was unsurprising that more young people voted in TV talent shows than turned out to vote in general elections.

The argument that more young people vote in shows like *Big Brother* than do in general elections has become a popular claim among journalists who use the figures as a way of highlighting what they often regard as apathy among the young electorate. This claim was criticized by the *BBC*'s political analyst Brian Wheeler. In the UK 2004 final of *Big Brother* 6.3 million people phoned to select a winning housemate. Wheeler suggests that if we want to argue that these voters are all in the 18–34 age range (the target audience), then we can compare them with 5.6 million 18–34 year-olds who voted in the 2005 general election. Of course there will be many people both older and younger who cast a vote, which will change the overall figures. More seriously, a significant number of voters cast multiple votes in a single week. Over the course of a *Big Brother* series, it has been argued that a significant number of people voted on up to 50 occasions and a minority voted between 50 and 100 times. In other words, the claim that more young people vote in *Big Brother* is almost certainly an exaggeration.

Adapted from *BBC News* © [2005] BBC http://news.bbc.co.uk/1/hi/uk-politics/4586995.stm (accessed 27 July 2011).

The youth vote will always be important because, in any general election, young first-time voters will make an initial decision about whether to vote and who to vote for. No party can afford to ignore this new segment of the electorate, especially as an initial voting preference may translate into a lifetime political loyalty. In a context where voter turnout has been declining among all age groups, there is also a worry about political mandates, the so-called 'democratic deficit', and about the long-term impact of not encouraging participation among young voters. In the UK, overall voter turnout at general elections has been declining since the 1950s. In

youth studies: an introduction

the general election of 2005, less than four in ten (37 per cent) 18–24 year-olds registered a vote, compared to an overall turnout of just over six in ten (61 per cent) (Marsh *et al.*, 2007). Figures for the 2010 election are based on survey results and therefore subject to a degree of error, but these show that less than one in two 18–25 year-olds voted compared to over eight in ten over 66 year-olds (Clarke *et al.*, 2011). Similar patterns exist in many other developed countries, including those where there are penalties for failing to vote, such as Australia. Compulsory voting certainly raises turnout among all sections of the electorate, but the experience in Australia is that younger people are still less likely to appear on the electoral register (Print *et al.*, 2004).

The lower level of involvement on the part of young people is partly explained by the way in which they are treated by the political classes. Marsh and colleagues (2007) argue that there is a tendency to treat young people as 'political apprentices' rather than as 'political agents' and that young people, in turn, regard themselves as being politically marginalized and as not being encouraged to play an active part in the political process. Henn and colleagues regard young people as political sceptics with little belief in the idea that 'political parties or representatives *genuinely* seek to further young people's interests or act upon their concerns' (2002: 178). Moreover, as Farthing argues, young people 'do not enjoy the same civil, political or social rights as adults' and it is 'common practice to reinforce hegemonic ideas about the marginal status of young people – that they are human beings awaiting full recognition of their humanity and citizenship' (2010: 184).

Generation and change

One of the key contemporary concerns about the low level of political participation among young people relates to the idea that the absence of younger people from political life cannot simply be explained as being part of a passing phase in the lifecycle. The fear is that today's youth will not necessarily 'grow into' traditional forms of adult participation as they age; their practice is a reflection of a new approach to politics whereby the low level of formal participation among this generation will be a defining feature of lives in the long term. The generational argument is underpinned by reference to broader theoretical approaches to processes of social change that come across as entirely credible. The problem is that it is very difficult to disentangle age and generational effects without the empirical evidence through which the changing practices of contemporary youth can be tracked (Henn *et al.*, 2002).

The theoretical case for a generational shift in approaches to political participation has roots in the work of Inglehart (1977), Giddens

(1991) and Beck (2001), with some later work by Inglehart and colleagues (2004) attempting to provide empirical backing for their original arguments through cross-national surveys of value changes. The core ideas they present, which have been elaborated by many other contributors, is that, across the developed world, there has been a shift from the collective politics of class to 'post-materialist' politics (Inglehart, 1977), 'life politics' (Giddens, 1991) or 'atomised citizenship' (Pattie et al., 2004). The weakening of the collective basis for political action draws on the idea of individualization, in that it carries the assumption that subjective attachments to social class have weakened as individuals increasingly see themselves as responsible for their own fate and face difficulties drawing parallels between the situations they face and the circumstances affecting others. The collective politics of class are seen here as rooted in an industrial age where workers clearly regarded their own security and material advancement as linked to the communal circumstances of their peers. In a collective context, wages and working conditions were to be improved by collective action through union membership, while economic and social advances were to be achieved through supporting parties of the left as representatives of the ordinary worker.

In many ways, the survival of collective politics is dependent on the existence of group identities, if not through a sense of belonging to a social class and sharing a set of conditions with others occupying the same class position, then certainly through a sense of belonging to a community of interests. Employment conditions are often thought of as providing the bedrock of collective identity and interests, perhaps expressed through trade union membership or more weakly through a trade association or even a shared professional or occupational identity. Take away the stability of employment, as careers are increasingly characterized by flexibility, and the foundation for collective identities are shaken (Sennett, 1998). In this context, Bang has argued that young people are not drawn towards ideological politics, but are involved with what he calls the 'micropolitics of becoming' (2004: 14). What Bang refers to as 'Everyday Makers' are individualistic, 'project orientated' and 'more fun-seeking than is usually associated with being civically engaged' (2004: 26). Indeed, as we suggested earlier, changes in education and employment and the increased fluidity of transitions does undermine social connection and makes it more difficult for individuals to identify others with whom they share a set of experiences. Collective party politics are based on the assumption that people can identify with others who share a core set of interests that can be translated into an agenda under which policies can be packaged and prioritized. Under the conditions of late modernity, for young people in particular, these packaged political agendas may hold little appeal and a pick-and-mix consumer model may be more attractive.

The politics of protest

Whereas young people may have a peripheral involvement with conventional politics, they should not be regarded as apathetic, as they are much more willing to get involved when it comes to single issues in areas that directly affect their lives or which reflect broad themes linked to social justice and global futures. Young people are often at the forefront of demonstrations, street protests and product boycotts, many of which provoke disproportionate reactions from the police and mainstream politicians. Recent examples are plentiful and include protests in 2011 against nuclear power in Tokyo, and in Germany where over 100,000 people are claimed to have turned out in Berlin alone. Well-attended protests in the UK against a sharp rise in student tuition fees, demonstrations in Greece against the proposed austerity packages proposed to meet IMF 'bail-out' conditions and large demonstrations in Spanish cities on the eve of elections over unemployment levels and the impact of economic policies all drew heavily on the support of youth. None of this is new of course; examples of youth activism focused on issues of concern were prominent in the 1960s where there was a strong focus on the war in Vietnam, on sexual politics and against racist policies. In the 1980s many countries witnessed direct action by young people focused on high levels of youth unemployment and changes in welfare regimes that had a disproportionate impact on young people. In the UK there were street battles with the police in many cities that were both linked to unemployment and poverty as well as to racist policing tactics. Anger among youth was reflected in the music of some of the key bands of the time: UB40 (named after the form used to claim unemployment payments) sang about the impact of unemployment, The Specials released 'Ghost Town', highlighting anger and frustration about levels of unemployment and government inaction, while the band Frankie Goes to Hollywood were associated with a T-shirt printed with the slogan 'Frankie says Arm the Unemployed'.

In 1981, Britain was in a state of crisis: the government was as unpopular as any since the war, unemployment was rampant and riots were breaking out across the country. Into this turbulent mix, the Specials released their doom-laden, highly political single, Ghost Town. Despairing of rising unemployment [...] it was not only a peculiarly unsettling record, but a uniquely prescient one. As Ghost Town reached number one, its lyrics were horribly borne out. 'Can't go on no more,' sang the Specials, 'the people getting angry.' As if on cue, the worst mainland rioting of the century broke out in Britain's cities and towns. For the first and only time, British pop music appeared to be commenting on the news as it happened.

(Petridis, 2002)

In many countries, young people have also been active participants in urban disorders. While many civil disorders can clearly be interpreted as political events in which participants are making a visible display about their disapproval of policies, forms of treatment or the situations they face, there is a tendency to describe them as riots, thus highlighting disorder, destruction and violence while downplaying political purpose (Akram, 2009). The disorders associated with the G8 protests in London, for example, were portrayed by the media as 'at best, the posturing of a bored youth, biting the hand that feeds them, or, at worst, criminal' (Marsh *et al*., 2007: 22–3). Tony Blair described their actions as 'mindless thuggery' (Marsh *et al*., 2007: 23). However, a sceptic may argue that people are happy to interpret an act as political if they approve of the outcomes or of the aims of the protesters (as in the Arab Spring or Tiananmen Square protests), and more likely to use the term riot if they disapprove of, or are unclear about, the aims. Akram (2009) has examined urban disorders through a political lens, arguing that while the triggers for action may be overtly political, as in the case of participation in, and reactions towards, neo-fascist demonstrations, they can also be linked to frustration, powerlessness, racism and perceived victimization. Urban disorders may involve criminal behaviour, but it tends not to be a key explanatory factor (Akram, 2009).

2005 was a difficult year for France, as it experienced some of the worst urban disorders it had ever known. France however, has a history of urban disorders dating back to the 1970s. The 1970s saw similar incidents occur in the banlieues, although compared to them, the urban disorders of 2005 were unprecedented in terms of their magnitude and geographical extent. The 1980s saw five large-scale urban disorders in the banlieues and the 1990s saw 48 large-scale urban disorders in addition to some 300 on a smaller scale, referred to as 'mini-riots'. The residential behaviour and status of Frances' [sic] ethnic minority population is central to understanding the disorders in France. Nearly all of the urban disorders of 2005 and of previous decades have taken place in social

youth studies: an introduction

housing neighbourhoods, nearly all of them in banlieues, and the
majority of the individuals involved have been non-white and
of North African and Black origin. The banlieues mostly consist
of high-rise social housing projects where a large proportion of
the country's ethnic minority populations live. The banlieues have
been disproportionately affected by very high unemployment following the economic crisis of the 1970s and the ensuing process
of economic restructuring. Levels of unemployment in these areas
are exacerbated by discriminatory employment practices within
the French labour market as well as relatively poor educational
outcomes for ethnic minorities (Akram, 2009: 318).

Young people often figure prominently in consumer boycotts, usually
oriented towards global capitalist enterprises. Recent targets have included
Nike for its alleged sweat-shop conditions and labour abuses in third world
countries, KFC over allegations of livestock conditions among key suppliers
and Starbucks for alleged anti-union activities and over a branch in Guan-
tánamo serving skinny lattes and muffins to military personnel associated
with torture and abuse. In South Africa the ANC Youth League organized
successful consumer boycotts against white-owned businesses accused of
racially motivated behaviour against young black consumers. In a study
of political participation among young people in several European countries, the number who had participated in consumer boycotts ranged from
32 per cent in Finland and 23 per cent in Italy, to 12 per cent in France and
4 per cent in the UK (Spannering, 2008). In this context, young people are
often seen as involved in what has been described as a 'movement society' (Tarrow, 1998; Marsh et al., 2007); participating in activities focused
on single and inter-linked issues of concern targeted as much towards the
institutions of global capitalism rather than representatives of the nation
state.

Young people's involvement in consumer action clearly highlights
Bang's (2004) ideas about Everyday Makers and micropolitics. Micropolitics relates to issues that directly impinge on lived experience and may
involve direct consumer action and finding imaginative ways of express-
ing strongly held views and opinions, along with a willingness to speak
out on issues of personal concern. For Marsh and colleagues this broader
definition of politics involves conceptualizing it 'less as an arena or set of
arenas, but rather as lived experience, in which, for example, individuals
who experience differing levels of inequalities may conceive of, and experience, politics differently' (2007: 21). Micropolitical issues may relate to

areas such as sexual politics, birth control or educational provision, which impinge directly on the lived experiences of young people but also extend to lifestyle choices reflected in decisions to boycott certain products (such as food grown on the occupied Palestinian territories) or to avoid activities that are seen as detrimental to the environment (long-haul air travel, or the purchase of certain species of fish). As one of the Italian participants in a European survey argued, 'What is personal is political and thus really...any choice is political...from what you buy in the supermarket, to any other choice.... The travel you decide to undertake, the philosophy you follow' (Spannering, 2008: 79). Micropolitics is not a compartmentalized set of activities, but is embedded in lifestyles and daily activities: it is about taking personal responsibility for change; doing change, rather than voting for change and therefore living politics (Farthing, 2010). As such, micropolitics can involve far greater commitment than participation in conventional politics.

Political extremes

Involvement by young people in the politics of protest can sometimes be interpreted as a challenge to democratic traditions or as promoted by extremist politics. While it is not difficult to find examples of street-based demonstrations of political extremism (such as those organized by the far-right British National Party), most young people who join political protests are middle class, well educated and rarely part of the 'far left' (Norris et al., 2005; Marsh et al., 2007). However, in many countries there are concerns about political extremism among young people, particularly with the activities of Islamic militants and factions of the extreme right.

Events such as 9/11, the Bali nightclub bombing of 2002, the train bombings in Madrid in 2004 and the London transport bombings in 2005 have triggered an interest by the police and media in Islamic extremism and the radicalization of young Muslims who are willing to take violent action in the name of jihad, holy war. While only a small minority of young Muslims support violent action, the ensuing moral panic has put the spotlight on the messages being promoted in mosques and the activities of Islamic societies in universities. The idea that the Koran legitimises terrorist action in Western societies as part of the struggle to defend Islam against infidels has been hotly disputed by prominent Islamic scholars who have unequivocally condemned terrorism as contrary to religious teachings. This is an interpretation that is upheld by the vast majority of Muslims in Western and non-Western countries. The Gallup Center for Muslim Studies has conducted a number of large-scale studies into the attitudes and values of Muslims, which clearly show that Muslims living in Western countries are comfortably able to reconcile Islamic religious identities with identities as European citizens. Moreover, Muslims living in London, Paris and Berlin expressed a strong preference for living in ethnically and religiously diverse neighbourhoods (Nyiri, 2007a). One of the Gallup polls asked respondents in London, Paris and Berlin to assess the acceptability of using violence to help secure a noble cause: in all of the cities, Muslims were more likely than the population at large to regard violent action as unacceptable (Nyiri, 2007a).

While Muslims living in Western societies are usually well-integrated citizens who share in the core political values of Western democracies, they frequently hold a set of beliefs that contrast with their non-Muslim neighbours. Indeed, the media frequently highlight what they portray as the clash of ideologies represented by Islamic conservatism on the one hand, and Western liberalism on the other. Surveys show that there are key areas where there are clear disagreements over values, such as over the acceptability of women wearing the hijab or burka in public or about the acceptability of homosexuality (Nyiri, 2007b), yet there is also much common ground and no evidence that value differences lead to extremism among young people.

In contemporary Western societies some of the most visible political extremism among young people relates to the activities of groups on the far right, some of which involves targeting Muslim and other immigrant communities and people who support liberal immigration policies. Many members of the extreme right are from lower working class communities in areas of high unemployment, who often hold the belief that their jobs have been taken by cheap immigrant labour. Politicians of the centre-left have often encountered difficulties in reconciling their own liberal views on immigration with those of their working class electorate who fear for their jobs or suspect that refugees and immigrants may be getting preferential treatment with regard to welfare benefits.

In the US, there has been a significant increase in 'white supremacist' groups since 2000, triggered by poor economic conditions and the election of Barack Obama (Leadership on Civil Rights Education Fund, 2009). Shortly before Obama was elected, two young people were arrested for allegedly planning to embark on a racially motivated killing spree, including the assassination of the presidential candidate. In Norway, the mass killings in Oslo and of young Labour Party supporters in Utøya Island by right-wing extremist Anders Breivik were triggered by his desire to see Muslims expelled from Europe and the extermination of European Marxists.

In Germany there is evidence of a growth in right-wing extremism among young people, despite strong efforts in schools to stimulate political tolerance (Miller-Idriss, 2009). Following interviews with working class

German youth and their teachers and many hours of classroom observation, Miller-Idriss (2009) argued that there were generational differences on the understanding of 'Germanness'. While the teachers' approach involved disseminating a sense of national shame associated with the Holocaust, young people frequently resented the expectation that they would share this sense of guilt and were drawn more towards right-wing ideologies as a way of establishing a sense of national pride.

Some implications for policy

While young people are criticized for failing to show a strong interest in conventional politics or to vote in elections, many of the efforts made to involve them are deeply patronizing and are underpinned by the idea that they are not fully responsible citizens and should not be trusted until they emulate the political practices of older generations. As citizens, young people are marginalized, yet they are expected to engage with the responsibilities of citizenship without being accorded full rights. While there are calls by some politicians to reduce the age at which young people are eligible to vote, there are no calls to give them full proportional representation in parliament. Youth parliaments have been established in some countries, but they are little more than adolescent debating chambers promoted by a condescending political elite.

Young people are political citizens who have real demands and priorities that are often very different from those expressed by older citizens. The political priorities of young people are often focused on big issues that will make a real difference to their lives both in the here and now and in the future: student funding, the impact of austerity measures on jobs for young people, unemployment, the environment and so on. Older voters often focus on their own priorities and place a low priority on the concerns of the young, to the extent that they are often willing to let the younger generation pick up the bill for their own excesses. Conventional politics favours the agendas of the older generation, leaving younger people to find alternative ways of making themselves heard.

In this context, it is little surprise that young people feel the need to take their protests to the streets and to confront the establishment head on. Parties rarely represent young people and packaged policies linked to collective identities often fail to appeal to a generation who are doing, and perhaps will continue, to 'do' politics differently in an atomized, post-materialist and individualized world order.

youth studies: an introduction

Summary points

1 Young people are often excluded from full rights of citizenship and are granted limited rights. There has been a tendency to restrict citizenship rights and make them more conditional.
2 While there has been a move to introduce citizenship education into schools, it tends to emphasize expectations regarding behaviour while underplaying political citizenship.
3 Young people tend to display relatively low levels of interest in conventional politics, which is understandable given their marginalization through the political establishment and by older voters.
4 While young people may not see the relevance of party politics, it is wrong to think of them as alienated or apathetic. They are frequently active in single-issue politics and the politics of protest.
5 There is some evidence to suggest that there has been a generational shift in approaches to political participation involving a weakening of collectivist responses and the emergence of a post-materialist politics shaped by individualized experiences.

Further questions

1 In what sense can young people be said to be excluded as citizens?
2 How can organizational membership promote active citizenship?
3 Would you consider young people to be politically marginalized, apathetic or alienated?
4 Is 'cool hunting' a genuine attempt to reach younger voters or is it opportunistic and patronizing?
5 Do you think there has been a generational shift in approaches to political participation?
6 Is urban disorder a legitimate way of participating politically?

Further reading

Akram, S. (2009) ' "Riots" or "urban disorders"? The case for re-politicizing urban disorders', in A. Furlong (ed.), *Handbook of Youth and Young Adulthood*, Abingdon: Routledge.

Farthing, R. (2010) 'The politics of youthful antipolitics: representing the "issue" of youth participation in politics', *Journal of Youth Studies*, 13 (2): 181–95.

Henn, M., Weinstein, M. and Wring, D. (2002) 'A generation apart? Youth and political participation in Britain', *British Journal of Politics and International Relations*, 4 (2): 167–92.

Marsh, D., O'Toole, T. and Jones, S. (2007) *Young People and Politics in the UK: Apathy or Alienation?* London: Palgrave Macmillan.

Internet links

This link takes you to the Crick Report, 'Education for citizenship':
www.teachingcitizenship.org.uk/dnloads/crickreport1998.pdf

The link below takes you to an interesting report on 'Young People, Politics and Popular Culture':
www.uea.ac.uk/mac/comm/media/press/2010/March/Young+people

This site contains some interesting surveys comparing the views of Muslims and non-Muslims:
www.gallup.com/se/127907/gallup-center-muslim-studies.aspx

chapter 11

Beyond the first world

Contents

Focusing on the majority

Confronting the literature on youth, including the contents of this book, one could well come away with the impression that Western youth form a majority while a largely invisible minority live in non-Western societies. Nothing could be further from the truth. The vast majority of young people live in developing countries: according to the UN, globally around 85 per cent of 15–24 year-olds live in developing countries, a figure projected to grow to 89.5 per cent by 2025 (UN, 2008). Moreover, this majority are extremely diverse: some live in rural areas but many inhabit the overcrowded metropolises of India, Asia and South America, some live traditional lives in tribal societies, while others participate in global youth cultures in ghetto contexts.

Many young lives in developing countries are defined by poverty, some suffer from famine and a lack of clean water, while involvement in armed conflict is all to common. Health problems are rife, especially due to the prevalence of HIV/AIDS in certain regions. The United Nations estimates that 200 million young people live in poverty, 130 million are illiterate and 10 million live with HIV/AIDS (UN, 2005). While in the West we talk about the protraction of youth, in some developing countries many will have died before reaching what we might regard as young adulthood. In some African countries, life expectancy is under 50 years: in Swaziland, for example, average life expectancy is under 40, an age some Westerners regard as part of young adulthood.

> There are currently over 1 billion youth in the second decade of life, and we know very little about the great majority of them. Most scholars of adolescence are in Western nations, and their research focuses almost entirely on youth in their corners of the globe. However, given increased global interaction and interdependency [...], it is essential that the field of adolescence awake from its parochialism and pay attention to the multiplicity of adolescents that make up the world community.
>
> (Larson and Wilson, 2004: 300)

The differences between the lives of those living in the global north and global south[1] are so profound that many of the theories we use to understand the lives of young people are meaningless in non-Western contexts (Nilan, 2011). Our discussions of employment and unemployment, for example, may be largely irrelevant in societies where much work is casual and linked to basic subsistence, while the idea of citizenship rights may hold little water in totalitarian regimes. Many of the interpretive frameworks that we treat as universally applicable are based on Western assumptions, and many observations have little currency outside of the economically advanced societies. Criticizing the Western-centrism of youth studies, Nilan argues that 'youth sociology...remains somewhat stuck in the very global status divisions of inequality that the sociological endeavour explicitly seeks to unsettle' (2011: 25). Indeed, she rightly suggests that

youth studies: an introduction

some of our key concepts, such as choice biographies and individualization, can be meaningless outside of the global north: in many non-Western societies, for example, collectivist traditions remain strong and family traditions and obligations continue to shape youth and young adulthood, while marriage and parenthood still define adulthood.

While the criticism of Western-centrism is hard to dispute, the 'Arab Spring' – the political unrest largely triggered by the frustrations of young people denied opportunities to make a reasonable income and living in contexts where their voices remain unheard – has started to focus attention on the experiences of young people in developing countries. The European Commission has recently placed social and political change in the Arab world onto its research agenda and, with high levels of unemployment affecting young people in Europe as well as much of the Middle East, there is a budding interest in exploring the frustrations of young people in countries outside of the global north.

Climate change

Global warming and climate change represent an acute threat to the lives of young people in many of the less developed parts of the world. Here White (2011) paints a vivid picture of the implications of climate change, predicting that it will trigger new conflicts and insecurities that impact on the lives of young people whose lives will become 'dominated by daily survival' (White, 2011: 16). Triggering disasters such as floods, drought and extreme weather, climate change will result in new conflicts between and within countries and will lead to new diasporas as people try to make a life for themselves under deteriorating environmental conditions. Young people affected by these disasters and conflicts may see migration as a way to improve their living conditions, although, as White argues, 'environmental refugees' may face the hostility of Western populations who tighten their borders and stigmatize those seeking refuge from global events triggered by Western excesses and irresponsibilities.

> Social inequality and environmental injustice will undoubtedly be the drivers of continuous conflict for many years to come as the most dispossessed and marginalised of the world's population suffer the brunt of food shortages, undrinkable water, climate-induced migration and general hardship in their day-to-day lives. The young and the old, the infirm and the disabled, will, in particular, suffer. Women will suffer more than men, and people of colour more than the non-indigenous and the non-migrant.
>
> (White, 2011: 13)

Climate change has been associated with extreme weather events which have increased markedly over recent years. The United Nations (2010) has shown that extreme weather events have doubled since 1980 and may increase by a further 50 per cent by 2015. Extreme weather events have had the greatest impact on parts of the world where large numbers of young people reside (such as South Asia, the Caribbean, Central America and islands in the Pacific), resulting in flooding and drought. Flooding can lead to water contamination in places where sanitation is primitive, leading to threats to health from cholera, typhoid and diarrhoea (UN, 2010). Drought can also restrict the availability of clean water with consequences for sanitation, agriculture and dehydration (UN, 2010).

Global warming has a range of other consequences that impact on young people in the less developed regions of the world. An increase in global temperatures, for example, has led to an increase in dengue fever, as the areas where the transmitting mosquito lives have expanded. Most of those who lose their lives as a result of dengue fever are children and young adults, with 600 million young people living in infested areas (UN, 2010).

The incidence of dengue has grown dramatically around the world in recent decades. Some 2.5 billion people – two fifths of the world's population – are now at risk from dengue. WHO currently estimates there may be 50 million dengue infections worldwide every year. In 2007 alone, there were more than 890,000 reported cases of dengue in the Americas, of which 26,000 cases led to a potentially lethal complication called dengue haemorrhagic fever (DHF).

The disease is now endemic in more than 100 countries in Africa, the Americas, the Eastern Mediterranean, South-east Asia and the Western Pacific. South-east Asia and the Western Pacific are the most seriously affected. Before 1970 only nine countries had experienced DHF epidemics, a number that had increased more than four-fold by 1995.

(WHO, 2009)

Climate change also seriously challenges food security in many parts of the world, hitting young people particularly hard. Here again extreme weather compromises health through crop failure and the reduction of agricultural productivity, or adversely impacts on supply chains, disrupting the distribution of food. The UN predicts that climate change could lead to a

youth studies: an introduction

fall in agricultural productivity in developing countries of between 9 and 21 per cent, with India, Pakistan and China (countries containing more than 40 per cent of the global population of young people) seriously affected by a decline in melt water from the Himalayas (UN, 2010).

These climate-induced changes are likely to increase conflict within and between countries as competition for scarce resources intensifies and are also likely to lead to an increase in migration as people seek to escape extreme poverty and hunger. Migration flows tend to show that those with few commitments and no dependents are the most mobile, with young males likely to be first to move (UN, 2010).

Health

Young people in the global south are faced with a wide range of health-related issues with strong spatial variations. These range from threats to health linked to a lack of food and inadequate nutrition, water and sanitation in some developing countries, to the risk of HIV/AIDS or of becoming a victim of war or civil disorder in others. These health risks lead to a situation where life expectancy in developing countries is around 35 years less than in industrialized countries (Blum and Nelson-Mmari, 2004).

Around a fifth of the world's population live in extreme poverty which significantly impacts on life expectancy: up to 420 million people experience chronic poverty which persists for several years, often across an entire lifetime, and manifest at times in a severe shortage of food (Chronic Poverty Research Centre, 2004). In parts of Africa, such as Angola and Swaziland as we have noted, life expectancy is less than 40 years (CIA, 2012). In some African countries, such as Malawi, more than three in four young people are deprived of shelter and lack sanitation. In countries such as Chad, the Congo, Bangladesh and Yemen, as a result of a lack of adequate food, more than one in four young people are underweight (UN, 2010). In these countries malnutrition is associated with a range of conditions that shorten lives, while other threats come from water-borne parasites and mosquitoes.

If we study the leading causes of death among young people, we find some striking differences. While in Europe unintentional injuries (usually involving road traffic accidents) are the leading cause of death, followed by suicide and self-inflicted injuries, in South America, the Caribbean and parts of Africa, homicide, war and other intentional injuries top the league tables, while in other parts of Africa HIV/AIDS is responsible for the majority of deaths among young people (Blum and Nelson-Mmari, 2004; UN, 2010).

The number of young people infected with HIV/AIDS is particularly high in Sub-Saharan Africa as well as in parts of the Caribbean. In Botswana,

South Africa and Zimbabwe HIV/AIDS affects more than a quarter of the youth population, with females most affected. In Botswana, which has the highest rate of infection, three in ten females between the ages of 15 and 24 are affected (Blum and Nelson-Mmari, 2004). Prevalence rates among females in parts of Africa are five times higher than among males, partly due to biological differences that make women significantly more vulnerable to infection, but also due to social and cultural factors which expose females to the risk of unprotected sex with promiscuous male partners (Mugisha, 2009). In many developing countries, condom use among young people remains low (although it is increasing), while the number of young people having premarital sex has increased. In countries such as Zimbabwe, the Dominican Republic and Guatemala, less than 2 per cent of unmarried, sexually active, 20–24 year-olds use condoms (Mugisha, 2009).

> In Sub-Saharan Africa, [...] where most infections are transmitted by heterosexual relations, young women generally face higher risks because they tend to have sex with older men, who are more likely to be infected than younger men. Some of these relationships are based on economic gain, that is, they involve the exchange of gifts or money for sex. There is now a great deal of research showing that power differentials inherent in such relationships make it difficult for young women to negotiate the use of condoms.
>
> (Mugisha, 2009: 345)

Development agencies and national governments have put considerable efforts into sex education programmes in order to try to reduce the risks associated with sexual activity, with such programmes becoming easier to implement due to increases in educational participation. Such interventions have had some success in reducing the numbers of young people participating in unprotected sex, although in many countries there is still a long way to go. In Brazil, for example, over the decade 1990 to 2000 the percentage of non-married, sexually active 20–24 year-olds using condoms increased from 0.3 to 4.1. On the other hand, some countries, such as Uganda, have been extremely successful in increasing condom use among 20–24 year-olds from virtually none to over a third (Mugisha, 2009).

Young women living in developing countries are also at risk of sexual violence, sexual slavery and enforced prostitution. Female refugees can be vulnerable to rape and sexual exploitation, while some conflicts, such as that in Rwanda, have been associated with mass rape, mutilation and

youth studies: an introduction

enforced pregnancy. Female genital mutilation remains common in parts of Africa, where up to half of all young women are ritually mutilated: the UN reports that, despite international efforts to halt the practice, there has been no significant decline and interventions are often met with local hostility (UN, 2005).

There are a wide range of health-related behaviours that impact on youth in developing countries, including some, like drinking and drug abuse, which make it more likely young people will engage in unsafe sexual practices. As in the West, the use of alcohol among young people has been increasing in developing countries and drug use has become more prevalent (UN, 2003). The number of injecting drug users in Central Asia, for example, is thought to be ten times higher than in the West, with one in four injecting users being under the age of 20 (UNAIDS Inter-Agency Task Team on Young People, 2004). Tobacco use among young people is also higher in developing countries and is increasing, especially among young women. Here multi-national tobacco companies are able to exploit new markets where there are few curbs on advertising to make up for profits lost due to increased regulation in the West.

Education

One of the key trends observed in education in the West – increasing participation – also underpins the experiences of young people in the developing world. However, in many countries the increase in participation is manifest in an expansion of primary education and in increased numbers making transitions from primary to secondary schooling. Levels of literacy remain low in many countries, and parents who rely on the labour of their children may be reluctant to allow them to attend school. In East and Mid Africa around one in four young males and three in ten females were illiterate in 2008 (UN, 2010). The level of primary school attendance is high in many countries (often in excess of 90 per cent), but large numbers fail to progress to secondary education. In Africa, around nine in ten young people attend primary school in Malawi and Zimbabwe (with attendance being marginally higher for females), while attendance in secondary schools falls to around 25 per cent in Malawi and 38 per cent in Zimbabwe (with attendance being slightly higher for males). Similarly, in Asia, around 85 per cent of young people attend primary school in Bangladesh, falling to around 42 per cent in secondary school (UN, 2010). As such, in many developing countries, secondary school attendance remains a minority experience.

While young people who lack basic skills may increasingly find themselves disadvantaged both in the labour market, as well as in their daily lives as they negotiate complex institutional contexts (Larson and Wilson,

2004), it can be difficult to motivate young people to learn where they lack any confidence that their efforts will pay off.

> What is the use of going to school? Even of we get better teachers, better materials, better schools, it will not change the living conditions of young people in this country. We are suppressed by powers that we cannot control: unemployment, violence, inequality, poverty.
>
> (young person in Brazil, quoted in Madsen, 2008: 157)

In schools, pedagogies can be primitive, dominated by rote learning and with few advanced educational tools. Where schools manage to procure modern facilities, such as computers, these are often shared by large numbers of people and lessons can be jeopardized by erratic power supplies.

Young people are motivated to engage with leaning through a variety of incentives; the promise of a job and a secure future often being paramount. However, in societies influenced by Confucianism, such as China, Korea and Japan, motivation may be influenced by the power of family expectations and the desire to maintain family honour, as well as through a tendency to regard education as a 'moral life enterprise' and as a pathway to enlightenment (Larson and Wilson, 2004).

Education has clear benefits for the individual, not only through increased wages and job security and through increased longevity; it also has a wide range of social benefits and can be linked to increased productivity, poverty reduction, democratization and social stability. Education for girls is regarded as a particularly sound investment, providing benefits that cross generations and can be linked to a wide range of health-related gains such as a reduction in fertility rates and protection from HIV/AIDS.

> Education is central to development. It empowers people and strengthens nations. It is a powerful 'equalizer', opening doors to all to lift themselves out of poverty. Moreover, education – especially girls' education – has a direct and proven impact on the goals related to child and reproductive health and environmental sustainability. Education also promotes economic growth, national productivity and innovation, and values of democracy and social cohesion.
>
> (World Bank, n.d.)

Of course national governments often regard educational policy as a tool for promoting broader political or ideological agendas. With educational systems in many developing countries rooted in their colonial past, these ideologies may be historically embedded and may restrict progress. In this context educational systems in parts of Africa were developed by British and French missionaries and aimed to produce obedient, God-fearing citizens who would not challenge the legitimacy of their colonial masters. In Brazil, in the aftermath of military rule, education was regarded as the means through which a fairer society could be established. 'Citizen Schools' were established to reach out to marginalized groups and the pedagogy shifted from one based on the promotion of 'discipline and obedience' to one that prioritized the nurturing of 'creativity, curiosity and the ability to think multiple alternatives to a given problem' (Madsen, 2008: 154).

Employment and entrepreneurship

Discussions about young people and employment in the global north frequently focus on rising unemployment and on the increase in precarious forms of employment, often characterized by low wages and the lack of formal contracts. While Beck (2000) argues that conditions in the West are undergoing a process of Brazilianization, a glance at conditions in the global south shows how far away the West is from these levels of casualization. In Ghana, for example, nearly eight in ten jobs are in the informal sector, and the International Labour Office argues that more than nine in ten new jobs in Africa will be in the informal sector, as will virtually all new jobs for young people in Latin America (UN, 2003). Due to poor wages and insecure conditions, the vast majority of informal workers in developing countries live in the slums: in Chad and Ethiopia, for example, 90 per cent of informal workers are slum residents (UN-HABITAT, 2006).

At the end of 2010, some 75 million young people globally were defined as unemployed, a rise of 4.6 million in a three-year period (ILO, 2011). While much of the increase was felt in the developed countries, part of the reason for this relates to the fact that in parts of the world, such as the Middle East and North Africa, youth unemployment has been consistently high for more than two decades (ILO, 2011). Commenting on the situation in the Middle East, the International Labour Office argues that:

> The collective frustration of a generation of youth that was granted the opportunity to gain an education but not given the same opportunity to gain decent employment was certainly a contributing factor behind mobilizing youth in support of the political protest movements in Bahrain, Egypt, Libyan Arab Jamahiriya, Syrian Arab Republic and Tunisia.
>
> (ILO, 2011: 5)

Furthermore, unemployment is a concept that has very limited use in much of the developing world. Where there is a lack of a welfare safety net and extreme poverty, people have to work to survive. This is not to say that they have jobs, but many scratch out a meagre living in the informal economy. In circumstances where families exist in conditions of chronic poverty, children may be expected to work from an early age and educational participation may be curtailed by the need to contribute to the family economy. Although governments in developing countries have made efforts to ban child labour, legislation is not always effective and may have unintended consequences. In Bangladesh, for example, legislative action resulted in the dismissal of large numbers of young people, mainly young girls, working in the garment industries. While some of these redundant workers enrolled in school, 'the great majority found new employment in the domestic, informal, and street economies – working as maids, stone crushers, welders, street hawkers and prostitutes – where work conditions and human rights violations are much worse' (Larson and Wilson, 2004).

Patwary and colleagues' (2012) study of young people engaged in medical waste scavenging in Dhaka provides a fascinating insight into the lives of young people living on the margins of Bangladeshi society, scavenging items such as used syringes, blades, bandages and saline bags from waste sites near hospitals for resale. Many of these young scavengers were from Dalit families and they frequently experienced abusive childhoods. Patwary and colleagues describe the way in which they learn from other workers and develop 'street capital' and 'street competencies' that enable them to perform as skilled scavengers.

With the lack of opportunities in the formal economy, young people in developing countries have to develop entrepreneurship skills in order to operate in hostile economic contexts. Sometimes this takes the form of low-level, dangerous, survival entrepreneurship, but can also include higher forms of enterprise through which they can make a reasonable, or even an exceptional, income. Indeed, given the limited capacity of the labour markets in developing countries to absorb young people and to provide them with the means of establishing a secure future, youth entrepreneurship is increasingly seen as sensible strategy. Entrepreneurial activity tends to be highest among young people who lack family and financial responsibilities and can afford to take risks; it is also highest in low-income countries where there may be few opportunities in the formal labour market (Schoof, 2006).

While the precarious situation of young people in the developing world is primarily a consequence of low demand for youth labour, there are also supply side issues, which, if addressed, may make it easier for young people to obtain more secure work. Among the skills that are in short supply in some countries are basic literacy and numeracy, as well as the lingual skills that have become increasingly important due to globalization. Education is

youth studies: an introduction

a key tool for addressing these deficits, although in some developing countries, especially in North Africa and the Middle East, young people are well educated and levels of graduate unemployment are high. Aside from skills, a lack of capital has tended to impede very poor people from making small-scale investments with life-changing potential. To address this problem, Muhammad Yunus set up a system of micro-credit in Bangladesh, making small loans available to poor people, including beggars, without collateral: the success of the scheme led to its replication in other countries and to the award of a Nobel Prize for Yunus.

Youth cultures

Given the very different life contexts and experiences of young people living in the global south from their northern contemporaries, it could be assumed that youth cultures would be constructed in distinct ways. In reality, many aspects of Western youth culture are manifest in developing countries. In part, this can be interpreted as a consequence of the marketing strategies of international corporations who attempt to sell Westernized identities, and the products that provide the props for such identities, to young people across the global south. Yet it would be wrong to present business as all-powerful and young people as cultural dopes pushed towards certain forms of consumption by forces beyond their control.

In explaining the globalization of youth cultures, Nilan and Feixa (2006) describe the ways in which youth cultures are adapted within local contexts, arguing that aspects of youth culture can originate in Western and non-Western contexts and are adapted globally through a process they refer to as 'hybridity'. Hybridity describes a process through which cultures are creatively manufactured through adapting something new to local contexts: it refers to 'cultural interactions between the local and the global' (Nilan and Feixa, 2006: 2). In other words, various aspects of global cultural identities are adapted in ways that help them become assimilated into a local cultural world.

Nilan (2006) illustrates the cultural hybridity of lifestyles through an examination of young Muslims in Indonesia. These young Indonesians were devout followers of Islam, yet found ways of synthesizing global cultural trends while maintaining and respecting their religious traditions. Muslim youth may drink non-alcoholic beer, possess iPhones with Koranic apps, purchase halal cosmetics and adapt their clothing in ways that reflect their desire to be modern.

In some cultural contexts these adaptations are fraught with difficulties. In some countries Muslims may hold anti-Western, or, specifically, anti-American, views, especially in the post-9/11 world. They may also abhor key components of Western youth cultures: sex outside of marriage, homosexuality, the use of drugs and alcohol. Their attempts to establish culturally hybrid lifestyles can put them into conflict with older members of their society who dislike their adaptations of traditions. In the 1960s, in Tanzania, Operation Vijana (operation youth) was launched as part of a major campaign to curb a trend towards the spread of 'indecent' aspects of modern youth culture. Popular Western dress, especially mini-skirts, tight dresses and wigs, were targeted and, in Dar es Salaam, there were numerous incidents involving attacks on young people regarded as indecently dressed by more conservative citizens (Ivaska, 2011).

> Since devout Islamic youth eschew western cultural hegemony, especially rampant hedonism and the location of sexuality and sexual activities in the realm of youth leisure rather than marriage, they constitute a ready market for a 'parallel world' of Muslim youth culture – a hybridized range of products and implied practices that follow the broad parameters of Islamic law.
>
> (Nilan, 2006: 107)

Clearly religious contexts can be central to the ways in which youth cultures are framed locally, but other factors, especially political factors, can be important. At an extreme, in North Korea, young people's scope for developing distinct youth styles is limited partly by the need to be seen to conform politically, but also as a result of relatively limited exposure to Western influences. In Vietnam, the trappings of Western-style youth culture are widespread, yet the Communist Youth Union does its best to provide 'politically correct leisure for young people' and to 'establish morally legitimate places for them' (Valentin, 2008: 77). For young people in Vietnam, the terms youth and union member are sometimes seen as synonymous, and the party plays a large part in the lives of young people. However, Vietnamese youth culture is also framed within Confucianist values under which respect and obedience towards older relatives are crucial (Valentin, 2008).

While young people are often able to accommodate youth cultures with seemingly conflictual dimensions of broader cultural identities, there are contexts in which clashes of values are inevitable. In contemporary Iran, for example, some reject and resent the Islamization of a society that was once relatively cosmopolitan. Following the Islamic revolution there were moves to "'cleanse" and "purify" the society from the alleged vices and evils of modernity and to bring up youth according to Islamic ideological and social values' (Shahabi, 2006: 113): a process that involved the banning of forms of entertainment that were regarded as non-Islamic and enforcing traditional dress codes. In response, a minority youth counter-culture

youth studies: an introduction

takes on an underground existence and banned, Western music, films and recreational drugs are traded and circulated (Shahabi, 2006).

In terms of music, many of the styles that have become popular in the West have roots in developing countries. Reggae, for example, came out of Jamaica in the 1960s, although it contained traces of traditional African music. Although blues and rock'n'roll have roots in black communities in the southern United States, they can also be traced back to African traditions, as can rap. Moreover, musical forms that have their origins in developing countries are frequently transformed and commercialized in Western contexts, then exported back to the developing world where they may undergo further transformation. 1960s Dar es Salaam, for example, had a thriving club scene centred on Westernized music, until soul music was banned in 1969 as part of a reaction against Western influences (Ivaska, 2011). In modern day Sénégal, there is a thriving hip-hop scene in Dakar, even though it is not well accepted in the wider community and is in some ways counter-cultural (Niang, 2006).

Some implications for policy

National governments and international organizations such as the UN and the World Bank share a concern for the well-being of young people in the global south. Young people today will shape the future of their own countries, as well as profoundly impacting on global relations. While experiencing diverse conditions of existence, youth cultures can permeate national boundaries and can help create the conditions for common ground and understandings.

Each of the areas covered in this chapter give rise to a number of pressing priorities for policies to improve the lives of young people and open up opportunities for a brighter future. Climate change is one of the areas where we in the West can help protect the lives of the most vulnerable, although of course some of the causes of global warming also stem from the rapid process of industrialization in countries such as China and India. Improving health often requires improved nutrition and the enhanced reliability of food supply chains, but also involves tackling disease and making modern drugs affordable to those who reside in poor countries. Enhanced education is also central to improving health, especially in the area of sexual health and the prevention of HIV/AIDS. Education is also the key to enhancing human capital and helping residents of the global south to compete in a global economy. Skill development is clearly important, but trade tariffs and the burden of debt can still make it difficult for developing countries to thrive.

The UN regularly publishes reports on youth that have a strong focus on young people in developing countries. These reports also monitor progress towards a wide range of targets in the fields covered by this chapter, as well as in related areas. While the international community has a duty to help improve the lives of young people in the developing world and to make us aware of progress and of shortcomings, we, as youth researchers, also have a duty to work towards an understanding of youth that is not dominated by a Western-centric perspective. This is not an area where we have performed well in the past, but hopefully it is an area that we can enthusiastically engage with better in the future.

Summary points

1 The vast majority of young people in the world today live in developing countries; by 2025 nine in ten young people will live in these regions.
2 Climate change will have a profound effect on the lives of young people in the global south, triggering disasters and conflicts and promoting new diasporas.
3 Although educational participation is increasing, in the global south many receive only basic schooling and may lack basic skills. Where employment opportunities are lacking, the incentive to participate in education may be low.
4 The majority of jobs in developing countries are in the informal sector; many young people work long hours to make a meagre living and often have to engage in risky activities.
5 Young people in the global south face a wide range of health risks, from chronic poverty, to HIV/AIDS, sexual violence, alcohol and drugs. These risks tend to be more extreme and life-threatening than in the global north.
6 Youth cultures in the global north and the global south often have much in common and there is a constant interplay through which lifestyles become globalized through complex processes of accommodation and transformation.

Further questions

1 In what ways can youth studies be thought of as Western-centric?
2 Explain some of the ways in which climate change may impact on the lives of young people in developing countries.

youth studies: an introduction

3 What are the main health risks faced by young people in developing countries?
4 Why are females more vulnerable to HIV/AIDS?
5 When discussing the labour market situations in the global south,
how useful is unemployment as a concept?
6 How do Confucian values affect the motivation to work at school?
7 What do Nilan and Feixa mean by the term 'hybridity'? How does
this explain the globalization of youth cultures?

Further reading

Hansen, K. T. (2008) (ed.) *Youth and the City in the Global South*,
Bloomington: Indiana University Press.
Mugisha, F. (2009) 'HIV and AIDS, STIs and sexual health among young
people', in A. Furlong (ed.), *Handbook of Youth and Young Adulthood*,
Abingdon: Routledge.
Nilan, P. and Feixa, C. (2006) (eds) *Global Youth? Hybrid Identities, Plural
Worlds*, Abingdon: Routledge.

Internet links

A link to a YouTube clip on a UN training programme for young people
living in slums:
www.unhabitat.org/categories.asp?catid=531#
This link takes you to the 2010 UN World Youth Report on climate change:
www.un.org/esa/socdev/unyin/documents/WYR2010Final%20online%20
version.pdf

chapter 12

Working with young people

Contents

Perspectives on youth work

With youth frequently portrayed as a period of 'storm and stress', with concerns about transitions from youth to adulthood, worries about the effective integration of young people and anxieties about perceived challenges to established value systems, there has been a long-standing tradition of providing additional support to young people in the form of youth work. In a range of different guises, youth work covers forms of support and intervention that include the provision of: casual youth clubs; more formal, sometimes uniformed, organizations; intensive work with young people identified as having specific problems; issue-based youth work intended to educate or raise awareness of specific areas of concern, such as drugs or sex; and street-based outreach programmes that aim to make contact with hard-to-reach youth. Broadly, youth work can be regarded as a form of informal education that aims to complement the established systems in the school setting by meeting young people on their own terms, addressing issues that concern them and providing them with a source of advice that is independent of the school, family and peer group.

With the field of youth work so broad, it would be wrong to think of it as underpinned by a consistent set of principles. In some areas, the agenda is clearly set by youth participants, and adult workers are largely regarded as facilitators; in other areas participation may be compulsory, with young people required to attend to address issues such as offending behaviour in a context clearly set by adults. There are also sectors that are linked closely to adult organizations and share their objectives: church groups, military groups and political groups, for example.

Although some of those who work in the youth sector are professionally qualified, there are a large number of volunteers in the sector, many of whom are unqualified. Unqualified workers tend to be more prevalent in the casual, leisure-based areas of youth work and are less prevalent in more intensive forms of youth work. State support for youth work is variable and traditionally the voluntary sector has played a large role. While youth work may be widely valued, informal education tends to be regarded as the poor relation of the statutory educational system and is vulnerable to cuts when budgets are tight. However, governments have often recognized the potential of youth work – broadly conceived – to deliver youth-related policy objectives. In the UK, for example, the youth service has been used as part of a strategy to reduce offending and teenage pregnancy and to address concerns relating to drug and alcohol misuse.

In the UK, as in many other countries, the motivation to work informally with young people was initially driven by concerns about moral standards and the desire to spread Christian ideology. In the UK many of the early youth organizations came into being in the mid-to-late nineteenth century and were clearly linked to Christian evangelism: the Young Men's Christian Association (YMCA), for example, was founded in 1844, and, like a number of contemporary organizations, aimed to ensure that the young people they worked with 'grew into "full Christian manliness" and were trained to be "good citizens" with "responsible roles in society"' (Evans, 1994: 180). Similarly, the Scout movement (founded in 1907) aimed to support young people's spiritual development, occupy them constructively and instil discipline into their lives. Other early youth groups were underpinned by a desire to provide political education (broadly conceived) and to provide

working with young people   243 education in informal settings to those whose family poverty blocked their access to formal education (Smith, 2002).

In the post-World War II era the breadth and direction of the youth service changed quite radically and the voluntary organizations that filled the pre-war landscape were supplemented with state-funded provision. In the UK there was a new emphasis on informal education designed to 'offer individual people in their leisure time, opportunities of various kinds, complementary to those at home, formal education and work, to discover and develop their personal resources of body, mind and spirit and thus better equip themselves to live the life of mature, creative and responsible members of a free society' (National Youth Bureau, 1990: 9). The post-war period also saw the introduction of training for youth leaders and the building of youth centres in many towns and cities.

Contemporary youth work is extremely varied both in the type of provision and underlying philosophies, to the groups that are targeted and the ways in which activities are funded. Youth workers themselves are also a heterogeneous group of workers with differing views about what constitutes youth work and whether or not it is possible to measure the effectiveness of their work. While a short chapter cannot hope to present youth work in all its complexity or offer advice on working with young people, it is possible to outline the main forms of youth work and their associated pedagogies and provide some evidence relating to its effectiveness.

Models of youth work

Although all forms of youth work stress the importance of personal and social development and place an emphasis on skills for life, youth work is a broad concept that encompasses numerous ways of working with young people built on a range of value systems (Williamson, 1997). Banks (1994) identifies four broad, overlapping categories of youth work:

- Personal and social development
- Preventative work
- Leisure-based work
- Youth social work

Cross-cutting these broad forms of youth work are distinct pedagogies, ranging from radical approaches that aim to promote change by helping young people identify the ways in which their experiences are shaped by social, economic and political structures, to approaches built around association and companionship, to those that aim to address perceived deficiencies in young people in order to equip them with the skills to find

youth studies: an introduction

individual solutions to problems. Here we can identify at least four models of youth work relating to underpinning pedagogies: these can be referred to under the headings of control, socialization, informal education and citizenship.

The assumption underpinning the control model is that young people are a threat to the prevailing social order and that youth organizations have a role to play in controlling behaviour and monitoring the activities of young people. These assumptions underpinned many of the early forms of youth work that developed in the early industrial and immediate post-Second World War era. The perceived threat was linked to the increase in leisure time and the emergence of youth cultures that were regarded as a threat to the prevailing moral order. Unstructured leisure was linked to bad habits and illegal or anti-social activities, and youth work was seen as the means through which acceptable, structured and healthy leisure use could be encouraged. Here Jeffs and Smith (1994) argued that youth work was seen by government as a means through which young people could be provided with structured activities and encouraged to engage in leisure pursuits regarded as constructive. In this context, Jephcott (1954) argued that in the 1950s many youth organizations adopted authoritarian modes of working and placed an emphasis on character building through discipline. Indeed, one of the early founders of youth clubs in the UK, Hannah More, thought that young people were corrupt with evil dispositions, with informal education being the means through which positive change could be achieved (Hendrick, 1990), and early youth workers regarded the control of the unruly working class youth as part of their role.

The socialization model shares many of the assumption of the control model: namely that youth work was a means through which young people could learn positive values and become responsible members of society, explore opportunities and develop their potential. While stressing the personal benefits associated with the constructive use of leisure, it is also concerned with the containment of youth (Jeffs, 1979; Davies, 1985). Describing youth work as a 'rescue mission for the disadvantaged' (1992: 18), Cockerill argues that the frequent emphasis of empowerment as a key objective in youth work masks a deficit view of youth as people lacking skills and in need of guidance. At the same time, within a socialization model, the need to control and contain young people's activities tends to remain implicit, while an emphasis is placed on preparation for adult roles, personal development and on encouraging young people to explore potential opportunities.

An emphasis on informal education often underpins youth work practice and is frequently highlighted in policy documents. Empowerment through involving young people in decision-making processes may be stressed and, through participation in their organization and the community at large, young people are expected to develop skills and grow in confidence. Informed by the work of Freire (1972), informal education is regarded as a means of liberation, through which oppressed or subordinate groups take responsibility for their own learning and regain their humanity. This approach tends to regard full participation and agenda setting by participants as important, and young people are expected to play a full and active role in the organization. The emphasis on empowerment and liberation in youth work was evident in some of the earliest organizations. Smith (2002), for example, draws attention to a club founded by two women later associated with the English Suffrage Union that provided social and political education to young women exploited in the West End dress trade. The focus on personal and social development tends to be stressed by youth workers themselves and by the youth services in local authorities. In a submission to the UK Parliament Education Select Committee, for example, representatives of Kent Youth Service argued that:

> At its core the aim of youth work is to support the personal and social development of young people through informal education and does so through the voluntary engagement of young people and their active involvement in the development of provision.
>
> (Kent Youth Service, 2010)

In another submission to the same Select Committee, a former government inspector of youth services and CEO of the UK National Youth Bureau drew attention to the ways in which youth work provision can promote social mobility through exposing young people to wider social networks.

The citizenship model of youth work tends to place a priority on facilitating access to health and social services, and promotes social integration. In contemporary contexts there is often an emphasis on helping young people to become active and responsible citizens. In the UK, the National Council for Voluntary Youth Services states that 'the key purpose of youth work is to work with young people to facilitate their personal, social, and educational development, and to enable them to gain a voice, influence, and place in society in a period of their transition from dependence to independence' (2008). However, the citizenship model also tends to stress voluntary participation and respect, which is far from universal. Indeed, in recent years a large amount of core funding for youth work has been linked to projects delivered to those seen as socially and economically disconnected, with an emphasis placed on re-engagement and re-integration. Some, but not all, of the projects delivered to those regarded as disconnected involve young people as unwilling participants who may be forced to work with a particular project as part of an employment or criminal justice project. Here it

youth studies: an introduction

should be noted that some youth work professionals would argue that voluntarism is a key component of youth work and therefore, by definition, any programme involving young people as unwilling or reluctant participants should not be regarded as youth work.

The practice of youth work

With youth work covering a wide range of activities in a broad variety of contexts, it is worth exploring the common principles that exist and outlining the different ways in which youth work is practised in a little more detail. In an influential paper published by the UK National Association of Youth Clubs, Fred Milson (1972) reflected on the goals and motives of youth workers. He argued that the first priority had to be individual personality development, forged in the context of social relationships and community involvement. In a similar vein, a UK government report (Department of Education and Science, 1987) on youth work highlighted the centrality of personal and social development in associational settings.

> The goals of youth work as a process of social and personal education are threefold; it aims to increase the ability of young people to:
>
> identify and develop their capacities – physical, intellectual, moral, spiritual, social and emotional;
> identify and accept their responsibilities, as individuals, citizens, group members;
> evaluate the contexts in which they live and act accordingly.
> (Department of Education and Science, 1987)

The emphasis on learning in associational contexts is what distinguishes youth work from youth social work. Youth work involves 'inter-personal interaction', and both involve 'young person with young person but also young person with adult' (Davies, 2005: 4). Offering a definition of youth work, Smith (2002) argues that ideally it must involve a focus on young people by experienced practitioners; participation should be voluntary; it should involve group activities and companionship; should be based on friendly relationships within an informal setting; and must have broad concerns with the welfare of participants. While Smith offers justification for the acceptance of these defining principles (that are also set out by Davies (2005) in what he refers to as a 'manifesto' for youth work), it is clear that they reflect a particular type of youth work rather than covering the broad waterfront of practice that is commonly referred to as youth work. Many qualified and experienced youth workers, for example, work in state-funded settings that are underpinned by a degree of compulsion or where there is a degree of formality to the organization.

Table 12.1 Bernard Davies' manifesto for youth work

Voluntary engagement	Where young people freely choose to become involved in a set of activities, they have power to influence the content of youth work and are likely to enjoy greater levels of respect.
Empowerment	Power in the organization should clearly be tipped in the direction of young people who should be fully involved in decision-making processes.
Accepting of young people as young people	Young people should be accepted as individuals at a particular stage of development with youth-specific sets of needs.
Meeting young people's expectations	Youth work takes place on territory and in temporal spaces 'owned' by young people, where they feel comfortable. However basic the facilities, young people need to be able to take ownership and be able to relax and have fun.
Focusing on the young person as an individual	The prime focus of youth work is on the young person as an individual underpinned by a commitment to help them fulfil their potential and overcome barriers.
Respectful of young people's peer networks	Peer groups are often important sources of identity and peer relations represent an arena where young people share interests and activities. Youth work must respect peer networks and work with them to achieve shared goals.
Respectful of young people's community and cultural identities	Youth work should help strengthen relationships to young people's community and culture and has to recognize the values and practices they share with others.
Broadening horizons	Youth work should help young people to become outward looking and creative and help them frame and realize their aspirations.
Concerned with young people's feelings	Youth work must be sensitive to young people's feelings, to how they feel about themselves, what they value and where they want to be.

In some respects it could be argued that the vision outlined by Davies (2005) and Smith (2002) is derived from a classic model of youth work with roots in a 'golden age' where state funding was more generous and youth workers were not expected to demonstrate 'hard' outcomes. Smith is certainly aware of policy shifts which, in the UK as well as elsewhere, have seen a move towards targeted, individualized work, particularly among those deemed to be in some way 'at risk'. In these new contexts, the voluntary principle has been eroded and the desired outcomes are framed by government rather than by young people as empowered participants. Contemporary youth work covers a spectrum where, at one end youth workers may supervise informal leisure activities and engage informally with voluntary participants, while at the other end they may be engaged in preventative work with vulnerable young people or offenders.

Although types of youth work overlap, it is useful to distinguish between four types of work: conventional youth work; issue and project-based youth work; intensive group work; and detached and outreach work.

Conventional youth work is the most common and familiar form of working, ranging from the traditional youth club where young people attend in the evening for varied activities, to youth cafes, uniformed groups such as the Scouts and Guides or cadet groups attached to the military, and faith-based groups associated with particular religions. While these groups have different objectives and, from the perspectives of the participants, may seem very different, they all typically provide young people with a safe environment in which they can participate in structured leisure activities or socialize informally with other participants. To the outside observer, it may be difficult to identify an educational element in these interactions, as young people may spend their time in conversation with peers, listening to music or playing pool. However, through participation young people may develop social skills and increase their confidence, they may value youth workers as a source of support and advice and may develop team-working skills through involvement in organizational agenda setting. In describing youth work as a 'playground for the learning of citizenship', Williamson (1997: 102) argues that involvement promotes 'self-confidence and creativity' and provides 'support, guidance and credible advice and information'.

Issue and project-based youth work is designed to help young people overcome specific problems and to provide them with the skills or information they need to deal effectively with the situations that face them. Issues may include relationships, unemployment, sexism and racism, health-related issues and behaviours or low self-esteem. Such programmes may involve a degree of compulsion and are frequently criticized for attempts to shape young people's views and behaviour in accordance with the position of the practitioner (Smith, 1988). When there is pressure on funds and where young people are seen to be involved in risky or threatening behaviour, there can be a shift away from conventional, open access forms of youth work to projects focused on issues like drugs, alcohol and sexual health. Issue and project work can take place in a club setting or may be set up as detached/outreach programmes targeting young people through to the most vulnerable.

Detached and outreach work involves youth workers going outside of institutional settings to engage directly with young people on the streets and in their communities. It tends to involve a focus on those who are not participating in traditional youth clubs, it can involve working on specific issues, such as health or gangs, and, in the case of outreach work, may aim to draw non-participants into traditional settings. While detached youth work can be an effective way of engaging with vulnerable populations, it is resource-intensive, and youth workers can take a long time to build up relationships. One of the strongest justifications for detached and out-reach work is that traditional youth work engages with a minority of young people, especially in older age ranges. Those who do not engage with more formal types of provision also have support needs and need to be approached on their own territory and at times that best suit their activities.

> **Granton Youth Centre Streetwork Programme** in Edinburgh focuses on young people drinking on the streets. Teams of youth workers go out on the streets on Friday and Saturday evenings to engage with young people who are drinking. They provide advice and information and direct young people to other services.
>
> Streetworkers wear a distinctive red jacket and top and are instantly recognisable. Their role is to engage with young people who don't access services and over time to steadily build up contact and relationship with the young people they meet. Street-workers get asked about a huge range of issues, and are often engaging with young people who have the highest support needs and who may be involved in antisocial behaviour.
>
> (www.grantonyouth.com/streetwork.html, accessed 5 January 2012)

Intensive group work tends to go a step beyond issue and project-based work. It often has strong links to the criminal justice system and atten-dance is frequently compulsory. Therefore, despite sharing some of the core objectives of mainstream youth work, such as skill enhancement and the development of self-confidence, it is not always recognized as youth work (Jeffs and Smith, 1988). Intensive youth work tends to focus on those in trouble or at risk, and aims to modify and control their behaviour. Inten-sive group work is often part of a set of targeted activities that include individually focused youth social work.

Evaluating youth work

Many youth workers are sceptical, even hostile, to the idea that their work can be evaluated. The results they achieve are seen as extremely varied, as young people themselves have very different needs and priorities and

youth studies: an introduction

come from different starting positions. Young people may develop in self-confidence, gain new relationships, new skills, may mature or may become more aware of their own strengths, desires and goals. Formally, these are difficult to assess and measure in an informal environment, and assessment of outcomes is not routinely measured. Indeed, one of the earliest commentators on youth work, Josephine Macalister Brew, made this point very explicit: 'a youth leader must try not to be too concerned about results' (Brew, 1957: 183, quoted in Smith, 2002).

In a climate of austerity, however sympathetic we are to these views, it is difficult to maintain a claim on public resources without being able to make a good case for effectiveness. If youth work supports personality development, provides effective guidance and helps young people negotiate barriers and fulfil their promise, then there is a good case for public support. Equally, if youth workers can reach those who are at risk or vulnerable and can help bring about positive behavioural change, then the service is clearly of value. However, rigorous evaluations of youth work are somewhat thin on the ground and existing studies provide contradictory results.

Perhaps one of the most robust studies to have been carried out in recent years was one based on the longitudinal British Birth Cohort surveys (Feinstein et al., 2006). In this study, the researchers focused on the impact of youth club participation at age 16 on outcomes at age 30: measures were available at both time points for around 6,000 people. After controlling for family disadvantage and poor educational attainments at age 16, the researchers discovered that youth club participation at age 16 was associated with social exclusion at age 30: youth club participants were more likely to be unemployed, to lack qualifications, to drink heavily and to have been involved in crime. The researchers argue that uniformed youth organizations that revolve around more structured activities are more clearly associated with positive outcomes and note that traditional youth clubs tend to attract young people from less advantaged families.

In a national evaluation of the effectiveness of youth work with vulnerable young people in Scotland, Furlong and colleagues (1997) were more positive about the benefits of youth work, especially outreach and detached work, which tended to focus on the most vulnerable. They noted that young people themselves tended to be very positive about their experience of youth work and of their relationships with youth workers. In particular, young people valued the opportunity for social contact provided by youth organizations and appreciated having a place where they could meet with friends and make new social contacts. Youth organizations were also seen as an important source of information and as providing an opportunity to learn new skills. At the same time relatively few young people (around one in twenty) said that they would be willing to discuss personal concerns with a youth worker. Attendance also tended to fall significantly with age and many young people felt that they had 'outgrown' youth groups, which had the greatest appeal to those under the age of 14.

A national evaluation of street-based youth work in England and Wales (Crimmens *et al.*, 2004) that focused on work with socially excluded youth was also positive about its benefits. The researchers argued that the street-based projects were a valuable source of information for those who were not in contact with other agencies and provided useful information on educational and occupational opportunities. They also argued that the projects helped young people make transitions back into education and into jobs and training. One of the problems they identified related to the concerns of the funders with meeting targets. Street-based youth workers argued that it could take a long time to establish a relationship with vulnerable young people (often over a year) and that a concern with targets effectively encouraged them to focus on those who were easiest to reach, rather than the difficult cases. There was also a concern that where funding was linked to crime reduction and community safety, relationships could be difficult to establish as youth workers came to be regarded as agents of social control.

> What working with young people in an outreach situation needs is sustained, long-term, work. You need time to engage the young people, get their trust and get to know them, what makes them tick and then to actually alter, or try and influence, their behaviour and activities, and you don't do that by jumping around from area to area.
> (street-based youth worker, quoted in Crimmens *et al.*, 2004: 3)

In the face of cuts to public spending triggered by the financial crisis in many Western countries, youth work is, on the one hand, an easy target for cuts, but, on the other, is viewed by some as an important control mechanism in helping keep jobless youth out of trouble and a lid on youth crime. Hence the street disorders in London in 2011 drew attention to the impact of cuts on young people living in disadvantaged inner-city areas. In the London borough of Haringey, for example, faced by a reduction in council funding of £41 million, the youth service budget was cut by 75 per cent, leading to the closure of many youth clubs and services and forcing young people to spend more time on the streets where they are subject to police surveillance and harassment. As one community activist put it, 'How do you create a ghetto? By taking away the very services that people depend upon to live, to better themselves' (*Guardian*, 2011d).

Ethics of youth work

As with professions like medicine or law, youth work practitioners establish a relationship with a client based on certain ethical understandings. In medicine and law, for example, there are established principles relating to what information can be passed on to a third party and what is understood to be sacrosanct. Although operating under a much loser regulatory framework that incorporates both unqualified volunteers and full-time qualified practitioners who may set agendas in their field, good youth work also operates within reasonably well-established ethical guidelines. Ethical youth work relates to the ways in which youth workers relate to the young person, to the checks put in place to ensure that those who work with young people are appropriately vetted and to the climate created in youth organizations to allow young people to develop and explore in an 'ethical climate' (McCulloch, 2007: 61).

In one of the most comprehensive books on youth work ethics, Sercombe (2010) develops a code of ethics that he originally drew up while working as a youth worker in Australia. Sercombe's starting point is that youth work is a relationship in which the young person is regarded as the 'primary client': young people should not be regarded as one of several competing stakeholders that may include funders, management committees, parents and so on. The young person should be able to expect that the youth worker will uphold their interests above all others. Other parts of the code include the obligation to work in non-discriminatory ways, to maintain transparent and truthful working practices, to avoid breaches of confidentiality and to set clear boundaries to the professional relationship, especially with respect to sexual relationships.

Confidentiality is a particularly sensitive area as there will tend to be limits to what a youth worker can be privy to without feeling the need to pass on the information to a third party. The most obvious example here is sexual abuse within the family, where the normal expectation of confidentiality clashes with the need to remove a young person from a dangerous and abusive situation. Where young people do not have confidence that confidentiality will be respected, they may decide not to come forward for help in the first place. Here good practice involves highlighting the limits to confidentiality and ensuring that young people have a clear awareness of what information will be protected and what might need to be passed on (Rixon and Turney, 2007).

Of course, unlike in the established professions, these ethical guidelines and others like them are voluntary and there is no professional regulatory body responsible for enforcing them. Moreover, many of those who work with young people are untrained and may have little awareness of what ethical practice entails. Even among professionally qualified youth workers, it is not possible to be 'struck off', and where a serious breach of established convention leads to the loss of employment, it is often possible to move onto another job.

While ethical youth work is clearly important, there is a view that, as a society, we have become overprotective. In the UK, those coming into regular contact with children and young people are subject to police vetting, even when this involves little more than volunteering at the school their own child attends on the odd occasion. It is argued here that the prevailing climate of protection derives from a small number of high-profile cases of abuse, leading to distrust and disincentivizing interaction between adults and young people. There is also a powerful argument that the focus on risk at the individual level can draw attention away from the ways in which conditions of poverty and exclusion contribute to abuse (Rixon and Turney, 2007).

Some implications for policy

The financial difficulties currently faced by many countries potentially lead to great challenges for youth work. Youth work may be regarded as an item of discretionary expenditure to be sacrificed when the pressure is on to maintain front-line services in the face of what can be savage cuts. There is also the risk that more informal programmes involving associative leisure experiences will be lost as resources are focused on targeted forms of youth work, especially programmes that address crime and anti-social behaviour: these practices could lead to the radical re-shaping of youth work agendas.

There is a good case to make for the benefits of youth work, which can provide vital support for young people, promote personal and social development, open up horizons and promote social mobility. In societies characterized by a process of individualization, the associative nature of youth work can help maintain communal values, build social capital and strengthen communities (Putnam, 2000). Governments that fail to provide adequate resources to promote youth development are extremely short-sighted.

At the same time, it would be wrong to defend current forms of provision uncritically. Certainly young participants and youth leaders can provide strong examples of the benefits of youth work, but many young people (including those in greatest need) are not attracted by current offerings, while some large-scale evaluations have not been able to demonstrate far-reaching impact. Youth work was developed in the industrial age and still bears many of its hallmarks. Youth transitions take much longer, but youth work has largely failed to attract older youth or support young people through protracted transitions. A new type of youth work needs to be developed to support the development of contemporary youth. A new agenda for youth work would involve helping young people navigate and make sense of complex transitions, building a firm associative base for social life, and strengthening citizenship and promoting political engagement. Indeed, youth work should be promoting a radical agenda and helping young people take control of the future.

Summary points

1 Youth work can be regarded as a branch of informal education, with roots in the nineteenth century, and which is now delivered in a wide variety of ways under diverse pedagogies.
2 While youth work might have a diverse range of objectives, personal and social development is often held to be paramount.
3 Although youth work can often be portrayed as a mechanism for social control, it can also be regarded as a form of empowerment and liberation.
4 While there are few comprehensive evaluations of the effectiveness of youth work, those that exist can tell quite different stories, some very positive, others somewhat negative.
5 A range of ethical principles, including confidentiality and the need to regard the young person as the 'primary client', underpins the relationship between youth workers and young people.

Further questions

1 Is youth work effectively a mechanism to control young people and reduce the 'threat' posed by unstructured, unsupervised, leisure?
2 How can we distinguish youth work from youth social work?
3 What are the essential features of youth work?
4 What potential benefits do young people derive from attending youth clubs?
5 Can the effectiveness of youth work be measured?
6 Does youth work need to be remodelled to meet the circumstances of the modern era?

Further reading

Harrison, R. and Wise, C. (eds) (2005) *Working with Young People*, London: Sage.

Sercombe, H. (2010) *Youth Work Ethics*, London: Sage.

Wood, J. J. and Hine, J. (eds) (2009) *Work with Young People: Theory and Policy for Practice*, London: Sage.

Internet links

www.infed.org/youthwork/b-yw.htm

Infed.org is a site dedicated to informal education. It contains a huge resource of contemporary and historical materials on all aspects of youth work.

This link takes you to a code of ethics for youth work developed in Australia:
www.yapa.org.au/youthwork/ethics/codetext.php

This link takes you to a Joseph Rowntree Foundation report on youth work by David Crimmens and colleagues:
www.jrf.org.uk/sites/files/jrf/654.pdf

Notes

1. Youth and the life course

1 Douglas Coupland regards the boomers as those born between 1946 and 1959 as he regards draft eligibility as a significant part of the experience of this generation.

4. Employment and unemployment

1 Austria, Belgium, Denmark, Finland, France, Germany, Greece, Ireland, Italy, Luxembourg, Netherlands, Portugal, Spain, Sweden and the UK.

2 Austria, Belgium, Cyprus, Czech Republic, Estonia, Denmark, Finland, France, Germany, Greece, Hungary, Ireland, Italy, Latvia, Lithuania, Luxembourg, Malta, Netherlands, Poland, Portugal, Slovenia, Slovak Republic, Spain, Sweden and the UK.

3 Some developed countries, such as Japan, were not hit by recession in the 1980s and levels of unemployment did not rise significantly.

4 In the US, unemployment among young people reached a post-war high of 19.25 in 2009 (Economic Policy Institute, 2010).

5 While the 1980s recession saw rates of unemployment reach their highest level since the 1930s, youth unemployment was significantly higher in the 1930s. While the all-age unemployment rate in the UK reached 22 per cent in 1932, if the rate were calculated using current definitions

it would have been somewhere in the region of 10–16 per cent (Hicks and Allen, 1999). As youth unemployment is likely to be two to three times higher, it may have been as high as 50 per cent.

5. Family, friends and living arrangements

1 Saito (1998) regards the *hikikomori* phenomenon as a psychological malaise, treatable with drugs and psychotherapy, rather than something triggered by social phenomena. In contrast, others (e.g. Furlong, 1998) argue that *hikikomori* do not form a homogeneous group and that social and economic factors provide at least a partial explanation.

8. Health and well-being

1 The number one cause of death among young people is accidental death, especially road accidents.

9. Crime and justice

1 Through an application to a magistrate sitting in a civil capacity.
2 The US has not ratified the UN Convention on the Rights of the Child; the only member state aside from Somalia (which lacked a working government) not to have signed.
3 Scottish slang: better a sore face than a red face.

11. Beyond the first world

1 The global north is a term frequently used by the United Nations and development agencies to refer to 57 countries that score highly on their Development Index: the majority of these are located in the northern hemisphere, although some, such as Australia, are located in the south. The global south refers to the remaining countries, most of which are developing countries in the southern hemisphere.

youth studies: an introduction

References

Aassve, A., Davia, M. A., Iacovou, M. and Mazzuco, S. (2005) 'Does leaving home make you poor? Evidence from 13 European countries', ISER Working Paper 2005–24, Colchester: University of Essex.

Abbott-Chapman, J. and Robinson, M. (2009) 'Leisure activities, place and identity', in A. Furlong (ed.), *Handbook of Youth and Young Adulthood*, Abingdon: Routledge.

ABC News (2011) 'Indigenous youth crime rates a "national crisis"', www.abc.net.au/news/2011-06-21/indigenous-youth-crime-rates-a-national-crisis/2765676 (accessed 9 August 2011).

Abrams, M. (1959) *The Teenage Consumer*, London: Press Exchange.

Akram, S. (2009) '"Riots" or "urban disorders"? The case for re-politicizing urban disorders', in A. Furlong (ed.), *Handbook of Youth and Young Adulthood*, Abingdon: Routledge.

Aldridge, S. (2001) *Social Mobility: A Discussion Paper*, London: Cabinet Office Performance and Innovation Unit, www.cabinetoffice.gov.uk/media/cabinetoffice/strategy/assets/socialmobility.pdf (accessed 5 April 2010).

Alexander, C., Duncan, S. and Edwards, R. (2010) 'Just a mum or dad: experiencing teenage parenting and work-life balances', in S. Duncan, R. Edwards and C. Alexander (eds), *Teenage Parenthood: What's the Problem?* London: Tufnell Press.

Ali, S. (2003) *Mixed-Race, Post-Race: Gender, New Ethnicities and Cultural Practices*, Oxford: Berg.

Altbach, P. G., Reisberg, L. and Rumbley, L. E. (2009) *Trends in Global Higher Education: Tracking an Academic Revolution*, Paris: UNESCO.

American College Health Association (2001) *National College Health Assessment*, Baltimore: American College Health Association.

Anderson, F., Worsley, R., Nunney, F., Maybanks, N. and Dawes, W. (2010) *Youth Survey 2009*, London: Youth Justice Board.

Anderson, S., Kinsey, R., Loader, I. and Smith, C. (1994) *Cautionary Tales: Young People, Crime and Policing in Edinburgh*, Aldershot: Averbury.

Arnett, J. J. (2004) *Emerging Adulthood: The Winding Road from the Late Teens through the Twenties*, New York: Oxford University Press.

Arnett, J. J., Kloep, M., Hendry, L. B. and Tanner, J. L. (2011) *Debating Emerging Adulthood: Stage or Process?* New York: Oxford University Press.

Arnot, M. (2002) *Reproducing Gender: Critical Essays on Educational Theory and Feminist Politics*, London: RoutledgeFalmer.

Arnot, M. and Mac an Ghaill, M. (eds) (2006) *Gender and Education*, Abingdon: Routledge.

Arulampalam, W. (2001) 'Is unemployment really scarring? Effects of unemployment on wages', *Economic Journal*, 111 (475): 585–606.

Ashton, D. N. (1986) *Unemployment Under Capitalism: The Sociology of British and American Labour Markets*, Brighton: Harvester.

Audit Commission (2010) *Against the Odds: Re-engaging Young People in Education, Employment or Training*, London: Audit Commission, www.audit-commission.gov.uk/SiteCollectionDocuments/Downloads/20100707-against-theoddsfull.pdf (accessed 10 October 2011).

Auer, P. and Cazes, S. (2003) *Employment Flexibility in an Age of Flexibility*, Geneva: International Labour Office.

Australian Bureau of Statistics (2008) *Living is for Everyone: Factsheet 3, Statistics on Suicide in Australia*, Canberra: Australian Government, Department of Health and Ageing.

Australian Institute of Criminology (2007) *Australian Crime: Facts and Figures 2006*, Canberra: Australian Institute of Criminology.

— (2011) *Australian Crime: Facts and Figures 2010*, Canberra: Australian Institute of Criminology.

Australian Institute of Family Studies (n.d.) 'Statistical information', www.aifs.gov.au/acssa/statistics.html (accessed 22 May 2012).

Australian Institute of Health and Welfare (2007) *Young Australians: Their Health and Wellbeing, 2007*, Canberra: Australian Institute of Health and Welfare.

Bagguley, P. and Mann, K. (1992) 'Idle thieving bastards? Scholarly representations of the "underclass"', *Work, Employment and Society*, 6 (1): 113–26.

Ball, S. J., Maguire, M. and Macrae, S. (2000) *Choice, Pathways and Transitions Post-16*. London: RoutledgeFalmer.

Bang, H. (2004) 'Everyday makers and expert citizens: building political, not social, capital', Working Paper, Canberra: Australian National University.

Banks, M. H. and Ullah, P. (1988) *Youth Unemployment in the 1980s: Its Psychological Effects*, London: Croom Helm.

Banks, S. (1994) 'Contemporary issues in youth work: editorial introduction', *Youth and Policy*, 46 (Autumn): 1–5.

Batchelor, S. (2005) '"Prove me the bam!": victimization and agency in the lives of young women who commit violent offences', *Probation Journal*, 52 (4): 358–75.

— (2009) 'Girls, gangs and violence: assessing the evidence', *Probation Journal*, 56 (4): 399–414.

Bauman, Z. (2000) *Liquid Modernity*, Cambridge: Polity.

BBC (2006a) 'ASBOs "demonising" young people', 23 April, http://news.bbc. co.uk/1/hi/uk/4935606.stm (accessed 11 August 2011).

— (2006b) 'Third "have sex below legal age"', 13 August, http://news.bbc.co.uk/ 2/hi/4784939.stm (accessed 24 June 2011).

— (2007) 'Police identify 169 London gangs', 21 February, http://news.bbc.co. uk/1/hi/england/london/6383933.stm (accessed 12 August 2011).

Beck, U. (1992) *Risk Society: Towards a New Modernity*, London: Sage.

— (2000) *The Brave New World of Work*, Cambridge: Polity.

— (2001) 'Freedom's children', in U. Beck and E. Beck-Gernsheim (eds), *Individualisation*, London: Sage.

Beck, U. and Beck-Gernsheim, E. (1995) *The Normal Chaos of Love*, Cambridge: Polity.

— (2002) *Individualization: Institutionalized Individualism and its Social and Political Consequences*, London: Sage.

Beder, S. (2000) *Selling the Work Ethic: From Puritan Pulpit to Corporate PR*, London: Zed Books.

Bell, D. N. F. and Blanchflower, D. G. (2010) *Youth Unemployment: Déjà Vu?* Stirling Economics Discussion Papers 2010–04, Stirling: University of Stirling.

Bellah, R., Madson, R., Sullivan, W. M., Swidler, A. and Tipton, S. M. (1985) *Habits of the Heart: Middle America Observed*, London: Hutchinson.

Bennett, A. (1999) 'Sub-culture or neo-tribes? Rethinking the relationship between youth, style and musical taste', *Sociology*, 33 (3): 599–617.

— (2009) 'Spectacular soundtracks: youth and music', in A. Furlong (ed.), *Handbook of Youth and Young Adulthood*, Abingdon: Routledge.

— (2011) 'The continuing importance of the "cultural" in the study of youth', *Youth Studies Australia*, 30 (3): 27–33.

— (forthcoming) *Growing Old Disgracefully? Popular Music, Ageing and Lifestyle*, Philadelphia: Temple University Press.

Bernstein, B. (1970) 'Education cannot compensate for society', *New Society*, 26 February, 15 (387): 344–7.

— (1971) *Class, Codes and Control, Volume 1*, London: Routledge and Kegan Paul.

Berrington, A., Hernandez, I. C., Ingham, R. and Stevenson, J. (2005) *Antecedents and Outcomes of Young Fatherhood: Longitudinal Evidence from the 1970 British Birth Cohort Study*, Final Report, Southampton: University of Southampton.

Bessant, J. (2008) 'Hard wired for risk: neurological science, "the adolescent brain" and developmental theory', *Journal of Youth Studies*, 11 (3): 347–60.

Best, A. L. (2009) 'Young people and consumption', in A. Furlong (ed.), *Handbook of Youth and Young Adulthood*, Abingdon: Routledge.

Biesta, G. (2009) 'Good education: what it is and why we need it', Inaugural Lecture 4 March, The Stirling Institute of Education, www.ioe.stir.ac.uk/documents/ GOODEDUCATION–WHATITISANDWHYWENEEDITInauguralLectureProf-GertBiesta.pdf (accessed 1 May 2012).

Biggart, A. (2002) 'Attainment, gender and minimum-aged school-leavers' early routes in the labour market', *Journal of Education and Work*, 15 (2): 145–62.

Biggart, A. and Furlong, A. (1996) 'Educating "discouraged workers": cultural diversity in the upper secondary school', *British Journal of Sociology of Education*, 17 (3): 253–66.

Blackman, S. (2007) 'See Emily play: youth culture, recreational drug use and normalisation', in M. Simpson, T. Shildrick and R. MacDonald (eds), *Drugs in Britain: Supply, Consumption and Control*, Basingstoke: Palgrave Macmillan.

— (2009) 'Young people, drugs and alcohol', in A. Furlong (ed.), *Handbook of Youth and Young Adulthood*, Abingdon: Routledge.

Black Mental Health UK (2008) *Mental Health Services and Ethnicity: The African Caribbean Experience*, London: BMH UK.

Blossfeld, H.-P., Klijzing, E., Pohl, K. and Roher, G. (1999) 'Why do co-habiting couples marry? An example of causal event history approach to independent systems', *Quality and Quantity*, 33 (3): 229–42.

Blum, R. W. (2005) 'Adolescents with disabilities in transition to adulthood', in D. W. Osgood, E. M. Foster, C. Flanagan and G. R. Ruth (eds), *On Your Own Without a Net: The Transition to Adulthood for Vulnerable Populations*, Chicago: University of Chicago Press.

Blum, R. W. and Nelson-Mmari, K. (2004) 'Adolescent health from an international perspective', in R. M. Lerner and L. Steinberg (eds), *Handbook of Adolescent Psychology*, Hoboken, NJ: John Wiley and Sons.

Blumer, H. (1937) 'Social psychology', in E. P. Schmidt (ed.), *Man and Society*, New York: Prentice-Hall.

Boaler, J. (2005) 'The "psychological prisons" from which they never escaped: the role of ability groupings in reproducing social class inequalities', *Forum*, 47 (2): 135–44.

Botting, B., Rosato, M. and Wood, R. (1998) 'Teenage mothers and the health of their children', *Population Trends*, 93 (Autumn): 19–28.

Bourdieu, P. (1974) 'The school as a conservative force: scholastic and cultural inequalities', in J. Eggleston (ed.), *Contemporary Research in the Sociology of Education*, London: Methuen.

— (1977) 'Cultural reproduction and social reproduction', in J. Karabel and A. H. Halsey (eds), *Power and Ideology in Education*, New York: Oxford University Press.

— (1984) *Distinction: A Social Critique of the Judgement of Taste*, Cambridge: Harvard University Press.

Breen, R. and Goldthorpe, J. H. (2001) 'Class, mobility and merit: the experience of two British birth cohorts', *European Sociological Review*, 17 (2): 81–101.

Brew, J. Macalister (1957) *Youth and Youth Groups*, London: Faber and Faber.

Bronfenbrenner, U. (1979) *The Ecology of Human Development: Experiments by Nature and Design*, Cambridge: Harvard University Press.

Brooks, R. (2002) 'Transitional friends? Young people's strategies to manage and maintain their friendships during a period of repositioning', *Journal of Youth Studies*, 5 (4): 449–67.

Buckingham, D. and Bragg, S. (2004) *Young People, Sex and the Media: The Facts of Life?* Basingstoke: Palgrave Macmillan.

Bühler, C. (1921) *Das Seelenleben*, quoted in J. Coleman and T. Husen (1985) *Becoming an Adult in a Changing Society*, Paris: OECD.

Bumpass, L. and Lu, H.-H. (2000) 'Trends in cohabitation and implications for children's family contexts in the United States', *Population Studies*, 54 (1): 29–41.

Bureau of Labor Statistics (2006) *100 Years of US Consumer Spending: Data from the Nation, New York City, and Boston*, Washington: US Bureau of Labor Statistics, www.bls.gov/opub/uscs/ (accessed 20 September 2011).

Bynner, J. (2005) 'Rethinking the youth phase in the lifecourse: the case for emerging adulthood?', *Journal of Youth Studies*, 8 (4): 367–84.

Byrne, D. (1999) *Social Exclusion*, Buckingham: Open University Press.

youth studies: an introduction

Campbell, I. (2004) *Casual Work and Casualisation: How Does Australia Compare?* Paper presented to a conference on 'Work Interrupted: Casual and Insecure Employment in Australia', University of Melbourne, August.

Casciani, D. (2008) 'Analysis: UK gun crime figures', *BBC News*, 31 January, http://news.bbc.co.uk/1/hi/uk/6960431.stm (accessed 5 August 2011).

CBS News (2006) 'CBS news poll: 55 percent of Americans pro-life, oppose most abortions', 16 January, http://ssbg.wordpress.com/2006/01/16/cbs-news-poll-55-percent-of-americans-pro-life-oppose-most-abortions/ (accessed 24 June 2011).

Cheal, D. (2008) *Families in Today's World: A Comparative Approach*, London: Routledge.

Child Poverty Action Group (2009) 'Ending child poverty: a manifesto for success', London: Child Poverty Action Group, www.cpag.org.uk/publications/extracts/CPAG_manifesto_0309.pdf (accessed 6 July 2010).

—— (2010) 'Poverty in the UK: a summary of facts and figures', London: Child Poverty Action Group, www.cpag.org.uk/povertyfacts/index.htm (accessed 6 July 2010).

Children and Young People Now (2009) 'Contraceptive use among young people on the rise', www.cypnow.co.uk/news/946964/Contraceptive-use-rise-among-young-people/?DCMP=ILC-SEARCH (accessed 24 June 2011).

Christensen, L., Dormor, D., Høeg, I. M., Ilg, W. and Niemelä, K. (2010) 'Protestant confirmation in European perspective', in S. Collins-Mayo and P. Dandelion (eds), *Religion and Youth*, Farnham: Ashgate.

Chronic Poverty Research Centre (2004) *Chronic Poverty Report, 2004–05*, Manchester: Institute for Development Policy and Management.

CIA (2012) *World Factbook*, Washington: CIA, www.cia.gov/library/publications/the-world-factbook/rankorder/2102rank.html (accessed 17 January 2012).

Clarke, H., Sanders, D., Stewart, M. and Whiteley, P. (2011) 'Measuring Turnout – Who Voted in 2010?' www.eprints.ncrm.ac.uk/1586/whiteley_measuring_turnout.ppt (accessed 15 July 2011).

Clarke, J., Hall, S., Jefferson, T. and Roberts, B. (1976) 'Subcultures, cultures and class: a theoretical overview', in S. Hall and T. Jefferson (eds), *Resistance Through Rituals: Youth Subcultures in Post-War Britain*, London: Hutchinson.

Cockerill, S (1992) 'Equality and empowerment', *Youth and Policy*, 36 (March): 17–22.

Cohen, P. (1972) 'Subcultural conflict and working class community', in Working Papers in Cultural Studies 2, Centre for Contemporary Cultural Studies, University of Birmingham, Spring, 5–51.

Cohen, S. (1972) *Folk Devils and Moral Panics*, London: MacGibbon and Kee.

Coleman, J. (1961) *The Adolescent Society: The Social Life of the Teenager and its Impact on Education*, New York: Free Press of Glencoe.

—— (1966) *Equality of Educational Opportunity*, Washington: US Office of Education.

—— (1974) *Youth: Transition to Adulthood*, Report of the Panel of the President's Science Advisory Committee on Youth, Chicago: University of Chicago Press.

Coleman, J. and Husén, T. (1985) *Becoming Adult in a Changing Society*, Paris: OECD.

Coleman, J. C. (2011) *The Nature of Adolescence*, 4th edn, London: Routledge.

Coleman, L. and Cater, S. (2006) ' "Planned" teenage pregnancy: perspectives of young women from disadvantaged backgrounds in England', *Journal of Youth Studies*, 9 (5): 593–614.

Coles, B. (1995) *Youth and Social Policy: Youth Citizenship and Young Careers*, London: UCL Press.

Collin, P. and Burn, J. (2009) 'The experience of youth in the digital age', in A. Furlong (ed.), *Handbook of Youth and Young Adulthood*, Abingdon: Routledge.

Collins-Mayo, S. (2010) 'Introduction', in S. Collins-Mayo and P. Dandelion (eds), *Religion and Youth*, Farnham: Ashgate.

Colosi, R. (2010) 'A return to the Chicago School? From the "subculture" of taxi dancers to the contemporary lap dancer', *Journal of Youth Studies*, 13 (1): 1–16.

Compas, B. E. (2004) 'Processes of risk and resilience during adolescence: linking contexts and individuals', in R. M. Lerner and L. Steinberg (eds), *Handbook of Adolescent Psychology*, 2nd edn, Hoboken, NJ: John Wiley and Sons.

Connell, R. W. (1987) *Gender and Power*, Oxford: Blackwell.

— (1995) *Masculinities*, Sydney: Allen and Unwin.

— (2000) *The Men and the Boys*, Oxford: Polity.

Cooley, C. H. (1902) *Human Nature and the Social Order*, New York: Scribner's.

Coordinating Council on Juvenile Justice and Delinquency Prevention (2000) 'Juveniles and the death penalty', www.ncjrs.gov/pdffiles1/ojjdp/184748.pdf (accessed 15 August 2011).

Copas, A. J., Wellings, K., Erens, B., Mercer, C. H., McManus, S., Fenton, K. A., Korovessis, C., Macdowell, W., Nanchahal, K. and Johnson, A. (2002) 'The accuracy of reported sensitive sexual behaviour in Britain: exploring the extent of change 1990–2000', *Sexual Transmission and Infection*, 78 (1): 26–30.

Corliss, C. L. (2011) *School Bullying in the Twenty-First Century*, MSc thesis, University of Glasgow, School of Education, Glasgow.

Côté, J. (2000) *Arrested Adulthood: The Changing Nature of Maturity and Identity*, New York: New York University Press.

— (2009) 'Youth-identity studies: history, controversies and future directions', in A. Furlong (ed.), *Handbook of Youth and Young Adulthood*, Abingdon: Routledge.

Côté, J. and Allahar, A. (1996) *Generation on Hold: Coming of Age in the Late Twentieth Century*, New York: New York University Press.

— (2006) *Critical Youth Studies: A Canadian Focus*, Toronto: Pearson.

Cotterell, J. (2007) *Social Networks in Youth and Adolescence*, Hove: Routledge.

Crick, B. (1998) *Education for Citizenship and the Teaching of Democracy in Schools: Final Report of the Advisory Group on Citizenship*, London: Qualifications and Curriculum Authority.

— (2002) 'Citizenship: citizenship must begin to replace ethos in the classroom', The *Independent*, 27 September, www.independent.co.uk/news/education/education-news/citizenship-bernard-crick-citizenship-must-begin-to-replace-ethos-in-the-classroom-607615.html (accessed 19 July 2011).

Crimmens, D., Factor, F., Jeffs, T., Pitts, J., Pugh, C., Spence, J. and Turner, P. (2004) *The Role of Street-Based Youth Work in Linking Socially Excluded Young People into Education, Training and Work*, York: Joseph Rowntree Foundation, www.jrf.org.uk/sites/files/jrf/654.pdf (accessed 5 January 2012).

Currie, C., Gabhainn, S. N., Godeau, E., Roberts, C., Smith, R., Currie, D., Picket, W., Richter, M., Morgan, A. and Barnekow, V. (2008) *Inequalities in Young People's Health: HBSC International Report from the 2005/2006 Survey*, Edinburgh: Child and Adult Health Research Unit.

youth studies: an introduction

Davies, B. (1985) *Threatening Youth: Towards a National Youth Policy*, Milton Keynes: Open University Press.

— (2005) 'Youth work: a manifesto for our times', *Youth and Policy*, 88 (Summer): 5–27.

Davies, B. (1989) *Frogs and Snails and Feminist Tales: Pre-School Children and Gender*, Sydney: Allen and Unwin.

Davis, E. C. and Friel, L. V. (2001) 'Adolescent sexuality: disentangling the effects of family structure and family context', *Journal of Marriage and Family*, 63 (3): 669–81.

de Gaston, J. F., Jensen, L. and Weed, S. (1995) 'A closer look at adolescent sexual activity', *Journal of Youth and Adolescence*, 24 (4): 465–79.

De Jong Gierveld, J., Liefbroer, A. C. and Beekink, E. (1991) 'The effect of parental resources on patterns of leaving home among young adults in the Netherlands', *European Sociological Review*, 7 (1): 55–71.

Delamont, S. (1980) *Sex Roles and the School*, London: Methuen.

Delaney, T. (2005) *American Street Gangs*, Upper Saddle River, NJ: Pearson/Prentice Hall.

Department for Children, Schools and Families (DCSF) (2007) *National Curriculum Assessment, GCSE and Equivalent Attainment and Post-16 Attainment by Pupil Characteristics in England*, London: Department for Children, Schools and Families.

Department of Culture, Media and Sport (DCMS) (2011) *Taking Part: The National Survey of Culture, Leisure and Sport, Statistical Release*, London: DCMS.

Department of Education and Science (1987) *Effective Youth Work: A report by HM Inspectors. Education Observed 6*, London: Department of Education and Science, www.infed.org/archives/gov_uk/effective_youth_work.htm (accessed 4 January 2012).

Deutsch, N. (2008) *Pride in the Projects: Teens Building Identities in Urban Contexts*, New York: New York University Press.

Diekstra, R. F. W., Kienhorst, C. W. M. and de Wilde, E. J. (1995) 'Suicide and suicidal behaviours among adolescents', in M. Rutter and D. J. Smith (eds), *Psychosocial Disorders in Young People: Time Trends and their Causes*, Chichester: John Wiley and Sons.

Driver, S. (2008) 'Introducing queer youth cultures', in S. Driver (ed.), *Queer Youth Cultures*, New York: State University of New York Press.

du Bois-Reymond, M. (1998) ' "I don't want to commit myself yet": young people's life concepts', *Journal of Youth Studies*, 1 (1): 63–79.

— (2009) 'Models of navigation and life management', in A. Furlong (ed.), *Handbook of Youth and Young Adulthood*, Abingdon: Routledge.

Duncan, A., Alexander, C. and Edwards, R. (2010) 'What's the problem with teenage parents?', in S. Duncan, R. Edwards and C. Alexander (eds), *Teenage Parenthood: What's the Problem?* London: Tufnell Press.

Dunham, C. C. (1998) 'Generation units and the life course: a sociological perspective on youth and the antiwar movement', *Journal of Political and Military Sociology*, 26 (2): 137–55.

Durkheim, E. (1952) *Suicide: A Study in Sociology*, London: Routledge and Kegan Paul.

Dwyer, P. and Wyn, J. (2001) *Youth, Education and Risk: Facing the Future*, London: RoutledgeFalmer.

Easterlin, R. A. (1980) *Birth and Fortune*, New York: Basic Books.

Eckersley, R. (2009) 'Progress, culture and young people's wellbeing', in A. Furlong (ed.), *Handbook of Youth and Young Adulthood*, Abingdon: Routledge.

Eckersley, R. and Dear, K. (2002) 'Cultural correlates of youth suicide', *Social Science and Medicine*, 55 (11): 1891–904.

Economic Policy Institute (2010) 'The kids aren't alright: a labor market analysis of young workers', EPI Briefing Paper No. 259, Washington: Economic Policy Institute.

Edmunds, J. and Turner, B. S. (2002) *Generations, Culture and Society*, Buckingham: Open University Press.

EGRIS (European Group for Integrated Social Research) (2001) 'Misleading trajectories: transitional dilemmas of young adults in Europe', *Journal of Youth Studies*, 4 (1): 101–19.

Elder, G. H Jr. (1974) *Children of the Great Depression: Social Change in Life Experience*, Chicago: University of Chicago Press.

— (1997) 'The life course as developmental theory', Presidential address to the Society for Research in Child Development, Washington DC, www.unc.edu/~elder/presentations/srcd-97.html (accessed 10 February 2009).

— (1998) 'The life course and human development', in R. E. Lerner (ed.), *Volume 1: Theories of Human Development: Contemporary Perspectives*, in W. Damon (editor-in-chief), *The Handbook of Child Psychology*, 5th edn, New York: Wiley.

Ellwood, D. (1982) 'Teenage unemployment: permanent scars or temporary blemishes?', in R. B. Freeman and D. A. Wise (eds), *The Youth Labour Market Problem: Its Nature, Causes and Consequences*, Chicago: University of Chicago Press.

Erikson, E. H. (1968) *Identity, Youth and Crisis*, New York: Norton.

Ermisch, J. and Francesconi, M. (1998) 'Cohabitation in Great Britain: not for long, but here to stay', Working Papers of the ESRC Research Centre on Micro-social Change, Paper 98–01, Colchester: University of Essex.

Esping-Anderson, G. (1990) *The Three Worlds of Welfare Capitalism*, Cambridge: Polity.

Euromonitor (2010) *Regional Focus: Youth Unemployment Remains High in Western Europe*, http://blog.euromonitor.com/2010/05/regional-focus-youth-unemployment-remains-high-in-western-europe.html (accessed 10 October 2011).

European Agency for Safety and Health at Work (2007) *European Risk Observatory Report: Young Workers – Facts and Figures*, Brussels: European Agency for Safety and Health at Work.

European Council (1997) *Luxembourg Employment Summit of the European Council*, www.eurofound.europa.eu/eiro/1997/11/feature/eu9711168f.htm (accessed 22 May 2012).

Eurostat (2004) *Work and Health in the EU: A Statistical Portrait, 1994–2002*, Luxembourg: Office for Official Publications of the European Communities.

— (2009a) *Youth in Europe: A Statistical Portrait*, Luxembourg: European Commission.

— (2009b) *Education in Focus: Key Statistics, 2007*, Luxembourg: European Commission.

— (2010) *Online Statistics*, table reference tps00055, http://epp.eurostat.ec.europa.eu/tgm/table.do?tab=table&init=1&language=en&pcode=tps00055&plugin=1 (accessed 27 January 2010).

— (2011) *Unemployment Statistics*, http://epp.eurostat.ec.europa.eu/statistics_explained/index.php?title=File:Table_youth_unemployment_MS.png&filetimestamp=20110930 132346 (accessed 10 October 2011).

Evans, K. (1994) 'Leisure patterns of young adults in Britain and the role of the youth service', *International Journal of Adolescence and Youth*, 4 (3–4): 179–94.

— (2002) 'Taking control of their lives? Agency in young adult transitions in England and the new Germany', *Journal of Youth Studies*, 5 (3): 245–69.

Evans, K. and Furlong, A. (1997) 'Metaphors of youth transitions: niches, pathways, trajectories or navigations', in J. Bynner, L. Chisholm and A. Furlong (eds), *Youth, Citizenship and Social Change in a European Context*, Aldershot: Ashgate.

Evans, K., Gerlach, C. and Kelner, S. (eds) (2007) 'The brain and learning in adolescence', in *Understanding the Brain: The Birth of a Learning Science*, Paris: Centre for Educational Research and Innovation (CERI).

Farrington, D. (1996) *Understanding and Preventing Youth Crime*, York: Joseph Rowntree Foundation.

— (2007) 'Childhood risk factors and risk-focused prevention', in M. Maguire, R. Morgan and R. Reiner (eds), *The Oxford Handbook of Criminology*, 4th edn, Oxford: Oxford University Press.

Farrington, D. and Welsh, B. (2007) *Saving Children from a Life of Crime*, Oxford: Oxford University Press.

Farthing, R. (2010) 'The politics of youthful antipolitics: representing the "issue" of youth participation in politics', *Journal of Youth Studies*, 13 (2): 181–95.

Fay, R. G. (1996) *Enhancing the Effectiveness of Active Labour Market Policies: Evidence from Programme Evaluations in OECD Countries*, Paris: OECD.

Feinstein, L., Bynner, J. and Duckworth, K. (2006) 'Young people's leisure contexts and their relation to adult outcomes', *Journal of Youth Studies*, 9 (3): 305–27.

Feinstein, L., Duckworth, K. and Sabates, R. (2008) *Education and the Family: Passing Success Across the Generations*, Abingdon: Routledge.

Fernandez, J. A., Walsh, M. R. J., Maller, M. G. and Wrapson, W. (2006) 'Police arrests and juvenile cautions: Western Australia 2006', Crime Research Centre, Perth: University of Western Australia, www.law.uwa.edu.au/-data/assets/pdf_file/0003/169248/Crime_and_Justice_Statistics_for_WA-2006-Police_Arrests_and_Juvenile_Cautions.pdf (accessed 8 August 2011).

Ferri, E., Bynner, J. and Wadsworth, M. E. (eds) (2003) *Changing Britain, Changing Lives: Three Generations at the End of the Century*, London: Institute of Education.

Feuer, L. S. (1969) *The Conflict of Generations*, New York: Basic Books.

Field, A. E., Cheung, L., Wolf, A. M., Herzog, D. B., Gortmaker, S. L. and Colditz, G. A. (1999) 'Exposure to the mass media and weight concerns among girls', *Pediatrics*, 103 (3): 54–60.

Field, J. (2003) *Social Capital*, London: Routledge.

Field, S., Kuczera, M. and Pont, B. (2007) *No More Failures: Ten Steps to Equity in Education*, Paris: OECD.

Flanagan, C. (2009) 'Young people's engagement and political development', in A. Furlong, (ed.), *Handbook of Youth and Young Adulthood*, Abingdon: Routledge.

Flory, R. and Miller, D. E. (2010) 'The expressive communalism of post-boomer religion in the USA', in S. Collins-Mayo and P. Dandelion (eds), *Religion and Youth*, Farnham: Ashgate.

Ford, N. (1989) 'Urban-rural variations in the level of heterosexual activity of young people', *Area*, 21 (3): 237–48.

Foucault, M. (1972) *The Archaeology of Knowledge*, London: Tavistock.

— (1981) *The History of Sexuality, Vol. 1*, London: Allen Lane.

Fouché, G. (2010) 'Danes show the way to get young people into work', *The Guardian*, 20 January, www.guardian.co.uk/society/2010/jan/20/youth-unemployment-jobcentre-vocational-courses (accessed 14 May 2010).

France, A. (2007) *Understanding Youth in Late Modernity*, Maidenhead: Open University Press.

— (2009) 'Young people and anti-social behaviour', in A. Furlong (ed.), *Handbook of Youth and Young Adulthood*, Abingdon: Routledge.

Frankel, R. (1998) *The Adolescent Psyche: Jungian and Winnicottian Perspectives*, London: Routledge.

Fraser, A. D. (2010) *Growing Through Gangs: Young People, Identity and Social Change in Glasgow*, PhD thesis, University of Glasgow, Glasgow.

Freire, P. (1972) *Pedagogy of the Oppressed*, New York: Continuum.

Freud, A. (1958) 'Adolescence', *The Psychoanalytic Study of the Child*, 13: 255–78.

Frosh, S., Phoenix, A. and Pattman, R. (2002) *Young Masculinities*, Cambridge: Polity.

Frost, L. (2003) 'Doing bodies differently: gender, youth, appearance and damage', in *Journal of Youth Studies*, 6 (1): 54–70.

Furlong, A. (1992) *Growing Up in a Classless Society? School to Work Transitions*, Edinburgh: Edinburgh University Press.

— (2006) 'Not a very NEET solution: representing problematic transitions among early school-leavers', *Work, Employment and Society*, 20 (3): 553–69.

— (2008) 'The Japanese hikikomori phenomenon: acute social withdrawal among young people', *The Sociological Review*, 56 (2): 309–25.

Furlong, A. and Cartmel, F. (1997) *Young People and Social Change: Individualization and Risk in Late Modernity*, Maidenhead: Open University Press.

— (2001) 'The relationship between youth unemployment and economic and social marginalisation: a comparative perspective', in B. Furaker (ed.), *Employment, Unemployment and Marginalisation*, Stockholm: Almqvist and Wiksell.

— (2004) *Vulnerable Young Men in Fragile Labour Markets*, York: York Publishing.

— (2007) *Young People and Social Change: New Perspectives*, 2nd edn, Maidenhead: Open University Press.

— (2009) *Higher Education and Social Justice*, Maidenhead: Open University Press.

— (2012) 'Social change and political engagement among young people: generation and the 2009/2010 British election survey', *Parliamentary Affairs*, 65 (1): 13–26.

Furlong, A. and Kelly, P. (2005) 'The Brazilianization of youth transitions in Australia and the UK?', *Australian Journal of Social Issues*, 40 (2): 207–25.

Furlong, A. and McNeish, W. (2000) *Integration Through Training*, Report to the European Commission, Glasgow: University of Glasgow.

Furlong, A., Cartmel, F., Biggart, A., Sweeting, H. and West, P. (2003) *Youth Transitions: Patterns of Vulnerability and Processes of Social Inclusion*, Edinburgh: Scottish Executive Social Research.

Furlong, A., Cartmel, F., Powney, J. and Hall, S. (1997) *Evaluating Youth Work with Vulnerable Young People*, Edinburgh: Scottish Council for Research in Education.

Furlong, A., Woodman, D. and Wyn, J. (2011) 'Changing times, changing perspectives: reconciling "transition" and "cultural" perspectives on youth and young adulthood', *Journal of Sociology*, 47 (4): 355–70.

Gallie, D. and Russell, H. (1998) 'Unemployment and life satisfaction', *Archives Européennes Sociologie*, 39: 3–35.

Gallie, D. and Vogler, C. (1994) 'Unemployment and attitudes to work', in D. Gallie, C. Marsh and C. Vogler (eds), *Social Change and the Experience of Unemployment*, Oxford: Oxford University Press.

Gallie, D. and White, M. (1993) *Employee Commitment and the Skills Revolution*, London: Policy Studies Institute.

George, S. and Dickerson, B. J. (1995) 'The role of the grandmother in poor single-mother families and households', in B. J. Dickerson (ed.), *African American Single Mothers: Understanding their Lives and Families*, Thousand Oaks, CA: Sage.

Giddens, A. (1991) *Modernity and Self Identity*, Oxford: Polity.

Goffman, E. (1959) *The Presentation of Self in Everyday Life*, Garden City: Anchor Books.

Goldacre, M., Seagrott, V. and Horton, K. (1993) 'Suicide after discharge from psychiatric in-patient care', *Lancet*, 342 (8866): 283–86.

Goldscheider, F. and Goldscheider, C. (1999) *The Changing Transition to Adulthood: Leaving and Returning Home*, Thousand Oaks, CA: Sage.

Goodwin, J. and O'Connor, H. (2005) 'Exploring complex transitions: looking back at the "golden age" of From School to Work', *Sociology*, 39 (2): 201–20.

Gorz, A. (1999) *Reclaiming Work: Beyond the Wage-Based Society*, Cambridge: Polity.

Graham, J. and Bowling, B. (1995) *Young People and Crime*, Home Office Research Study 145, London: Home Office.

Green, A., Wolf, A. and Leney, T. (1999) *Convergence and Divergence in European Education and Training Systems*, Bedford Way Papers, No. 7, London: Institute of Education.

Grossman, C. L. (2010) 'Survey: 72% of Millennials "more spiritual than religious"' *USA Today*, 14 October, www.usatoday.com/news/religion/2010-04-27-1Amillfaith27_ST_N.htm (accessed 27 April 2011).

Guardian, The (2004) 'Young Muslims "made scapegoats" in stop and search', 3 July, www.guardian.co.uk/uk/2004/jul/03/terrorism.race (accessed 1 May 2012).

— (2011a) 'Where cuts fall, the gangs flourish', 30 July, p. 13.

— (2011b) 'UK riots: Cameron looks for lessons from LA to tackle home-grown gangs', 11 August, www.guardian.co.uk/uk/2011/aug/11/uk-riots-gang-crackdown (accessed 15 May 2012).

—(2011c) 'Data Journalism reading the riots: what we know. And what we don't', www.guardian.co.uk/news/datablog/2011/dec/09/data-journalism-reading-riots (accessed 16 May 2012).

— (2011d) 'Farewell youth clubs, hello street life and gang warfare', 29 July, www.guardian.co.uk/uk/2011/jul/29/young-people-gangs-youth-clubs-close (accessed 22 May 2012).

Guest, D. (2000) 'Management and the insecure workforce: the search for a new psychological contract', in E. Heery and J. Salmon (eds), *The Insecure Workforce*, London: Routledge.

Gunter, A. (2010) *Growing Up Bad: Black Youth, Road Culture and Badness in an East London Neighbourhood*, London: Tufnell Press.

Hagedorn, J. (2008) *A World of Gangs: Armed Young Men and Gangsta Culture*, Minneapolis: University of Minnesota Press.

Hall, G. S. (1904) *Adolescence: Its Psychology and its Relations to Physiology, Anthropology, Sociology, Sex, Crime, Religion and Education*, New York: Appleton.

Hall, S. and Jefferson, T. (eds) (1976) *Resistance Through Rituals: Youth Subcultures in Post-War Britain*, London: Hutchinson.

Halsey, K. and White, R. (2009) *Young People, Crime and Public Perceptions: A Review of the Literature*, Slough: National Foundation for Educational Research, www.socialscienceforschools.org.uk/Image/Young%20people,%20crime%20 and%20-public%20perceptions_tcm11-9026.pdf (accessed 8 August 2011).

Hansen, R. S. (n.d.) 'Surviving and moving beyond low-wage jobs: solutions for an invisible workforce in America', www.quintcareers.com/surviving_low-wage_jobs.html (accessed 22 May 2012).

Harrington, V. and Mayhew, B. (2001) *Mobile Phone Theft*, Home Office Research Study 235, London: Home Office.

Harris, J., Howard, M., Jones, C. and Russell, L. (2005) *Great Expectations: How Realistic is the Government Target to get 60 Per Cent of Young Mothers into Education, Employment or Training?* Oxford: YWCA.

Havighurst, R. J. (1948) *Development Tasks and Education*, New York: David McKay.

Hawkes, D. (2010) 'Just what difference does teenage motherhood make? Evidence from the Millennium Cohort Study', in S. Duncan, R. Edwards and C. Alexander (eds), *Teenage Parenthood: What's the Problem?* London: Tufnell Press.

Hawton, K. (1987) 'Assessment of suicide risk', *British Journal of Psychiatry*, 150 (February): 145–53.

Hayes, J. and Nutman, P. (1981) *Understanding the Unemployed: The Psychological Effects of Unemployment*, London: Tavistock.

Hazel, N. (2008) *Cross-national Comparison of Youth Justice*, London: Youth Justice Board, www.yjb.gov.uk/publications/Resources/Downloads/Cross_national_final.pdf (accessed 9 August 2011).

Heath, S. and Kenyon, L. (2001) 'Single young professional and shared household living', *Journal of Youth Studies*, 4 (1): 83–100.

Heaven, P. C. L. (1994) *Contemporary Adolescence: A Psychological Approach*, Melbourne: Macmillan.

Hébert, Y. (2001) 'Identity, diversity and education: a critical review of the literature', *Canadian Ethnic Studies*, 33 (3): 155–85.

Hebson, G. (2009) 'Renewing class analysis in studies of the workplace: a comparison of working-class and middle-class women's aspirations and identities', *Sociology*, 43 (1): 27–44.

Heikkinen, M. (2001) 'Social networks of the marginal young: a study of young people's social exclusion in Finland', *Journal of Youth Studies*, 3 (4): 389–407.

Heinz, W. R. (2009) 'Youth transitions in an age of uncertainty', in A. Furlong (ed.), *Handbook of Youth and Young Adulthood: New Perspectives and Agendas*, Abingdon: Routledge.

Hellgren, J., Sverke, M. and Isaksson, K. (1999) 'A two-dimensional approach to job insecurity: consequences for employee attitudes and well-being', *European Journal of Work and Organizational Psychology*, 8 (2): 179–95.

Henderson, S. (1999) 'The question of gender', in N. South (ed.), *Drugs: Cultures, Controls and Everyday Life*, London: Sage.

Henderson, S., Holland, J., McGrellis, S., Sharpe, S. and Thomson, R. (2007) *Inventing Adulthoods: A Biographical Approach to Youth Transitions*, London: Sage.

Hendrick, H. (1990) *Images of Youth: Age, Class and the Male Youth Problem 1880–1920*, Oxford: Clarendon Press.

Hendry, L. B. and Kloep, M. (2010) 'How universal is emerging adulthood? An empirical example', *Journal of Youth Studies*, 13 (2): 169–79.

Hendry, L., Shucksmith, J., Love, J. G. and Glendinning, A. (1993) *Young People's Leisure and Lifestyles*, London: Routledge.

Henn, M., Weinstein, M. and Forrest, S. (2005) 'Uninterested youth? Young people's attitudes towards party politics in Britain', *Political Studies*. 53 (3): 556–78.

Henn, M., Weinstein, M. and Wring, D. (2002) 'A generation apart? Youth and political participation in Britain', *British Journal of Politics and International Relations*, 4 (2): 167–92.

Hesmondhalgh, D. (2005) 'Subcultures, scenes or tribes? None of the above', *Journal of Youth Studies*, 8 (1): 21–40.

Hess, R. and Holloway, S. D. (1984) 'Family and school as educational institutions', in R. D. Parke (ed.), *Review of Child Development Research, Vol.7: The Family*, Chicago: University of Chicago Press.

Hicks, J. and Allen, G. (1999) *A Century of Change: Trends in UK Statistics Since 1900*, House of Commons Library, London: Social and General Statistics.

Hills, J., Brewer, M., Jenkins, S., Lister, R., Lupton, R., Machin, S., Mills, C., Modood, T., Rees, T. and Riddell, S. (2010) *An Anatomy of Economic Inequality in the UK: Report of the National Equity Panel*, London: Government Equalities Office.

Hoare, C. (2009) 'Identity and spiritual development in the papers of Erik Erikson', *Identity*, 9 (3): 183–200.

Hodkinson, P. (2002) *Goth: Identity, Style and Subculture*, London: Berg.

—— (2009) 'Young people's fashion and style', in A. Furlong (ed.), *Handbook of Youth and Young Adulthood*, Abingdon: Routledge.

Hofer, B. K. and Moore, A. S. (2010) *The iConnected Parent: Staying Close to Your Kids in College (and Beyond) While Letting Them Grow Up*, New York: Free Press.

Holland, J., Ramazanoglu, C., Sharpe, S. and Thomson, R. (2004) *The Male in the Head: Young People, Heterosexuality and Power*, London: Tufnell Press.

Hollands, R. (2002) 'Division in the dark: youth cultures, transitions and segmented consumption spaces in the night-time economy', *Journal of Youth Studies*, 5 (2): 153–73.

—— (2009) 'Young adults and the night-time economy', in A. Furlong (ed.), *Handbook of Youth and Young Adulthood*, Abingdon: Routledge.

Holligan, C. P. and Deuchar, R. (2009) 'Territorialities in Scotland: perceptions of young people in Glasgow', *Journal of Youth Studies*, 12 (6): 731–46.

Home Office (1998) *Crime and Disorder Act*, London: Stationary Office.

Horkheimer, M. and Adorno, T. (1972) *Dialectic of Enlightenment*, New York: Herder and Herder.

Horrocks, C. (2002) 'Using life course theory to explore the social and developmental pathways of young people leaving care', *Journal of Youth Studies*, 5 (3): 325–36.

Hough, M. and Roberts, J. V. (2004) *Youth Crime and Youth Justice: Public Opinion in England and Wales*, Bristol: Policy Press.

Howe, N. and Strauss, W. (1991) *Generations: The History of America's Future, 1584–2069*, New York: Perennial.

—— (1993) *13th Gen: Abort, Retry, Fail?* New York: Vintage.

—— (1997) *The Fourth Turning: What the Cycles of History Tell Us About America's Next Rendezvous with Destiny*, New York: Broadway Books.

—— (2000) *Millennials Rising: The Next Great Generation*, New York: Vintage Books.

Hughes, M. (2009) *Social Trends 39*, London: Palgrave Macmillan.

— (2010) *Social Trends 40*, London: Office for National Statistics.

Hughes, M., Church, J. and Zealey, L. (eds) (2009) *Social Trends 39*, London: Office for National Statistics.

Iacovou, M. (2002) 'Regional differences in the transition to adulthood', *The Annals of the American Academy of Political and Social Science*, 580 (1): 40–69.

Independent Commission on Youth Crime and Antisocial Behaviour (2009) *Responding to Youth Crime and Antisocial Behaviour: A Consultation Paper*, London: Nuffield Foundation.

— (2010) *The Case for a Fresh Start: The Report of the Independent Commission*, London: Nuffield Foundation, www.youthcrimecommission.org.uk/attachments/076_FreshStart.pdf (accessed 11 August 2011).

Inglehart, R. (1977) *The Silent Revolution: Changing Values and Political Styles Among Western Publics*, Princeton: Princeton University Press.

Inglehart, R., Basáñez, M., Díez-Medrano, J., Halman, L. and Luijkx, R. (2004) *Human Beliefs and Values: A Cross-cultural Sourcebook based on the 1999–2002 Values Surveys.* Mexico: Siglo Veintiuno Editores.

Institute for the Study of Civil Society (2010) 'Factsheet: youth crime in England and Wales', London: Institute for the Study of Civil Society, www.civitas.org.uk/crime/factsheet-YouthOffending.pdf (accessed 8 August 2011).

International Labour Office (2011) *Global Employment Trends for Youth: 2011 Update*, Geneva: International Labour Office.

Inui, A. (2007) Personal communication.

— (2009) 'NEETs, freeters and flexibility: reflecting precarious situations in the new labour market', in A. Furlong (ed.), *Handbook of Youth and Young Adulthood*, Abingdon: Routledge.

Ipsos MORI (2006) *Attitudes Towards Teenagers and Crime*, London: Ipsos MORI, www.ipsos-mori.com/researchpublications/researcharchive/poll.aspx?oItemId=287 (accessed 1 May 2012).

Ivaska, A. (2011) *Cultured States: Youth, Gender, and Modern Style in 1960s Dar es Salaam*, Durham: Duke University Press.

Jackson, C. (2003) 'Motives for "laddishness" at school: fear of failure and fear of the feminine', *British Educational Research Journal*, 29 (4): 581–98.

Jackson, P. (2004) *Inside Clubbing: Sensual Experiments in the Art of Being Human*, Oxford: Berg.

Jackson, S. and Scott, S. (2010) *Theorizing Sexuality*, Buckingham: Open University Press.

Jahoda, M., Lazarsfeld, P. F. and Zeisel, H. (1933) *Marienthal: The Sociography of an Unemployed Community* (English translation 1972), London: Tavistock.

Järvinen, M. and Gundelach, P. (2007) 'Teenage drinking, symbolic capital and distinction', *Journal of Youth Studies*, 10 (1) 55–71.

Jeffs, A. J. (1979) *Young People and the Youth Service*, London: Routledge and Kegan Paul.

Jeffs, T. (1979) *Young People and the Youth Service*, London: Routledge and Kegan Paul.

Jeffs, T. and Smith, M. (1994) 'Young people, youth work and a new authoritarianism', *Youth and Policy*, 46 (Autumn) 17–33.

Jeffs, T. and Smith, M. (eds) (1988) *Welfare and Youth Work Practice*, London: Macmillan.

Jephcott, P. (1954) *Some Young People*, London: Allen and Unwin.

Jones, G. (1995) *Leaving Home*, Buckingham: Open University Press.

— (2005) 'Social protection policies for young people: a cross-national comparison', in H. Bradley and van J. Hoof (eds), *Young People in Europe: Labour Markets and Citizenship*, Bristol: Policy Press.

— (2009) *Youth*, Cambridge: Polity.

— (n.d.) *Enjoying and Achieving: The Implications for Youth Work of Every Child Matters*, Research Programme Series Book 4, Leicester: National Youth Agency, www.nya.org.uk/dynamic_files/research/enjoying and achieving.pdf (accessed 8 April 2010).

Jones, G., O'Sullivan, A. and Rouse, J. (2006) 'Young adults, partners and parents: individual agency and the problems of support', *Journal of Youth Studies*, 9 (4): 375–92.

Jonsson, J. O. (1993) 'Persistent inequalities in Sweden?', in Y. Shavit and H.-P. Blossfeld (eds), *Persistent Inequality, Changing Educational Attainment in Thirteen Countries*, Boulder: Westview.

Karabanow, J. and Naylor, T. D. (2010) 'Being hooked up: exploring the experiences of street youth and information technologies', in E. D. Looker and T. D. Naylor (eds), *Digital Diversity: Youth, Equity and Information Technology*, Waterloo: Wilfred Laurier Press.

Kehily, M. J. (2007a) 'A Cultural perspective', in M. J. Kehily (ed.), *Understanding Youth: Perspectives, Identities and Practices*, London: Sage.

— (2007b) 'Playing', in M. J. Kehily (ed.), *Understanding Youth: Perspectives, Identities and Practices*, London: Sage.

Keniston, K. (1968) *Young Radicals: Notes on Committed Youth*, New York: Harcourt Brace.

Kent Youth Service (2010) 'Written evidence submitted by Kent Youth Service' to the Education Select Committee, www.publications.parliament.uk/pa/cm201012/cmselect/cmeduc/744/744vw104.htm (accessed 4 January 2012).

Kiernan, K. (1992) 'The impact of family disruption in childhood on transitions made in young adult life', *Population Studies*, 46 (1992) 213–24.

Kintrea, K., Bannister, J., Pickering, J., Reid, M. and Suzuki, N. (2008) 'Young people and territoriality in British cities', York: Joseph Rowntree Foundation, www.jrf.org.uk/sites/files/jrf/2278-young-people-territoriality.pdf (accessed 17 August 2011).

Kroger, J. (2004) *Identity in Adolescence*, 3rd edn, London: Routledge.

Kupchick, A. (2006) *Judging Juveniles: Prosecuting Adolescents in Adult and Juvenile Courts*, New York: New York University Press.

Lantz, S. (2005) 'Students working in the Melbourne sex industry: education, human capital and the changing patterns of the youth labour market', *Journal of Youth Studies*, 8 (4): 385–401.

Lareau, A. (1989) *Home Advantage: Social Class and Parental Intervention in Elementary Schools*, London: Falmer.

Larson, R. and Wilson, S. (2004) 'Adolescence across place and time: globalization and the changing pathways to adulthood', in R. M. Lerner and L. Steinberg (eds), *Handbook of Adolescent Psychology*, 2nd edn, Hoboken, NJ: John Wiley and Sons.

Laufer, M. and Laufer, M. E. (1984) *Adolescence and Developmental Breakdown: A Psychoanalytic View*, New Haven: Yale University Press.

Lawy, R., Quinn, J. and Diment, K. (2010) 'Responding to the "needs" of young people in jobs without training (JWT): some policy suggestions and recommendations', *Journal of Youth Studies*, 13 (3): 335–52.

Leadership Conference on Civil and Human Rights, The (2000) 'Justice on trial: racial disparities in the American criminal justice system', Leadership Conference on Civil and Human Rights, www.protectcivilrights.org/pdf/reports/justice.pdf (accessed 9 August 2011).

Leadership on Civil Rights Education Fund (2009) 'Confronting the new faces of hate: hate crimes in America', Leadership on Civil Rights Education Fund, www.protectcivilrights.org/pdf/reports/hatecrimes/lccref_hate_crimes_report.pdf (accessed 1 August 2011).

Lee, I.-L. (2010) *Self-Destructive Behaviour Among Taiwanese Young People*, PhD thesis, University of Glasgow.

Lerner, R. M. and Steinberg, L. (2004) 'The scientific study of adolescent development: past, present and future', in R. M. Lerner and L. Steinberg (eds), *Handbook of Adolescent Psychology*, 2nd edn, Hoboken, NJ: John Wiley and Sons.

Levin, H., Belfield, C., Muennig, P. and Rouse, C. (2007) 'The costs and benefits of an excellent education for all of America's children, www.cbcse.org/media/download_gallery/Leeds_Report_Final_Jan2007.pdf (accessed 17 August 2011).

Levine, J. (2002) *Harmful to Minors: The Perils of Protecting Children from Sex*, Minneapolis: University of Minnesota Press.

Levitas, R. (1998) *The Inclusive Society: Social Exclusion and New Labour*, London: Macmillan.

Levitas, R., Pantazis, C., Fahmy, E., Gordon, D., Lloyd, E. and Patsios, D. (2007) *The Multi-Dimensional Analysis of Social Exclusion*, London: Cabinet Office.

Lopez, N. (2002) 'Race-gender experiences and schooling: second generation Dominican, West Indian and Haitian youth in New York City', *Race, Ethnicity and Education*, 5 (1): 67–89.

Loughran, H. (2010) 'Eighteen and celebrating: birthday cards and drinking cultures', *Journal of Youth Studies*, 13 (6): 631–45.

Mac an Ghaill, M. (1994) *The Making of Men: Masculinities, Sexualities and Schooling*, Buckingham: Open University Press.

McAra, L. and McVie, S. (2007a) 'Youth Justice? The impact of system contact on patterns of desistence from offending', *European Journal of Criminology*, 4 (3): 315–45.

— (2007b) 'Criminal Justice Transitions', Edinburgh Study of Youth Transitions and Crime, Working Paper No. 14, Edinburgh: University of Edinburgh.

McCulloch, K. (2007) 'Ethics, accountability and the shaping of youth work practice', in R. Harrison, C. Benjamin, S. Curran and R. Hunter (eds), *Leading Work with Young People*, London: Sage.

McDermott, E. and Graham, H. (2005) 'Resilient young mothering: social inequalities, late modernity and the "problem" of "teenage" motherhood', *Journal of Youth Studies*, 8 (1): 59–79.

MacDonald, R. (ed.) (1997) *Youth, the 'Underclass' and Social Exclusion*, London: Routledge.

— (2009) 'Precarious work: risk, choice and poverty traps', in A. Furlong (ed.), *Handbook of Youth and Young Adulthood*, London: Routledge.

MacDonald, R. and Marsh, J. (2005) *Disconnected Youth? Growing Up in Britain's Poor Neighbourhoods*, Basingstoke: Palgrave Macmillan.

youth studies: an introduction

MacDonald, R., Shildrick, T. and Simpson, M. (2007) 'Drugs in Britain: discussion and conclusions', in M. Simpson, T. Shildrick and R. MacDonald (eds), *Drugs in Britain: Supply, Consumption and Control*, Basingstoke: Palgrave Macmillan.

MacDonald, S. and Telford, M. (2007) 'The use of ASBOs against young people in England and Wales: lessons from Scotland', *Legal Studies*, 27 (4): 604–29.

McDowell, L. (2003) *Redundant Masculinities: Employment Change and White Working Class Youth*, Oxford: Blackwell.

— (2009) 'New masculinities and femininities: gender divisions in the new economy', in A. Furlong (ed.), *Handbook of Youth and Young Adulthood*, Abingdon: Routledge.

McLeod, J. and Yates, L. (2006) *Making Modern Lives: Subjectivity, Schooling and Social Change*, Albany: State University of New York Press.

Madsen, U. A. (2008) 'Toward eduscapes: youth and schooling in a global era', in K. T. Hansen (ed.), *Youth and the City in the Global South*, Bloomington: Indiana University Press.

Maffesoli, M. (1995) *The Time of the Tribes: The Decline of Individualism in Mass Society*, London: Sage.

Maguire, S. (2010) ' "I just want a job" – what do we really know about young people in jobs without training?', *Journal of Youth Studies*, 13 (3): 317–33.

Mail Online (2010) 'Tories will clamp down on "sexualisation" of children, vows Cameron', 19 February, www.dailymail.co.uk/news/article-1251908/David-Cameron-Tories-clamp-sexualisation-children.html (accessed 3 November 2010).

Mannheim, K. (1952) 'The problem of generations', in K. Mannheim, *Essays on the Sociology of Knowledge*, London: RKP.

Marcenko, M. O., Fishman, G. and Friedman, J. (1999) 'Re-examining adolescent suicidal ideation: a developmental perspective applied to a diverse population', *Journal of Youth and Adolescence*, 28 (1): 121–38.

Markus, H. and Nurius, P. (1986) 'Possible selves', *American Psychologist*, 41 (9): 954–69.

Marsh, D., O'Toole, T. and Jones, S. (2007) *Young People and Politics in the UK: Apathy or Alienation?* London: Palgrave Macmillan.

Marshall, T. H. (1963) *Sociology at the Crossroads*, London: Heinemann.

Marx, K. (1947) *The German Ideology*, New York: International Publishers.

Marx, K. and Engels, F. (1848) *The Manifesto of the Communist Party*, London: Communist League.

Mascherrini, M., Jungblut, J.-M. and Salvatore, L. (2011) *Young People and NEETs in Europe*, Dublin: Eurofound.

Mason, D. (ed.) (2003) *Explaining Ethnic Differences: Changing Patterns of Disadvantage in Britain*, Bristol: Policy Press.

Mattinson, J. and Mirrlees-Black, C. (2000) *Attitudes to Crime and Criminal Justice: Findings from the 1998 British Crime Survey*, Research Findings No. 111, London: Home Office.

Matza, D. (1964) *Delinquency and Drift*, New York: Wiley.

Mead, G. H. (1934) *Mind, Self, Society*, Chicago: University of Chicago Press.

Mental Health Foundation (1999) *Bright Futures: Promoting Children and Young People's Mental Health*, London: Mental Health Foundation.

Michael, R. T., Gagnon, J. H., Laumann, E. O. and Kolata, G. (1995) *Sex in America: A Definitive Survey*, New York: Warner.

Miles, R. (1989) *Racism*, London: Routledge.

Miles, S. (2000) *Youth Lifestyles in a Changing World*, Buckingham: Open University Press.

Miliband, D. (2006) *Social Exclusion: The Next Steps Forward*, London: Office of the Deputy Prime Minister.

Miller-Idriss, C. (2009) *Blood and Culture: Youth, Right-Wing Extremism, and National Belonging in Contemporary Germany*, Durham: Duke University Press.

Milson, F. (1972) 'Why am I a youth worker? An examination of the goals and motives of youth workers', London: National Association of Youth Clubs, www.infed.org/archives/nayc/milson_why.htm (accessed 4 January 2012).

Mind (2011) 'Statistics 2: suicide', http://mind.org.uk/help/research_and_policy/statistics_2_suicide (accessed 22 June 2011).

Modood, T. (1997) 'Culture and identity', in T. Modood, R. Berthoud, J. Lakey, J. Nazroo, P. Smith, S. Virdee and S. Beisham (eds), *Ethnic Minorities in Britain*, London: Policy Studies Institute.

Moore, J. W. (1998) 'Understanding youth gangs: economic restructuring and the urban underclass', in M. Watts (ed.), *Cross-cultural Perspectives on Youth and Violence*, Stamford: JAI Press.

Mørch, S. (1997) 'Youth and action theory', in J. Bynner, L. Chisholm and A. Furlong (eds), *Youth, Citizenship and Social Change in a European Context*, Aldershot: Ashgate.

MORI (2008) *MORI Youth Survey 2008: Young People in Mainstream Education*, London: Youth Justice Board.

Mortimer, J. (2009) 'Changing experiences of work', in A. Furlong (ed.), *Handbook of Youth and Young Adulthood*, Abingdon: Routledge.

Muggleton, D. (1997) 'The post-subculturalist', in S. Redhead, D. Wynne and J. O'Connor (eds), *The Club Cultures Reader*, Malden: Blackwell.

Mugisha, F. (2009) 'HIV and AIDS, STIs and sexual health among young people', in A. Furlong (ed.), *Handbook of Youth and Young Adulthood*, Abingdon: Routledge.

Mulder, C. H. (2009) 'Leaving the parental home in young adulthood', in A. Furlong (ed.), *Handbook of Youth and Young Adulthood*, Abingdon: Routledge.

Mulder, C. H. and Clark, W. A. V. (2000) 'Leaving home and leaving the state: evidence from the United States', *International Journal of Population Geography*, 6 (6): 423–37.

Muncie, J. (2009) *Youth and Crime*, 3rd edn, London: Sage.

Murray, C. (1990) *The Emerging British Underclass*, London: Institute of Economic Affairs.

Nairn, K., Higgins, J., Thompson, B., Anderson, M. and Fu, N. (2006) 'It's just like the teenage stereotype, you go out and drink and stuff: hearing from young people who *don't* drink', *Journal of Youth Studies*, 9 (3): 287–304.

Nakanishi, Y. (2003) 'Making sense of Japanese juvenile crime statistics: beyond an economic approach and policy implications', *Radical Statistics*, 81 (Spring): 34–50.

National Center for Children in Poverty (2010) 'Topics: child poverty' www.nccp.org/topics/childpoverty.html (accessed 6 July 2010).

National Council for Voluntary Youth Services (2008) *National Occupational Standards for Youth Work*, www.ncvys.org.uk/index.php?page=284#NOS (accessed 20 September 2011).

National Youth Bureau (1990) *Danger or Opportunity?* Leicester: National Youth Bureau.

youth studies: an introduction

Nayak, A. (2006) 'Displaced masculinities: chavs, youth and class in the post-industrial city', *Sociology*, 40 (5): 813–31.

Newcombe, R. (2007) 'Trends in the prevalence of illicit drug use in Britain', in M. Simpson, T. Shildrick and R. MacDonald (eds), *Drugs in Britain: Supply, Consumption and Control*, Basingstoke: Palgrave Macmillan.

Niang, A. (2006) 'Bboys: hip-hop culture in Dakar, Sénégal', in P. Nilan and C. Feixa (eds), *Global Youth? Hybrid Identities*, Plural Worlds, Abingdon: Routledge.

Nilan, P. (2006) 'The reflexive youth culture of devout Muslim youth in Indonesia', in P. Nilan and C. Feixa (eds), *Global Youth? Hybrid Identities*, Plural Worlds, Abingdon: Routledge.

— (2011) 'Youth sociology must cross cultures', *Youth Studies Australia*, 30 (3): 20–6.

Nilan, P. and Feixa, C. (2006) 'Youth hybridity and plural worlds', in P. Nilan and C. Feixa (eds), *Global Youth? Hybrid Identities*, Plural Worlds, Abingdon: Routledge.

Noon, M. and Blyton, P. (2002) *The Realities of Work*, 2nd edn, London: Palgrave.

Norris, P., Walgrave, S. and Von Aelst, P. (2005) 'Who demonstrates? Antistate rebels, conventional participants or everyone?' *Comparative Politics*, 37 (2): 89–2005.

Nyiri, Z. (2007a) 'Muslims in Europe: basis for greater understanding already exists', *Gallup Special Report: Muslims in Europe*, Princeton, NJ: Gallup, www.gallup.com/se/127907/gallup-center-muslim-studies.aspx (accessed 1 August 2011).

— (2007b) 'Values questions set European Muslims apart', *Gallup Special Report: Muslims in Europe*, Princeton, NJ: Gallup, www.gallup.com/se/127907/gallup-center-muslim-studies.aspx (accessed 1 August 2011).

Oakley, A. (1981) *Subject Woman*, Oxford: Martin Robertson.

OECD (Organisation for Economic Co-operation and Development) (2009) *Education at a Glance, 2009*, Paris: OECD.

Offer, D. (1969) *The Psychological World of the Teenager*, New York: Basic Books.

Office for National Statistics (2007) *Statistics on Drug Misuse, England, 2007*, London: ONS.

Office of Juvenile Justice and Delinquency Prevention (2011) *Statistical Briefing Book*, www.ojjdp.gov/ojstatbb/default.asp (accessed 8 August 2011).

O'Higgins, N. (2001) *Youth Unemployment and Employment Policy: A Global Perspective*, Geneva: International Labour Office.

Oliver, M. and Barnes, C. (1998) *Disabled People and Social Policy: From Exclusion to Inclusion*, Harlow: Longman.

Omole, T. (2011) 'Drug use', in E. Fuller (ed.), *Smoking, Drinking and Drug Use Among Young People in England in 2010*, London: NHS Information Centre for Health and Social Care, www.ic.nhs.uk/pubs/sdd10fullreport (accessed 17 August 2011).

O'Reilly, J. and Yau, M. (2009) *2008 Parent Census, Kindergarten to Grade 6*, Etobicoke: Toronto District School Board.

Osgerby, B. (1998) *Youth in Britain Since 1945*, Oxford: Blackwell.

Owens, R. E. Jr. (1998) *Queer Kids: The Challenges and Promise for Lesbian, Gay, and Bisexual Youth*, New York: Harrington Park Press.

Paechter, C. (2007) *Being Boys, Being Girls: Learning Masculinities and Femininities*, Maidenhead: Open University Press.

Pahl, R. (2000) *On Friendship*, Cambridge: Polity.

Panel on Fair Access to the Professions (2009) *Unleashing Aspiration: Summary and Recommendations of the Full Report*, London: Cabinet Office, www.cabinetoffice.gov.uk/media/227105/fair-access-summary.pdf (accessed 1 May 2012).

Panel on Juvenile Crime (2001) *Juvenile Crime, Juvenile Justice*, Washington: National Academy Press.

Park, A. (2004) 'Has modern politics disenchanted the young?', in A. Park, J. Curtice, K. Thompson, C. Bromley and M. Phillips (eds), *British Social Attitudes, the 21st Report*, London: Sage.

Parker, H., Measham, F. and Aldridge, J. (1995) *Drugs Futures: Changing Patterns of Drug Use Amongst English Youth*, London: Institute for the Study of Drug Dependence.

— (1998) *Illegal Leisure: The Normalisation of Adolescent Drug Use*, London: Routledge.

Pascall, G. and Hendey, N. (2004) 'Disability and the transition to adulthood: the politics of parenting', *Critical Social Policy*, 24 (2): 165–86.

Pattie, C., Seyd, P. and Whiteley, P. (2004) *Citizenship, Democracy and Participation in Contemporary Britain*, Cambridge: Cambridge University Press.

Patwary, M. A., O'Hare, W. T., Karim, S. A. and Sharker, M. H. (2012) 'The motivation of young people moving into medical waste scavenging as a street career', *Journal of Youth Studies*, 15 (5): 591–604.

Peach, C. (1996) *Ethnicity and the 1991 Census*, Vol. 2, London: Office of Populations, Censuses and Surveys.

Petridis, A. (2002) 'Ska for the madding crowd', *The Guardian*, 8 March, www.guardian.co.uk/culture/2002/mar/08/artsfeatures.popandrock (accessed 28 July 2011).

Pendleton, L., Smith, C. and Roberts, J. (1991) 'Drinking on television: a content analysis of recent alcohol portrayal', *Addiction*, 86: 769–74.

Phillips, A. and Chamberlain, V. (2006) *MORI Five-Year Report: An Analysis of Youth Survey Data*, London: Youth Justice Board for England and Wales.

Pilcher, J. (1994) 'Mannheim's sociology of generations: an undervalued legacy', *The British Journal of Sociology*, 45 (3): 481–95.

Pitts, J. (2001) *The New Politics of Youth Crime: Discipline or Solidarity?* Lyme Regis: Russell House Publishing.

Platt, S. (1994) 'Unemployment and suicide behaviour', *Social Science and Medicine*, 149: 401–5.

— (2000) 'Suicide risk among young adults in Scotland: examining the evidence, explaining the trends and reviewing options for prevention', in A. Morton and J. Francis (eds), *The Sorrows of Young Men: Exploring the Increasing Risk of Suicide*, Edinburgh: Centre for Theology and Public Issues, University of Edinburgh.

Pleace, N. and Fitzpatrick, S. (2004) *Centrepoint Youth Homelessness Index: An estimate of Youth Homelessness for England*, York: Centre for Housing Policy, University of York.

Plummer, K. (2006) 'Identity', in W. Outhwaite (ed.), *The Blackwell Dictionary of Modern Social Thought*, Oxford: Blackwell.

Polhemus, T. (1994) *Streetstyle: From Sidewalk to Catwalk*, London: Thames and Hudson.

Pollock, G. (1997) 'Uncertain futures: young people in and out of work since 1940', *Work, Employment and Society*, 11 (4): 615–38.

youth studies: an introduction

— (2002) 'Ignoring the past: underemployment and risk in late modernity', in M. Cieslik and G. Pollock (eds), *Young People in Risk Society*, Aldershot: Ashgate.

Powell, M. (2000) 'The hidden history of social citizenship', www.essex.ac.uk/ecpr/events/jointsessions/paperarchive/copenhagen/ws6/powell.PDF (accessed 19 July 2011).

Prince's Trust (2010) *YouGov Youth Index 2010*, London: Prince's Trust.

Print, P., Saha, L. J. and Edwards, K. (2004) *Youth Electoral Study – Report 1: Enrolment and Voting*, Sydney: Australian Electoral Commission.

Putnam, R. (1995) *Bowling Alone: America's Declining Social Capital*, New York: Simon and Schuster.

Putnam, R. D. (2000) *Bowling Alone: The Collapse and Revival of American Community*, New York: Simon and Schuster.

Puuronen, V., Sinisalo, P., Miljukova, I. and Shvet, L. (2000) *Youth in a Changing Karelia*, Aldershot: Ashgate.

Quinn, J., Lawy, R. and Diment, K. (2008) 'Dead end kids in dead end jobs: reshaping debates on young people in jobs without training', *Research in Post-Compulsory Education*, 13 (2): 185–94.

Raftery, A. E. and Hout, M. (1993) 'Maximally maintained inequality: expansion, reform and opportunity in Irish Education 1921–75', *Sociology of Education*, 66 (1): 41–62.

Rattansi, A. and Phoenix, A. (1997) 'Re-thinking youth identities: modernist and post-modernist frameworks', in J. Bynner, L. Chisholm and A. Furlong (eds), *Youth, Citizenship and Social Change in a European Context*, Aldershot: Ashgate.

Reay, D. (2005) 'Who goes where in higher education: an issue of class, ethnicity and increasing concern', London: Institute for Policy Studies in Education, London Metropolitan University.

Redhead, S. (1997) *Subcultures to Clubcultures: An Introduction to Popular Cultural Studies*, Oxford: Blackwell.

Regales, J. (2008) 'My identity is fluid as fuck: transgender zine writers constructing themselves', in S. Driver (ed.), *Queer Youth Cultures*, Albany, NY: State University of New York Press.

Reynolds, S. (1997) 'Rave culture: living dream or living death', in S. Redhead, D. Wynne and J. O'Connor (eds), *The Clubcultures Reader: Readings in Popular Cultural Studies*, Oxford: Blackwell.

Reynolds, T. (2007) 'Friendship networks, social capital and ethnic identity: researching the perspectives of Caribbean young people in Britain', *Journal of Youth Studies*, 10 (4): 383–98.

Riddell, S. (2009) 'Disability, exclusion and transition to adulthood', in A. Furlong (ed.), *Handbook of Youth and Young Adulthood*, London: Routledge.

Rifkin, J. (2004) *The End of Work: The Decline of the Global Labor Force and the Dawn of the Post-Market Era*, New York: Tarcher/Penguin.

Rinnie, R., Mikko, A., Kivirauma, J. and Simola, H. (2003) *Adolescents Facing Education Politics of the 21st Century*, Turku: Finnish Educational Research Association.

Rixon, A. and Turney, D. (2007) 'Safeguarding', in M. Robb (ed.), *Youth in Context: Frameworks, Settings and Encounters*, London: Sage.

Robb, M. (2007a) 'Gender', in M. J. Kehily (ed.), *Understanding Youth: Perspectives, Identities and Practices*, London: Sage.

— (2007b) 'Wellbeing', in M. J. Kehily (ed.), *Understanding Youth: Perspectives, Identities and Practices*, London: Sage.

Robbins, M. and Francis, L. (2010) 'The teenage religion and values survey in England and Wales', in S. Collins-Mayo and P. Dandelion (eds), *Religion and Youth*, Farnham: Ashgate.

Roberts, D. F., Henriksen, L. and Foehr, U. G. (2004) 'Adolescents and media', in R. M. Lerner and L. Steinberg (eds), *Handbook of Adolescent Psychology*, 2nd edn, Hoboken, NJ: John Wiley and Sons.

Roberts, K. (1975) 'The developmental theory of occupational choice: a critique and an alternative', in G. Esland, G. Salaman and M. Speakman (eds), *People and Work*, Edinburgh: Holmes McDougall.

— (2004) *The Leisure Industries*, Basingstoke: Palgrave Macmillan.

— (2007) 'Youth transitions and generations: a response to Wyn and Woodman', *Journal of Youth Studies*, 10 (2): 263–9.

— (2009) *Youth in Transition: Eastern Europe and the West*, Basingstoke: Palgrave Macmillan.

Roberts, K., Pollock, G., Rustamova, S., Mammadova, Z. and Tholend, J. (2009) 'Young adults' family and housing life-stage transitions during post-communist transition in the South Caucasus', *Journal of Youth Studies*, 12 (2): 151–66.

Rosenthal, R. and Jacobson, L. (1968) *Pygmalion in the Classroom*, New York: Irvington.

Rousseau, D. M. (1995) *Psychological Contracts in Organizations: Understanding Written and Unwritten Agreements*, Thousand Oaks, CA: Sage.

Rugg, J., Ford, J. and Burrows, R. (2004) 'Housing advantage? The role of student renting in the construction of housing biographies in the United Kingdom', *Journal of Youth Studies*, 7 (1): 19–34.

Rustin, M. and Chamberlayne, P. (2002) 'Introduction: from biography to social policy', in P. Chamberlayne, M. Rustin and T. Wengraf (eds), *Biography and Social Exclusion in Europe*, Bristol: Policy Press.

Rutter, M. and Smith, D. J. (eds) (1995) *Psychosocial Disorders Among Young People: Time Trends and their Causes*, Chichester: John Wiley and Sons.

Saavedra, J. D. (2010) 'Just the facts: a snapshot of incarcerated hispanic youth', Washington, DC: National Council of La Raza, http://njjn.org/uploads/digital_library/resource_1529.pdf (accessed 9 August 2011).

Saito, T. (1998) *Shakaiteki Hikikomori: Owaranai Shishunki (Social Withdrawal: Unfinished Puberty)*, Tokyo: PHP-Kenkyujo.

Sampson, R. J. and Laub, J. H. (1995) *Crime in the Making: Pathways and Turning Points Through Life*, Cambridge: Harvard University Press.

— (2003) 'Life-course desisters? Trajectories of crime among delinquent boys followed to age 70', *Criminology*, 41 (3): 319–39.

Savage, M. (2000) *Class Analysis and Social Transformation*, Buckingham: Open University Press.

Savin-Williams, R. C. and Diamond, L. M. (2004) 'Sex', in R. M. Lerner and L. Steinberg (eds), *Handbook of Adolescent Psychology*, 2nd edn, Hoboken, NJ: John Wiley and Sons.

Scarpetta, S., Sonnet, A. and Manfredi, T. (2010) *Rising Youth Unemployment During the Crisis: How to Prevent Negative Long-Term Consequences on a Generation*, Paris: OECD.

Schneider, J. (2000) 'The increasing financial dependency of young people on their parents', *Journal of Youth Studies*, 3 (1): 5–20.

youth studies: an introduction

Schofield, G. (1994) *The Youngest Mothers*, Aldershot: Avebury.

Schoof, U. (2006) *Stimulating Youth Employment: Barriers and Incentives to Enterprise Start-Ups by Young People*, Geneva: International Labour Office.

Schuller, T. (2007) 'Social capital and young people', in H. Helve and J. Bynner (eds), *Youth and Social Capital*, London: Tufnell Press.

Self, A. and Zealey, L. (eds) (2007) *Social Trends, 37*, London: Office for National Statistics.

Sennett, R. (1998) *The Corrosion of Character: The Personal Consequences of Work in the New Capitalism*, New York: Norton.

Sercombe, H. (2010) *Youth Work Ethics*, London: Sage.

SEU (1999) *Teenage Pregnancy: Report by the Social Exclusion Unit*, London: Stationary Office.

Shahabi, M. (2006) 'Youth subcultures in post-revolution Iran', in P. Nilan and C. Feixa (eds), *Global Youth? Hybrid Identities, Plural Worlds*, Oxford: Routledge.

Sharpe, S. (1976) *Just Like a Girl*, London: Penguin.

Shavit, Y. and Müller, W. (2000) 'Vocational secondary education: where diversion and where safety net?', *European Societies*, 2 (1): 29–50.

Shildrick, T. (2002) 'Young people, illicit drugs and the question of normalisation', *Journal of Youth Studies*, 5 (1): 35–48.

Shildrick, T., MacDonald, R., Furlong, A., Riden, J. and Crowe, R. (2012) *Intergenerational Cultures of Worklessness: A Qualitative Exploration in Glasgow and Middleborough*, York: Joseph Rowntree Foundation.

Shiner, M. (2009) *Drug Use and Social Change: The Distortion of History*, Basingstoke: Palgrave Macmillan.

Simpson, M., Dawkins, J. and Maddern, G. (1997) 'Casual employment in Australia: incidence and determinants', *Australian Economic Papers*, 36 (69): 194–204.

Sloam, J. (2007) 'Rebooting democracy: youth participation in politics in the UK', *Parliamentary Affairs*, 60 (4): 548–67.

Smart, D., Richardson, N., Sanson, A., Dussuyer, I., Marshall, B., Toumbourou, J. W., Prior, M. and Oberklaid, F. (2005) *Patterns and Precursors of Adolescent Antisocial Behaviour, Outcomes and Connections*, Melbourne: Australian Institute of Family Studies.

Smith, M. K. (1988) *Developing Youth Work, Informal Education, Mutual Aid and Popular Practice*, Milton Keynes: Open University Press.

— (2002) 'Youth work: an introduction', in *The Encyclopaedia of Informal Education*, www.infed.org/youthwork/b-yw.htm (accessed 4 January 2012).

Smith, R. J. and Maughan, T. (1998) 'Youth culture and the making of the post-Fordist economy: dance music in contemporary Britain', *Journal of Youth Studies*, 1 (2): 211–28.

Spannering, R. (2008) 'Understanding (non-) participation: forms, meanings and reasons', in R. Spannering, G. Ogris and W. Gaiser (eds), *Youth and Political Participation in Europe*, Opladen: Barbara Budrich.

Sparrow, P. R. and Cooper, C. L. (2003) *The Employment Relationship: Key Challenges for HR*, Oxford: Butterworth-Heinemann.

Standing, G. (2011) *The Precariat: The New Dangerous Class*, London: Bloomsbury.

Stephen, D. E. (2000) 'Young women construct themselves: social identity, self-concept and psychosocial well-being in homeless facilities', *Journal of Youth Studies*, 3 (4): 445–60.

Sullivan, K., Cleary, M. and Sullivan, G. (2004) *Bullying in Secondary Schools*, London: Paul Chapman.

Tarrow, S. (1998) *Power in Movement: Social Movement and Contentious Politics*, Cambridge: Cambridge University Press.

Thompson, P. (1975) *The Edwardians: The Remaking of British Society*, London: Weidenfield.

Thornton, S. (1995) *Club Cultures: Music, Media and Subcultural Capital*, Oxford: Polity.

Thresher, F. (1927) *The Gang: A Study of 1313 Gangs in Chicago*, Chicago: University of Chicago Press.

Tiggemann, M. and Pickering, A. S. (1996) 'Role of television in adolescent women's body dissatisfaction and drive for thinness', *International Journal of Eating Disorders*, 20 (2): 199–203.

Times, The (2008) 'Children's commissioner calls for ban on mosquito, ultrasonic anti-teen device', 12 February, www.timesonline.co.uk/tol/news/uk/article3356157.ece (accessed 13 May 2011).

Tönnies, F. (2001) *Community and Civil Society*, Cambridge: Cambridge University Press.

Topel, R. and Ward, M. (1992) 'Job mobility and the careers of young men', Working Paper No. 2649, Cambridge: National Bureau of Economic Research.

Townsend, P. (1979) *Poverty in the United Kingdom: A Survey of Household Resources and Standards of Living*, London: Penguin.

Trinca, H. and Fox, C. (2004) *Better than Sex: How a Whole Generation Got Hooked on Work*, Milsons Point: Random House Australia.

Turffrey, B. (2010) *The Human Cost: How the Lack of Affordable Housing Impacts on all Aspects of Life*, London: Shelter.

Turner, K. M. (2004) 'Young women's views on teenage motherhood: a possible explanation for the relationship between socio-economic background and teenage pregnancy outcome', *Journal of Youth Studies*, 7 (2): 221–38.

Tyyskä, V. (2009) *Youth and Society: The Long and Winding Road*, 2nd edn, Toronto: Canadian Scholars' Press.

UNAIDS Inter-Agency Task Team on Young People (2004) *At the Crossroads: Accelerating Youth Access to HIV/AIDS Interventions*, New York: UNFPA.

UNESCO (2009) *Global Education Digest, 2009*, Montreal: UNESCO.

UN-HABITAT (2006) *The State of the World's Cities 2006-7: Facts on Youth*, www.unhabitat.org/downloads/docs/3974_95355 (accessed 18 January 2012).

UNICEF (2006) *Behind Closed Doors: The Impact of Domestic Violence on Children*, UNICEF, New York, www.unicef.org/protection/files/BehindClosedDoors.pdf (accessed 17 August 2011).

United Nations (1995) 'The world programme of action for youth on leisure-time activities' (A/RES/50/81), www.un.org/esa/socdev/unyin/wpayleisure.htm#WPAY (accessed 5 May 2011).

— (1998) 'Use and application of United Nations standards and norms in crime prevention and criminal justice', Report of the Secretary General E/CN.15/1998/8/Add.1, Geneva: United Nations.

— (2003) *World Youth Report, 2003*, New York: United Nations.

— (2005) *World Youth Report, 2005*, New York: United Nations.

— (2008) *Youth and the United Nations*, www.org/esa/socdev/unyin/qanda.htm (accessed 22 December 2008).

youth studies: an introduction

— (2010) 'The world youth report: youth and climate change', New York: United Nations, www.un.org/esa/socdev/unyin/documents/WYR2010Final%20online%20version.pdf (accessed 17 January 2012).

US Census Bureau (2000) *America's Families and Living Arrangements, 2000*, Washington: US Census Bureau.

— (2007) *America's Families and Living Arrangements, 2007*, Washington: US Census Bureau.

US Department of Justice (2007) *National Crime Victimization Survey: Indicators of School Crime and Safety* http://bjs.ojp.usdoj.gov/index.cfm?ty=pbdetail&iid=1762 (accessed 9 August 2011).

Valentin, K. (2008) 'Politicized leisure in the wake of *doi moi*: a study of youth in Hanoi', in K. T. Hansen (ed.), *Youth and the City in the Global South*, Bloomington: Indiana University Press.

Vickerstaff, S. (2003) 'Apprenticeship in the "golden age": were youth transitions really smooth and unproblematic back then?' *Work, Employment and Society*, 17 (2): 269–87.

Wacquant, L. (2008) *Urban Outcasts: A Comparative Sociology of Advanced Marginality*, Cambridge: Polity.

Wade, A. and Beran, T. (2011) 'Cyber bullying: the new era of bullying', *Canadian Journal of School Psychology*, 26 (1): 44–61.

Waites, M. (2005) *The Age of Consent: Young People, Sexuality and Citizenship*, Basingstoke: Palgrave.

Waiton, S. (2001) *Scared of the Kids: Curfews, Crime and Regulation of Young People*, Leicester: Perpetuity Press.

Walkerdine, V., Lucey, H. and Melody, J. (2001) *Growing Up Girl: Psychosocial Explorations of Gender and Class*, London: Palgrave.

Watson, I., Buchanan, J., Campbell, I. and Briggs, C. (2003) *Fragmented Futures: New Challenges in Working Life*, Annandale, NSW: Federation Press.

Webster, C. (2009) 'Young people, "race" and ethnicity', in A. Furlong (ed.), *Handbook of Youth and Young Adulthood*, Abingdon: Routledge.

Webster, C., Simpson, D., MacDonald, R., Abbas, A., Cieslik, M., Shildrick, T. and Simpson, M. (2006) *Poor Transitions: Social Exclusion and Young Adults*, Bristol: Policy Press.

West, A., Lewis, J. and Currie, P. (2009) 'Students' Facebook "friends": public and private spheres', *Journal of Youth Studies*, 12 (6): 615–27.

West, D. J. and Farrington, D. P. (1977) *The Delinquent Way of Life*, London: Heinemann.

West, P. (1997) 'Health inequalities in the early years: is there equalisation in youth?', *Social Science and Medicine*, 44: 833–58.

— (2009a) 'Health in youth: changing times and changing influences', in A. Furlong (ed.), *Handbook of Youth and Young Adulthood*, Abingdon: Routledge.

— (2009b) 'Health related behaviours in context', in A. Furlong (ed.), *Handbook of Youth and Young Adulthood*, Abingdon: Routledge.

Westergaard, J. (1992) 'About and beyond the underclass: some notes on influences of social climate on British sociology', *Sociology*, 26 (4): 575–87.

White, R. (2011) 'Climate change, uncertain future and the sociology of youth', *Youth Studies Australia*, 30 (3): 13–19.

White, R. and Wyn, J. (2004) *Youth and Society: Exploring the Social Dynamics of Youth Experience*, Melbourne: Oxford University Press.

Wilkinson, R. and Pickett, K. (2010) *The Spirit Level: Why Equality is Better for Everyone*, London: Penguin.

Williamson, H. (1997) 'Youth work and citizenship', in J. Bynner, L. Chisholm and A. Furlong (eds), *Youth and Citizenship in a European Perspective*, Aldershot: Avebury.

— (2004) *The Milltown Boys Revisited*, London: Berg.

Willis, P. (1977) *Learning to Labour*, Farnborough: Saxon House.

Wilson, B. (2006) *Fight, Flight or Chill: Subcultures, Youth, and Rave into the Twenty-First Century*, Montreal: McGill-Queen's University Press.

Wood, R. T. (2006) *Straightedge Youth: Complexity and Contradictions of a Subculture*, New York: Syracuse University Press.

Woodman, D. (2010) *The Post-Secondary School Transition and the Desynchronisation of Everyday Life*, Unpublished PhD Thesis, Melbourne: The University of Melbourne.

Woodward, D. (2003) *Nursery Class Children's Formation of Gender Perspectives*, Unpublished M.Phil Thesis, Milton Keynes: Open University Press.

World Bank (n.d.) 'Education and development', http://go.worldbank. org/F5K8Y429G0 (accessed 18 January 2012).

World Health Organization (2004) 'Suicide huge but preventable public health problem', www.who.int/mediacentre/news/releases/2004/pr61/en/index.html (accessed 22 June 2011).

— (2009) 'Dengue and dengue haemorrhagic fever', Fact sheet No. 117, www.who. int/mediacentre/factsheets/fs117/en/ (accessed 16 January 2012).

Wotherspoon, T. (2004) *The Sociology of Education in Canada: Critical Perspectives*, 2nd edn, Don Mills: Oxford University Press.

Wyn, J. (2009a) 'Educating for late modernity', in A. Furlong (ed.), *Handbook of Youth and Young Adulthood*, Abingdon: Routledge.

— (2009b) *Youth Health and Welfare: The Cultural Politics of Education and Wellbeing*, Melbourne: Oxford University Press.

Wyn, J. and White, R. (1997) *Rethinking Youth*, Sydney: Allen and Unwin.

Wyn, J. and Woodman, D. (2006) 'Generation, youth and social change in Australia', *Journal of Youth Studies*, 9 (5): 495–514.

— (2007) 'Researching youth in a context of social change: a reply to Roberts', *Journal of Youth Studies*, 10 (3) 373–81.

Yardley, E. (2008) 'Teenage mothers' experience of stigma', *Journal of Youth Studies*, 11 (6): 671–84.

Zielenziger, M. (2006) *Shutting out the Sun: How Japan Created its Own Lost Generation*, New York: Nan A. Talese.

Author index

youth studies: an introduction

youth studies: an introduction

Subject index

youth studies: an introduction